QUIZ WHIZ

KINGFISHER

BOSTON

KINGFISHER
a Houghton Mifflin Company imprint
222 Berkeley Street
Boston, Massachusetts 02116
www.houghtonmifflinbooks.com

First published in 2008
10 9 8 7 6 5 4 3 2 1
1TR/1107/WKT/PICA/140MA/C

FOR KINGFISHER:
Senior editor: Hannah Wilson
Coordinating editor: Stephanie Pliakas
Picture research manager: Cee Weston-Baker
Artwork archivist: Gina Weston-Baker
Senior production controller: Teresa Wood
DTP coordinator: Catherine Hibbert

FOR TOUCAN:
Editor: Hannah Bowen
Designer: Bob Burroughs

LIBRARY OF CONGRESS CATALOGING-IN-PUBLICATION DATA
Jackson, Tom.
  Quiz whiz / Tom Jackson and Sean Callery—1st ed.
    p. cm.
  Includes index.
  ISBN-13: 978-0-7534-6173-0
  1. Questions and answers—Juvenile literature. I. Callery,
Sean. II. Title.
  GV1507.Q5J33 2008
  030—dc22

                            2007031845

ISBN 978-0-7534-6173-0

Printed in China

CONTENTS

How this book works

Read all about it first! Start with the introduction and follow the boxes across the pages from left to right and top to bottom. Look at the pictures, too, because sometimes the answers can be found there. Then it is time to tackle the questions . . .

1. Eight questions

The questions are on the far left of each page. In addition to general questions, there are true or false options, and sometimes you have to unscramble letters to find the answer!

2. Follow the numbers!

All of the answers are somewhere on the pages. If you do not know the answer right away, each question has a matching number in an orange or blue circle to help you find the right place to start reading.

3. Find the answer

When you have answered all of the questions, turn to the back of the book to see if you were right!

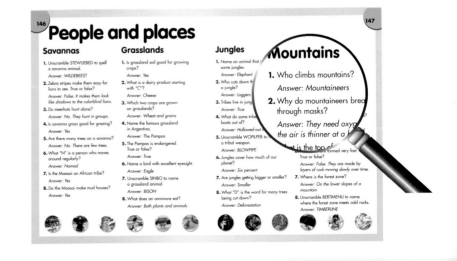

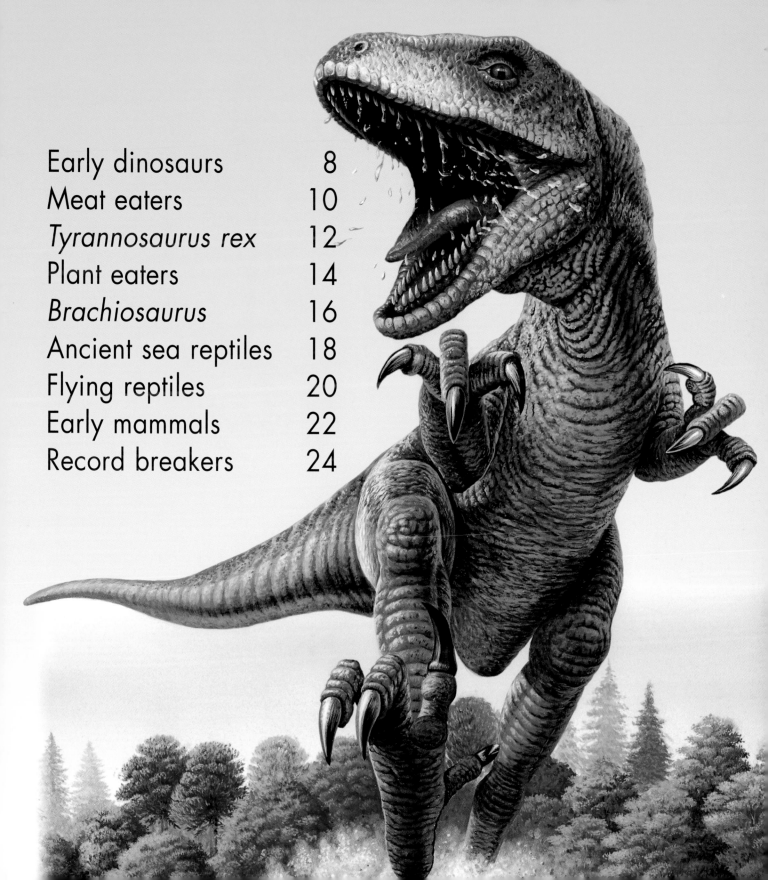

Chapter One

DINOSAURS

Early dinosaurs

The dinosaurs were a group of large reptiles. The first dinosaur lived around 245 million years ago. The last ones died out 65 million years ago.

1. What does *dinosaur* mean?

2. All dinosaurs were small. True or false?

3. How many types of dinosaurs were there?

4. Did dinosaurs lay eggs?

5. Unscramble DOOPRSAU to spell a type of dinosaur.

6. What were meat-eating dinosaurs called?

7. Did crocodiles live at the same time as dinosaurs?

8. How did a *Coelophysis* move?

Terrible name   1 2 3

The word *dinosaur* means "terrible lizard." There were probably around 10,000 types of dinosaurs. Many of them were much larger than any reptiles alive today.

Ancient life 4 5 6 7

Dinosaurs laid eggs and had scaly skin. There were two main types of dinosaurs. Theropods were meat eaters and had clawed feet. Sauropods were giant plant eaters. Other reptiles, such as crocodiles and lizards, lived at the same time.

pterosaur (flying reptile)

sauropod

theropod

crocodile

lizard

Coelophysis

Two feet 8

One of the earliest hunting dinosaurs was *Coelophysis*. It ran on its back legs and snapped up small reptiles in its long jaws.

long jaw

Meat eaters

Dinosaurs are among the largest and fiercest hunters that have ever lived. Some of them would have towered over elephants and giraffes!

1. Where did *Allosaurus* live?

2. What did *Allosaurus* use to kill prey?

3. When did *Albertosaurus* live?

4. How did *Albertosaurus* kill its victims?

5. *Deinonychus* moved slowly. True or false?

6. Did *Deinonychus* ever hunt in groups?

7. What does "*Deinonychus*" mean?

8. Unscramble the word WALC.

Dagger teeth　　　1　2

Allosaurus was a huge hunter that lived in North America around 150 million years ago. It killed prey with its jagged teeth.

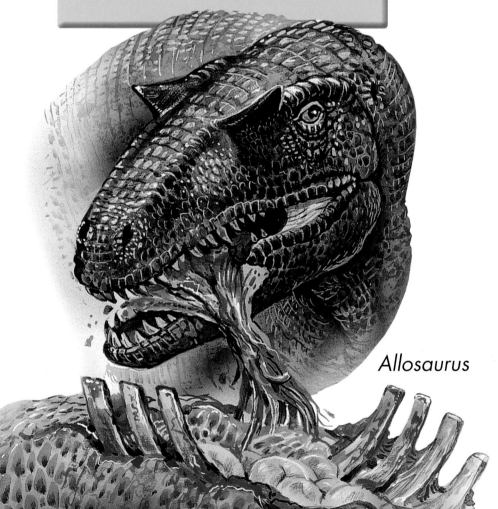

Allosaurus

Neck crusher 3 4

Albertosaurus hunted around 70 million years ago. It chased prey by running on its back legs. It killed its victims with a bite to the back of the neck.

Deinonychus

Albertosaurus

Runner 5 6

Deinonychus was a fast-running hunter from North America. It killed giant plant eaters, possibly working in groups like wolves do today.

Hooked claws 7 8

The name *Deinonychus* means "terrible claw." The hunter's largest claw was on its second toe and was used to slash prey.

Tyrannosaurus rex

The most famous dinosaur of all, *Tyrannosaurus rex*, was as tall as a house and had teeth that were as long as your feet! It was a very skilled hunter.

1. *Tyrannosaurus rex* ate dead bodies. True or false?

2. How did *T. rex* find dead bodies?

3. Did *T. rex* stand on four legs?

4. Was *T. rex* fast?

5. Unscramble GGEDAJ ETEHT to name something used by *T. rex* when hunting.

6. What does "*Tyrannosaurus rex*" mean?

7. When did *T. rex* live?

8. Where have most *T. rex* fossils been found?

Flesh feast   1   2

Tyrannosaurus rex (*T. rex*) scavenged for food, sniffing out the bodies of animals that had died naturally and then eating them!

Weapons 3 4 5

T. rex stood on two legs. It could not run very fast and attacked prey by surprise. It used its long, jagged teeth and the claws on its feet to rip flesh off a dead body. Its tiny arms were not used in hunting.

Lizard king 6 7 8

The name *Tyrannosaurus rex* means "king of the tyrant lizards"—a tyrant is a cruel ruler. *T. rex* lived around 70 million years ago. Its teeth were the size of bananas! Most *T. rex* fossils have been found in North America.

Plant eaters

The largest types of dinosaurs ate plants. They chewed leaves and branches, and they swallowed stones in order to grind up the food inside their stomachs!

1. *Apatosaurus* was bigger than a blue whale. True or false?

2. What is another name for *Apatosaurus*?

3. Unscramble SUROTUESGAS.

4. What were the plates on a *Stegosaurus* used for?

5. What was on a *Stegosaurus*'s tail?

6. What does "*Triceratops*" mean?

7. What were the horns of a *Triceratops* used for?

8. What protected a *Triceratops*'s neck?

Monster leaf eater ① ②

Apatosaurus was one of the largest-ever dinosaurs. It was almost as large as today's blue whale. *Apatosaurus* is also known as *Brontosaurus*.

Apatosaurus

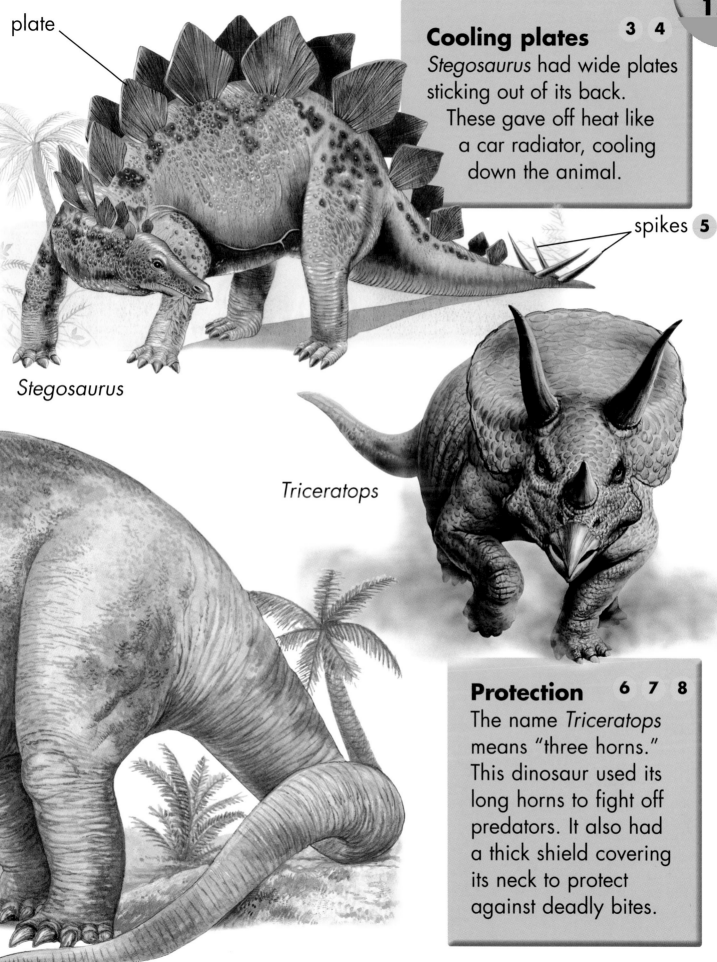

plate

Cooling plates 3 4
Stegosaurus had wide plates sticking out of its back. These gave off heat like a car radiator, cooling down the animal.

spikes 5

Stegosaurus

Triceratops

Protection 6 7 8
The name *Triceratops* means "three horns." This dinosaur used its long horns to fight off predators. It also had a thick shield covering its neck to protect against deadly bites.

Brachiosaurus

Brachiosaurus lived around 140 million years ago. Like a giraffe, it had long legs and a long neck for reaching leaves high up in the trees.

1. Unscramble ELAESV to spell food eaten by a *Brachiosaurus*.

2. What made a *Brachiosaurus*'s teeth blunt?

3. Where were a *Brachiosaurus*'s nostrils?

4. Nostrils may have helped a *Brachiosaurus* smell. True or false?

5. What else may the nostrils have been used for?

6. How heavy was a *Brachiosaurus*?

7. Which is taller, a *Brachiosaurus* or a telephone pole?

8. How long was a *Brachiosaurus*?

Crushing jaw 1 2

Brachiosaurus was a plant eater with many teeth, which it used to crush leaves and woody branches. This tough food often made its teeth blunt (dull).

Head holes [3] [4] [5]

Brachiosaurus had nostrils on a ridge along the top of its head. These might have given the dinosaur a powerful sense of smell, or they could have been used to make loud calls.

nostril

Size me up [6] [7]

Brachiosaurus weighed 77 tons—the same as ten double-decker buses! It was a very long dinosaur, and it was taller than a telephone pole.

teeth

8

72 feet long

Ancient sea reptiles

While dinosaurs ruled the land, other types of reptiles ruled the oceans. Most of these sea creatures are now extinct. Only turtles have survived.

1. When did *Archelon* live?

2. What did *Archelon* eat?

3. How long was *Archelon*?

4. Which sea reptile looked like a dolphin?

5. Plesiosaurs had long necks. True or false?

6. What did *Placodus* eat?

7. What did *Globidens* crush?

8. Unscramble SAUROTHON to spell an ocean reptile with sharp teeth.

Giant shell 1 2 3

Archelon was an early turtle that lived 220 million years ago. It was as long as a car and ate shellfish.

Archelon

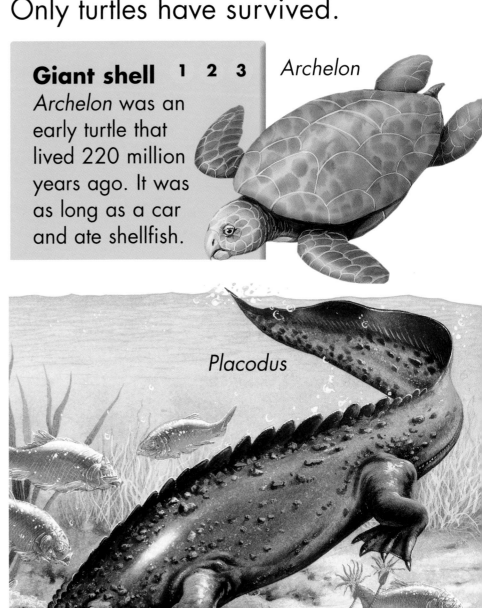

Placodus

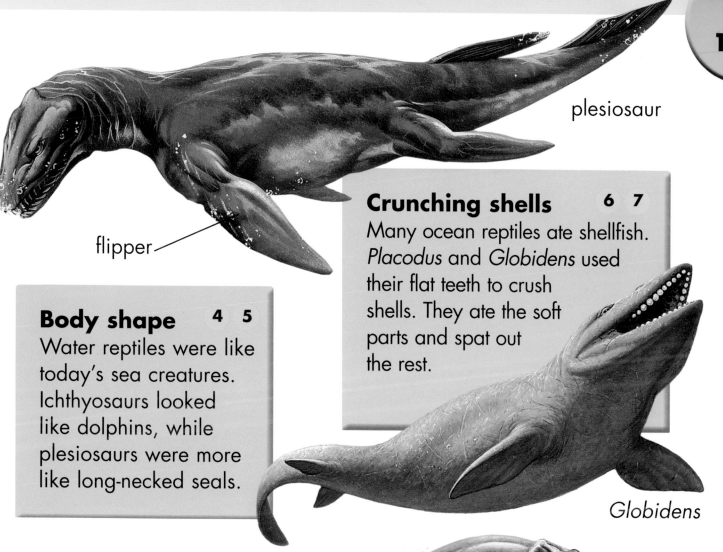

plesiosaur

flipper

Crunching shells   6 7

Many ocean reptiles ate shellfish. *Placodus* and *Globidens* used their flat teeth to crush shells. They ate the soft parts and spat out the rest.

Body shape   4 5

Water reptiles were like today's sea creatures. Ichthyosaurs looked like dolphins, while plesiosaurs were more like long-necked seals.

Globidens

8 nothosaur

ichthyosaur

Flying reptiles

Pterosaurs were relatives of the dinosaurs. Although they looked similar to birds, pterosaurs had no feathers and were not early types of birds.

1. What does *pterosaur* mean?

2. Was a pterosaur's wing made of skin?

3. A pterosaur's wing contained a long finger. True or false?

4. Were pterosaurs very good at flying?

5. How did cliff-living pterosaurs catch their food?

6. Was *Dimorphodon* a fast runner?

7. Unscramble TCSNIE to spell a food eaten by *Dimorphodon*.

8. Was the largest flying animal a pterosaur?

Finger wing 1 2 3
The word *pterosaur* means "winged lizard." The wing was made of skin that stretched out behind a superlong finger.

Pteranodon

Dimorphodon

Cliff jumpers   4 5

Pterosaurs were not great fliers. They found it difficult to get up into the air. Some jumped off sea cliffs to do so. They swooped over the water, scooping up fish. Then they rode warm, rising air before gliding back to their perches.

Little snapper   6 7

Dimorphodon could fly, but it was also a fast runner. It snapped up flying insects with its large jaws, and it also caught small animals on the ground.

Largest ever!   8

Many pterosaurs were the size of sparrows, but the largest pterosaur was the biggest animal ever to fly. Each wing was as long as a soccer goal.

Early mammals

Mammals are not related to dinosaurs. Instead, they come from an even older type of reptile. The first mammals lived around 100 million years ago.

1. Unscramble SPARUMILAS.

2. Where do marsupial babies stay after birth?

3. Where do most marsupials live today?

4. Mammals lived at the same time as dinosaurs. True or false?

5. What happened when dinosaurs became extinct?

6. Did mammals eat dinosaur eggs?

7. Dinosaurs had hair. True or false?

8. Does a mammal's hair keep it warm?

Pocket baby   1 2 3

Many early mammals were marsupials. Marsupials give birth to tiny babies, which then continue to grow inside a pouch on their mother's belly. Today marsupials are rare. Most of them live in Australia.

baby in pouch

tyrannosaur

Survivors 4 5

Small mammals lived alongside dinosaurs. They were often preyed on by dinosaurs. When dinosaurs died out, mammals took over.

Egg feasts 6

Dinosaur eggs were full of protein and nutrients, so they were good food. Some early mammals may have been big enough to break into the eggs to eat them!

Hairy coats 7 8

Unlike dinosaurs, mammals have hair on their bodies. The hair keeps the animals warm. Mammals can survive in much colder weather than dinosaurs.

DINOSAURS
Record breakers

1. Dinosaurs became extinct after a six-mile-wide meteor hit Mexico 65 million years ago.

2. The first dinosaur fossil was identified in 1841.

3. When dinosaurs roamed Earth, the continents were connected in a huge area of land called Pangaea.

4. The largest meat-eating dinosaur was *Spinosaurus*. It was almost 70 feet long.

5. The biggest dinosaur ever discovered was *Amphicoelias*. It weighed 122 tons.

6. Biologists know that not all dinosaurs died out. Some evolved into the birds that we see today.

7. The most ancient types of reptiles are turtles and tortoises. They evolved 280 million years ago.

8. The smallest dinosaurs were around the size of chickens.

9. The largest-ever dinosaur bone found was five feet long and weighed one ton.

10. The most intelligent dinosaur was *Troodon*. It had the largest brain compared to its body size.

Chapter Two
LAND ANIMALS

Elephants

The African elephant is the biggest land animal. Asian elephants are slightly smaller. Elephants are endangered. They are hunted for their tusks.

1. What is a group of elephants called?

2. Are male elephants in charge of a herd?

3. What is an elephant's tusk made of?

4. Can you train an elephant to work?

5. Unscramble NALABINH to spell a famous general's name.

6. Do elephants eat leaves and grasses?

7. Elephants eat for 16 hours each day. True or false?

8. Are plants a high-energy food?

Hannibal's army

ivory tusk **3**

All in the family **1** **2**

Elephants live in big groups called herds. Female elephants are in charge of life in an elephant family. Elephant babies drink their mother's milk.

At war **4** **5**

Young elephants are smart and easy to train. They have worked with people for thousands of years. In 218 B.C., Hannibal, a great general, took some elephants across the snowy Alps to fight the Romans.

Hungry **6** **7** **8**

An elephant reaches up into a tree to pull down leaves. Elephants eat grasses, too. Plants are not a high-energy food, so elephants must eat a lot of them. They eat for 16 hours each day.

Lions

The lion is a powerful type of cat. Almost all lions live in Africa on grassland called the savanna. Lions hunt large animals such as zebras. They kill with a bite to the neck.

1. What is the thick hair on a lion's neck called?

2. Male and female lions are the same size. True or false?

3. What is a group of lions called?

4. Who rules a group of lions?

5. What are baby lions called?

6. Which member of a pride always eats first?

7. Unscramble SENOSIL to figure out who raises a baby lion.

8. What does a male lion do if he meets another male lion?

King of the beasts ①②
A male lion has a thick mane of hair on his neck. Male lions are larger, heavier, and stronger than female lions.

Family 3 4 5 6

Lions live in groups called prides. Prides are ruled by a single male. The other members are lionesses (females) and cubs (baby lions). Lionesses do the hunting, but the male gets to eat first!

Keeping control 7 8

Lionesses work together to raise their cubs. The male doesn't help much. Instead, he spends his time fighting off rival males that come to take over the pride.

rival male

Tigers

1. Why do tigers have stripes?

2. Do tigers make much noise when they walk?

3. Unscramble RIGESTS to give the word for a female tiger.

4. How long does a tiger cub stay with its mother?

5. Tigers live in large groups. True or false?

6. How do tigers keep their claws sharp?

7. How does a tiger get close to its prey?

8. How do tigers kill their prey?

The tiger is the world's largest cat. It lives in the jungles of Asia. Tigers hunt deer and other wild animals such as boar. They attack people only if they cannot find anything else to eat.

Surprise attack   1   2

Tigers are best known for their stripes. Dark stripes on orange fur help a tiger stay hidden among the shadows. A tiger can walk almost silently on its soft, wide feet.

Growing up (3)(4)

A tigress (female tiger) gives birth to around six cubs every three years. Only one or two of the cubs will survive. They live with their mother for two years and learn how to hunt.

Living alone (5)(6)

Tigers live alone. They scratch long marks into tree trunks. This keeps their claws razor sharp, and the scratches also warn other tigers to stay away.

In for the kill (7)(8)

A tiger hides in the undergrowth and creeps up on its prey. It then charges out of its hiding place and runs into the victim, knocking it over. The tiger breaks the prey's neck swiftly with its mighty jaws.

stalking   charging   the catch

Wolves

The wolf is the largest wild dog in the world. It is the ancestor of all breeds of pet dogs. Wolves live in groups called packs. Most live in the forests of Canada and Siberia (Russia).

1. Which small animal might a wolf catch?

2. When do wolves hunt as a team?

3. Unscramble NURNGIN to name something wolves are very good at.

4. How far can a wolf run in one day?

5. A group of wolves is called a flock. True or false?

6. How many pack members have cubs each year?

7. Why do wolves howl?

8. How far away can you hear a wolf howling?

Hunting team ① ②
During the summer, wolves hunt by themselves for hares, which are similar to rabbits, and other small animals. During the winter, wolf packs work as a team to kill bigger animals such as deer.

Star runner 3 4

A wolf's body is built to run long distances. A wolf has big lungs and a strong heart, so it does not get tired quickly. A wolf can run 125 miles in one day.

Pair up 5 6

A wolf pack is organized according to strict rules. Only one male and one female in the pack have cubs, but the other wolves in the pack help care for the young.

Midnight howler 7 8

People once thought that wolves howled at the moon. In fact, howling tells other wolves where they are and warns them to stay away! A howl can be heard up to ten miles away.

Flightless birds

Not all birds can fly. In fact, the world's largest birds are too heavy to leave the ground. Their wings are very small, and they have long legs that are used for running fast.

1. Cassowaries live in deserts. True or false?

2. Unscramble SQAECU to name the bone on a cassowary's head.

3. What is a cassowary's casque used for?

4. What is the largest bird in the world?

5. Where do ostrich live?

6. How does an ostrich escape from danger?

7. How did the emu get its name?

8. How does an emu find fresh food?

Bone head   1 2 3

The cassowary lives in the forests of New Guinea in Asia. It has a bone spike on its head called a casque. The bird pushes branches out of the way with its casque.

casque

cassowary

Giant runner 4 5 6

The ostrich is the world's largest bird—it can grow to nine feet tall. Ostrich live in Africa. They stay out of danger by running away. Ostrich can reach speeds of 43 miles per hour.

emu

ostrich

Rain bird 7 8

The largest bird in Australia is the emu. It gets its name from the call it makes. Emus eat shoots and flowers that sprout after it rains. The birds follow rain clouds to find fresh food.

Bears

Bears are the world's biggest land predators. A predator is an animal that hunts other animals for food. Most bears live in the forests of North America and Asia.

1. How do bears climb trees?

2. How long are the claws of a brown bear?

3. Unscramble EVEEBIH to find the place where bears get honey.

4. Bears never eat fish. True or false?

5. Where do bears often gather to catch fish?

6. Bears can catch fish with their teeth. True or false?

7. Do bears like to eat nuts and berries?

8. How do bears eat honey?

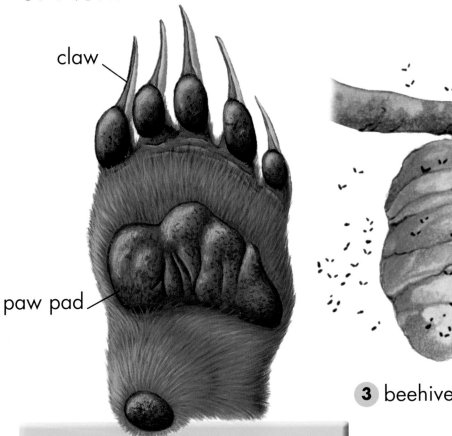

claw

paw pad

3 beehive

Slash and grab   1 2

Bears have long claws for slashing prey, digging dens, and gripping bark when climbing trees. Brown bears have the biggest claws. They are four inches long.

Catching fish 4 5 6

Bears like to catch salmon and trout from rivers. The bears gather around waterfalls where these fish are easy to find. They knock the prey out of the water with their huge paws or catch them with their sharp teeth.

Yummy! 7 8

Bears also like to eat nuts and berries. They love honey, too. Small bears climb trees and rip open beehives. They lick the honey out with their tongues, and they even eat the bees!

Pandas

1. Why do pandas have white faces with black eyes and ears?

2. Unscramble OBAMOB to find the plant that pandas eat.

3. Where do pandas sleep?

4. What sticks out of a panda's wrist?

5. How long does it take for a panda cub to grow up?

6. Which country do pandas live in?

7. How many pandas live in the wild?

8. Do pandas live on mountains?

The giant panda is a type of bear. It eats bamboo, which doesn't provide much energy. Pandas must eat a lot in order to stay alive. They can sleep for only four hours before waking up hungry again!

Black eyes 1
Pandas are known for their black-and-white fur. The black eyes and ears make it easier for them to see one another in a forest.

bamboo 2

Living in a forest 3 4 5

Pandas do not have dens—they sleep out in the open. They hold bamboo using a sixth "finger," which sticks out from each wrist. Pandas have cubs every two years. A cub takes around four years to grow up.

Wild ones 6 7 8

Pandas are very rare. They live only in China, where around 1,000 wild pandas live in small patches of bamboo forests on mountainsides.

Polar bears

The polar bear is the world's largest bear. Males are as large as family-size cars. For most of the year, polar bears hunt for food in the frozen seas that surround the North Pole.

1. Is a polar bear's fur white?

2. Why do polar bears have a layer of fat under their skin?

3. Unscramble END to name the place where cubs are born.

4. How long do cubs stay in a den?

5. What does a polar-bear mother eat when she is in a den with her cubs?

6. What do polar bears hunt?

7. Where do polar bears wait for their prey?

8. Polar bears catch seals with fishing rods. True or false?

Life on ice 1 2

A polar bear's fur looks white, but the hairs are actually see-through. Each bear has a layer of fat under its skin so that it can survive if it cannot find food.

Snow mother 3 4 5
Polar bears give birth during the winter inside a den under the snow. The cubs stay there for three months, living on their mother's milk. The mother will not eat at all until she and the cubs leave in the spring.

large paw

Fierce hunter 6 7 8
Polar bears hunt seals by lying in wait for them beside holes in the ice. Then the bears kill them with a blow of the paw.

Jungle animals

Many interesting and different animals live in jungles. Jungles grow where it is very hot and wet all year round. That is why jungles are also called rainforests.

1. Why are jungles being cut down?

2. Why are some jungle animals rare?

3. Unscramble VAJNA to spell the name of a rare rhino.

4. How many horns does a Javan rhino have?

5. How do toucans crack nuts?

6. How long is a quetzal's tail?

7. What would happen if someone touched a red frog?

8. Where does an ocelot hunt?

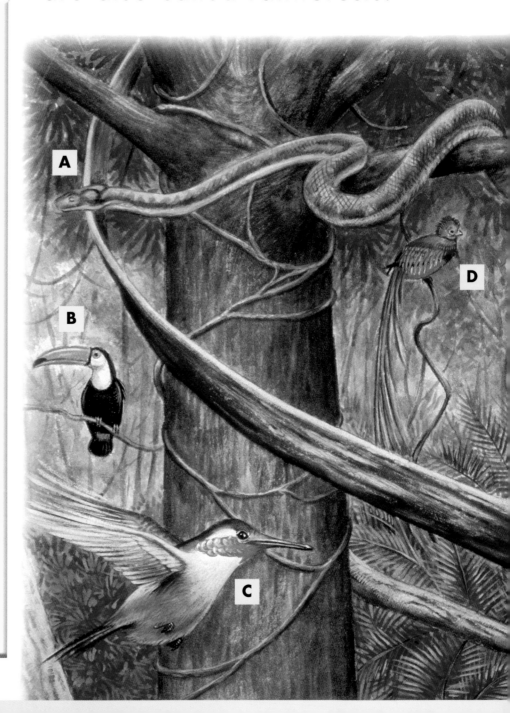

A

B

C

D

Rare creatures 1 2 3 4

Large areas of jungles are being cut down to make room for farms. Jungle animals are now rare because they have few places to live. One of the rarest of all is the Javan rhino (left). Unlike most other rhinos, this type has only one horn.

Amazon 5 6 7 8

These animals live in South America's Amazon rainforest:

A Tree snake

B Toucan. It cracks nuts with its big beak.

C Hummingbird

D Quetzal. Its tail is four times longer than the rest of its body.

E Howler monkey

F Sloth. It hangs upside down.

G Vampire bat

H Red frog. Its skin is poisonous.

I Ocelot. It hunts in the undergrowth.

Apes and monkeys

People often get confused between monkeys and apes, but they are different in many ways. Monkeys are small and have tails, while apes are big and don't have tails.

1. Where could you find a wild gorilla?

2. Which ape lives in Southeast Asia?

3. What is the most common type of ape in the world?

4. When do howler monkeys call?

5. How far away can a howler monkey's call be heard?

6. Where is a howler monkey's voice box?

7. Unscramble DRIMLALN to spell the name of the largest monkey.

8. Where do mandrills live?

Rare relatives   1 2 3

Apes include the gorillas and chimpanzees of Africa and the orangutans of Southeast Asia. All of these animals are very rare. The only common ape is the human— you and me!

orangutan

Wake up! 4 5 6

Howler monkeys bellow loudly in the morning. The calls can be heard almost two miles away. Their calls are so loud because of the large voice box in their bulging throats.

Funny face 7 8

The mandrill is the biggest monkey in the world. It lives deep in the jungles of Africa. Male mandrills have colorful faces and sharp fangs to frighten off their enemies.

Bugs and beetles

There are 500,000 types of bugs and beetles! Bugs suck their food, while beetles bite theirs. Ladybugs and weevils are common beetles, while cicadas and pond skaters are types of bugs. Bugs are types of insects.

1. What do bugs have instead of bones?

2. How do bugs breathe?

3. A water bug has hairy legs to stay warm. True or false?

4. How do water bugs catch fish?

5. What do stag beetles use their pincers for?

6. Unscramble NATENANE to give another word for insect feelers.

7. How many legs does a bug have?

8. Where do beetles keep their wings?

Outer skin 1 2

A bug does not have bones. Instead, it has a hard skin that gives the body its shape. The bug breathes air through holes in its skin.

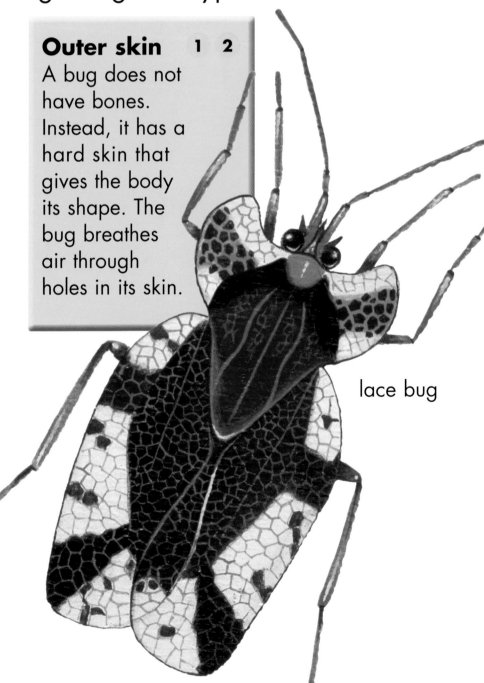

lace bug

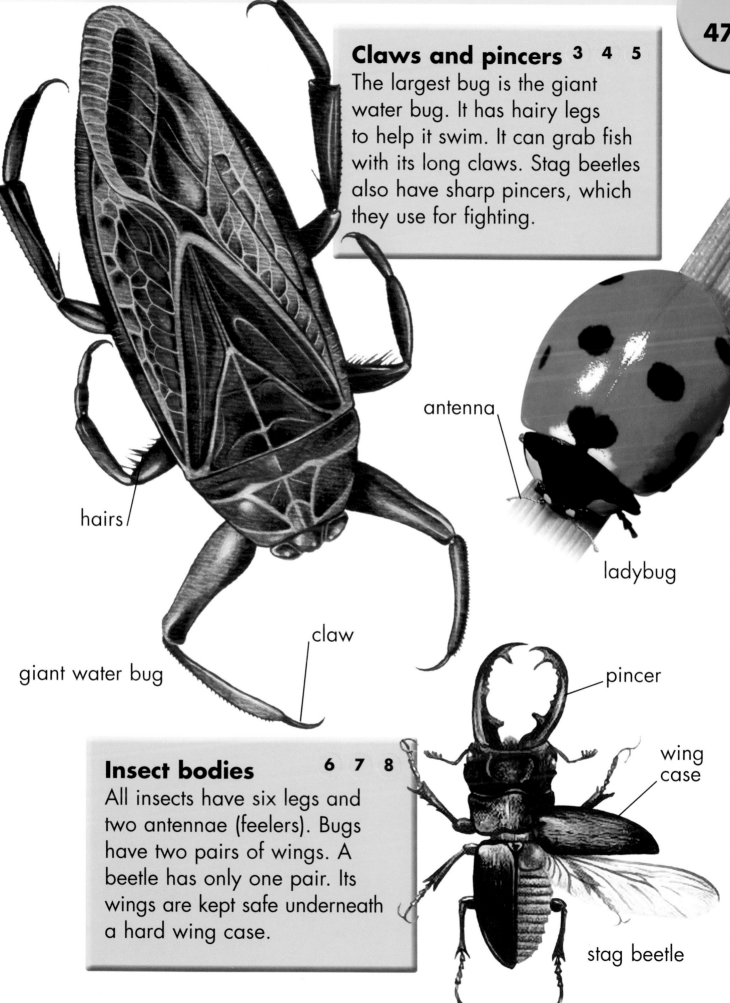

Claws and pincers 3 4 5

The largest bug is the giant water bug. It has hairy legs to help it swim. It can grab fish with its long claws. Stag beetles also have sharp pincers, which they use for fighting.

antenna

ladybug

hairs

claw

giant water bug

pincer

wing case

Insect bodies 6 7 8

All insects have six legs and two antennae (feelers). Bugs have two pairs of wings. A beetle has only one pair. Its wings are kept safe underneath a hard wing case.

stag beetle

Ants

Thousands of ants live together inside nests. Each nest has one queen ant, and only she can lay eggs. Most of the eggs hatch into female ants, which spend their lives working for the queen.

1. Where do weaver ants live?

2. Baby ants are called larvae. True or false?

3. What do larvae make to glue leaves together?

4. Which ants defend a nest?

5. Soldier ants are armed with sharp jaws and what other weapons?

6. Where might you find an ant's nest?

7. Which types of ants gather food?

8. Unscramble UPAPE to find the name for ant cocoons.

Leaf nests

1 2 3

Weaver ants build a nest of leaves for the queen and her young. The ants hold the leaves together and grip larvae (baby ants) in their jaws. The larvae make sticky silk that glues the leaves together.

adult ant holds larva

Defense force 4 5

Most nests have a force of fierce soldier ants to keep the queen safe. They have sharp jaws for biting and stingers in their tails.

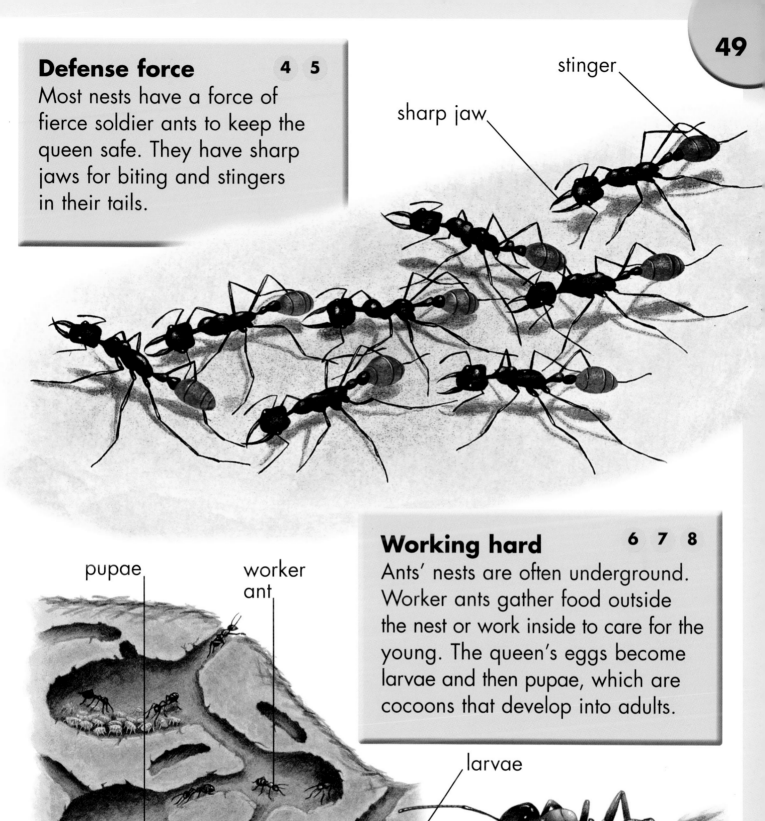

stinger

sharp jaw

pupae

worker ant

Working hard 6 7 8

Ants' nests are often underground. Worker ants gather food outside the nest or work inside to care for the young. The queen's eggs become larvae and then pupae, which are cocoons that develop into adults.

larvae

Butterflies and moths

Large and colorful, butterflies are very delicate insects. They are seen most often during the summer, fluttering around flowers in parks and gardens.

1. What hatches from a butterfly egg?

2. What do caterpillars eat?

3. What is the name of the silk bag that a caterpillar spins?

4. Unscramble CRAMNOH to spell the name of a common butterfly.

5. Moths fly at night. True or false?

6. Which are more colorful, moths or butterflies?

7. How many wings do butterflies have?

8. What is the mouthpart of a butterfly called?

Stages of life 1 2 3

A butterfly egg hatches into a caterpillar. It eats leaves and fruit and then spins a silk bag (cocoon) around itself. Once inside, the caterpillar grows wings and changes into a butterfly. The butterfly emerges from the cocoon.

caterpillar

monarch 4

red admiral

Colorful wings 5 6

Moths are similar to butterflies, but they fly at night instead. They are dull in color so that they can hide in the dark. Butterflies come out during the day, so their wings are brightly patterned to match the flowers.

Camberwell beauty

eggs

peacock

Flying insects 7 8

Butterflies have four wings (two pairs). Each front wing is hooked to a back wing so that they work like a single big wing. Butterflies eat only liquids. They suck their food through a long, tube-shaped mouthpart called a proboscis.

Farm animals

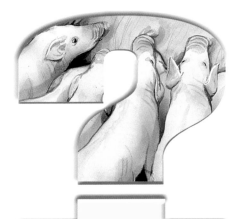

The animals on farms provide us with milk, eggs, and, of course, meat. These animals produce other things, too. Their skins become leather and their fat is used in lotions and skin creams.

1. Roosters lay eggs. True or false?

2. What is a female chicken called?

3. Where does wool come from?

4. Which breed of cattle is best for producing milk?

5. Unscramble FROHEERD to spell the name of a cattle breed.

6. What is special about Highland cattle?

7. Ham, pork, and what other meat comes from a pig?

8. What is a female pig called?

hen   rooster

Chickens 1 2
Eggs are laid by female chickens, or hens. A male chicken is called a rooster. Roosters are larger than hens and have more colorful feathers.

sheep

53

sheep

Curls and chops 3

Sheep are raised for their meat, called lamb or mutton, and their coats. Their curly hair is used to make wool.

Jersey

Breeds 4 5 6

Each breed, or type, of cattle is raised for a special reason. Jersey cows produce creamy milk, and Herefords are raised for their meat. Highland cattle have long, thick hair to keep them warm during the winter.

Hereford

Highland

New life 7 8

Pigs are raised for their meat, which is sold as bacon, pork, and ham. Every year, sows (female pigs) give birth to several piglets. They are killed for their meat at six months old.

Dogs

Dogs make good pets because they are friendly, loyal, and soon become part of the family. All types of dogs are relatives of wolves.

1. What does *carnivore* mean?

2. What does a dog use its teeth for?

3. Dogs have no sense of smell. True or false?

4. How many puppies can a female dog produce?

5. How long does it take puppies to become adults?

6. When did dogs start to live with people?

7. What is a mongrel?

8. Unscramble GOBDULL to spell a breed of dog.

Meat eaters 1 2 3
Like their wild relatives, dogs are carnivores (meat eaters). They have strong jaws and sharp teeth for chewing. Dogs often have long noses and a very good sense of smell.

Shetland sheepdog

Puppies 4 5
Female dogs might give birth to as many as 12 puppies in a single litter. It takes two or three years for a puppy to grow to full size.

Breeds 6 7
Dogs have lived with people for 15,000 years. Since then, people have bred them into different types, or breeds. Each breed is suited to certain jobs—Border collies are good sheepdogs. A dog that is a mixture of breeds is called a mongrel.

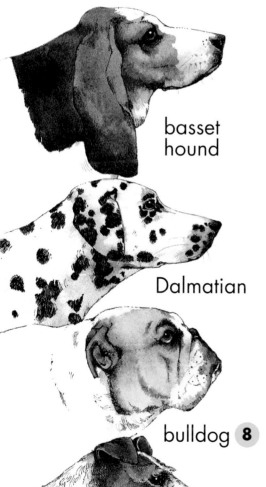

basset hound

Dalmatian

bulldog 8

fox terrier

Border collie

Cats

1. Cats hunt for birds. True or false?

2. Where are a cat's claws stored?

3. How does a mother cat clean her kittens?

4. What does a happy cat do?

5. Which wild animals are pet cats closely related to?

6. Some cats are black and white. True or false?

7. What are cats with spots and blotches called?

8. Unscramble SNAPIER to spell the name of a cat breed.

A few thousand years ago, people welcomed cats into their homes to catch mice and rats. The cats never left, and they are now much-loved pets—but they still enjoy hunting!

Little hunter   1 2

Just like a lion or a tiger, a pet cat is an expert hunter. It stalks birds and mice before pouncing on them. A cat has a claw on each toe. The claws are stored inside sheaths to keep them sharp.

Bengal

tabby

Bundles of fur 3 4

Cats give birth to up to five babies, or kittens. After birth, the mother licks the kittens clean and then feeds them milk. Kittens like to play with balls and soft toys. These games help kittens learn how to hunt. Cats purr when they are happy.

Breeds 5 6 7

Pet cats are close relatives of African wildcats, but they look very different. Pet cats come in many types, or breeds. They have either long or short hair. Most pet cats are white, black, red, or gray. Cats with spots and blotches are called tabbies.

longhair

8 Persian

LAND ANIMALS
Record breakers

1. The heaviest land animal is the African elephant.
It weighs up to six tons.

2. The tallest animal in the world is the giraffe.
Males are around 18 feet tall.

3. Scientists think that there are ten billion billion
individual insects alive at any one time.

4. The largest colony of ants is in southern Europe.
It spreads into three countries and is home
to seven billion ants.

5. The fastest land animal is the cheetah.
It can run up to 43 miles per hour.

6. The smallest reptile of all is the Jaragua sphaero
(dwarf gecko), a type of lizard. It is less than
one inch long.

7. The longest-living land animals are giant tortoises.
They can live for 200 years.

8. The rarest mammal in the world is a ground
squirrel that lives in Canada. There are only 29 left!

9. The largest hunter on land is the polar bear.

10. The smallest breed of horse is the Falabella pony.
It is only 31 inches tall!

Chapter Three
SEA CREATURES

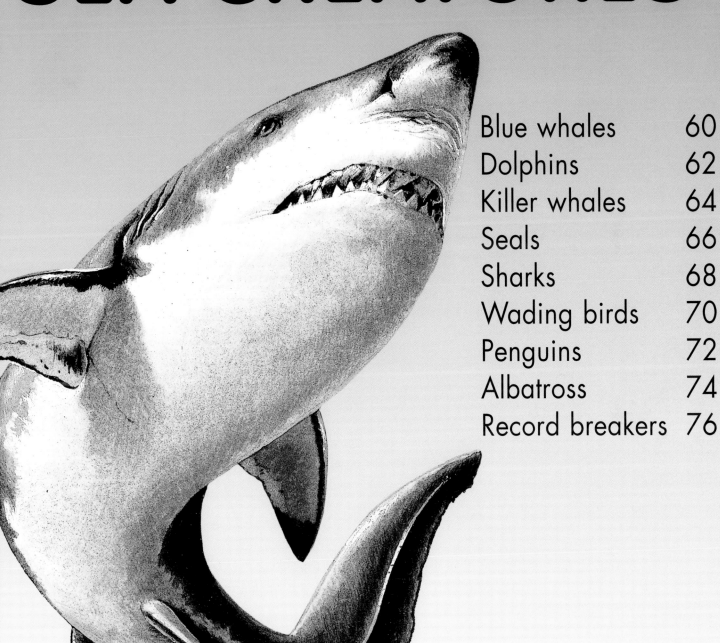

Blue whales

The blue whale is the biggest animal that has ever lived on Earth. Its eyes are the size of grapefruit, and its huge mouth could swallow a minibus!

1. Blue whales are a type of fish. True or false?

2. What is the flat part of a whale's tail called?

3. What is a blue whale as long as?

4. How much can a blue whale eat in one day?

5. What does a blue whale eat?

6. Unscramble LENABE TALSEP to name the bristles in a blue whale's mouth.

7. What is a baby whale called?

8. Name the word for a whale's nostril.

fluke

Fishy tail 1 2
Blue whales live in oceans, but they are not fish. They need to breathe air just like we do. Instead of legs, blue whales have two long flippers and a tail with two flat flukes.

Giant of the sea 3 4
A blue whale is as long as a tennis court and weighs twice as much as a train engine. This whale can eat four tons of food in one day.

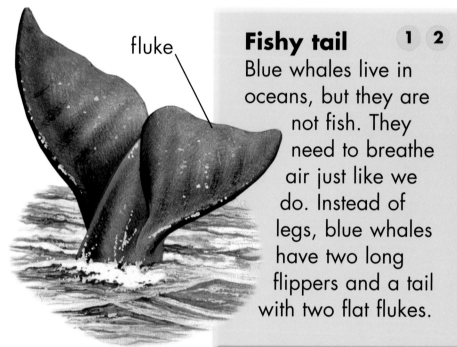

baleen plates

Gulping food ⑤ ⑥

Blue whales eat krill, which are like tiny shrimp. They take a gulp of water and sieve out the krill with bristles inside their mouths. The bristles are called baleen plates.

blowhole

Breeding ⑦ ⑧

A baby whale, or calf, is born underwater. Its mother must push it to the surface so that it can breathe through its huge nostrils, or blowholes.

Dolphins

There are 32 types of dolphins. Most live in groups, or pods, in warm parts of the world, far out at sea. However, a few types of dolphins live in rivers.

1. Where is a dolphin's "melon"?

2. A dolphin's melon contains oil. True or false?

3. What does a dolphin use its melon for?

4. What is another name for a dolphin's snout?

5. What do dolphins have instead of legs?

6. Unscramble SOLRAD INF to give the name of part of a dolphin.

7. Dolphins breathe air. True or false?

8. Dolphins never catch fish to eat. True or false?

Sound system ① ② ③
Dolphins have an oil-filled lump, known as a melon, inside their rounded heads. The melon helps them pick up sounds underwater.

common dolphin

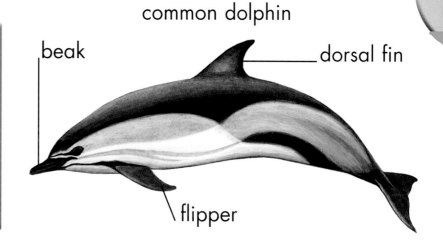

beak

dorsal fin

flipper

Body parts 4 5 6

A dolphin has a long snout, or beak, and flippers instead of legs. A fleshy dorsal fin sticks out of its back.

High jump 7 8

Dolphins often leap up out of the water. They do this to breathe air and possibly show off, too. Dolphins hunt fish in groups.

Killer whales

Orcas, or killer whales, are actually very large and powerful types of dolphins. They live in all of the world's oceans.

1. Do killer whales hunt for other types of whales?

2. What is the name of a group of whales?

3. Whale pods never contain females. True or false?

4. Which type of killer whale has a curved dorsal fin?

5. What shape is the dorsal fin of a male killer whale?

6. What happens if a whale's fin is very tall?

7. How does a whale look around?

8. Unscramble PSY PHPOGIN.

Hungry! ① ② ③

Killer whales hunt for seals, fish, sea birds, and even other whales. Females and young whales live in groups called pods. Adult males usually live alone.

Fin facts 4 5 6

Female killer whales have curved dorsal fins, but adult males have tall, pointed fins. Sometimes the fins are so tall that they flop over to one side.

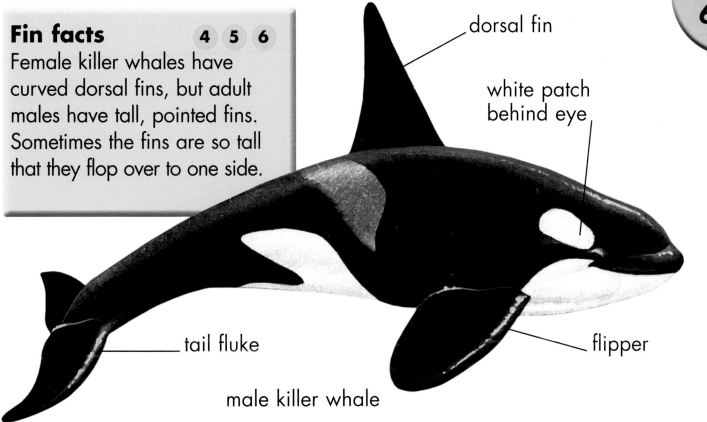

dorsal fin

white patch behind eye

tail fluke

flipper

male killer whale

Look out! 7 8

A killer whale pokes its head out of the water so that it can look around and check where it is. This is called spy hopping.

Seals

With its flippers and rounded body, a seal can only wiggle around on land. In the water, it becomes an expert swimmer.

1. Can baby seals swim?

2. Why is a baby seal's fur white?

3. Name the world's largest type of seal.

4. What is the word for a male seal?

5. Elephant-seal cows are larger than the bulls. True or false?

6. Where do harp seals hunt?

7. Unscramble LESHIFLSH to name something that harp seals eat.

8. What do seals use to sense water currents made by their prey?

Hiding out 1 2

Baby seals cannot swim, and they stay on land or the ice until they grow up. Their warm white fur keeps them hidden in the snow.

Sea elephants ③ ④ ⑤

The largest seal is the elephant seal. Male elephant seals, or bulls, are as big as jeeps. A bull is three times larger than a female seal, or cow.

Water hunter ⑥ ⑦ ⑧

Harp seals hunt under the ice of the Arctic Ocean. They snap up fish and shellfish. The seals' whiskers detect currents in the water made by fish.

Sharks

Sharks are the fiercest fish in the world. Many of them must swim all the time. If they stopped, they would sink to the bottom of the ocean and drown.

1. What do killer sharks have in their mouths?

2. What is the largest killer shark called?

3. What does a remora use to stick itself to a shark?

4. What do pilot fish eat?

5. Can sharks detect electricity?

6. Hammerheads have pointed snouts. True or false?

7. Where do blue sharks live?

8. Unscramble DQISU to spell something eaten by a shark.

Killer fish ① ②

Most sharks are hunters. They are armed with large, pointed teeth. The biggest killer of all is the great white shark. It can grow as long as a bus.

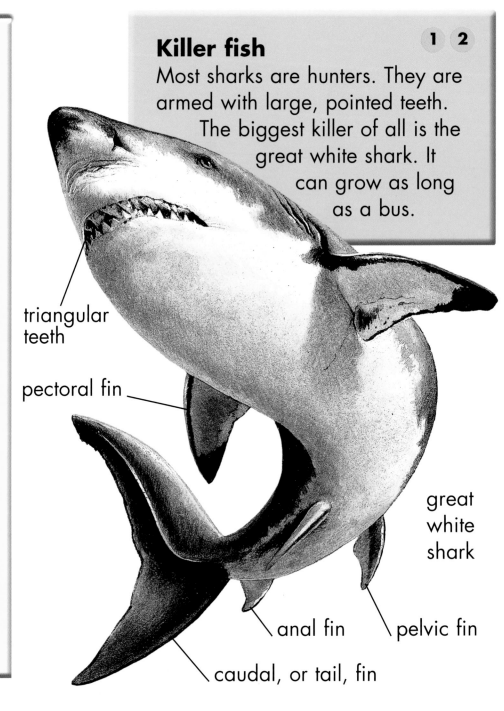

triangular teeth

pectoral fin

great white shark

anal fin

pelvic fin

caudal, or tail, fin

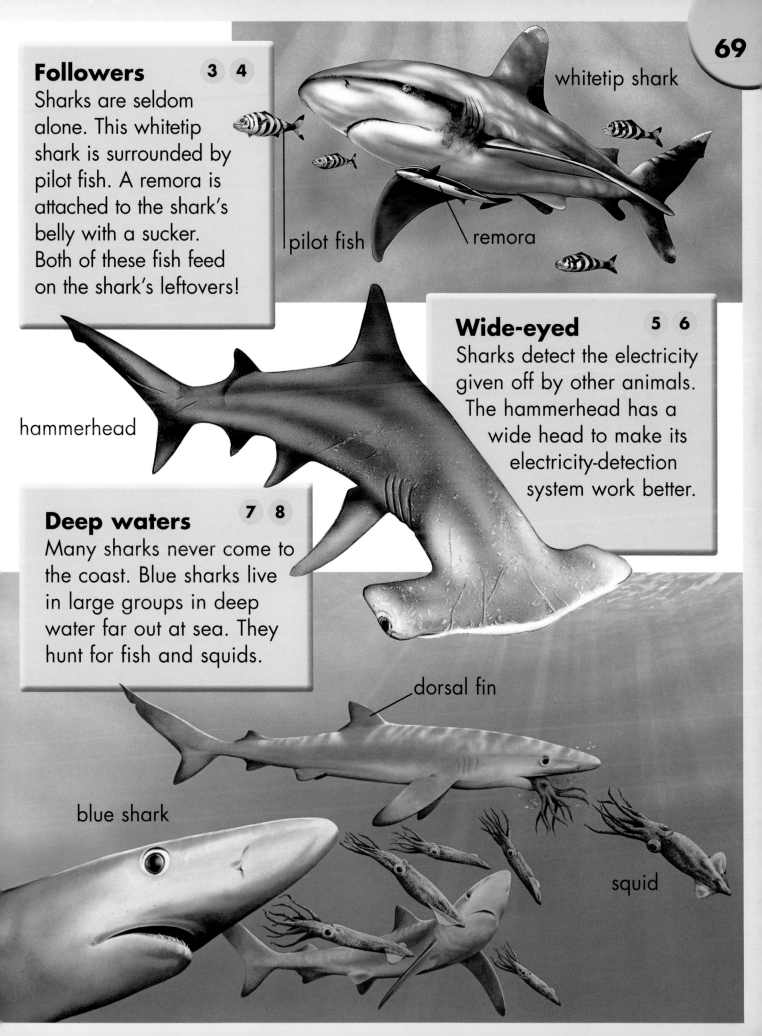

Followers 3 4
Sharks are seldom alone. This whitetip shark is surrounded by pilot fish. A remora is attached to the shark's belly with a sucker. Both of these fish feed on the shark's leftovers!

whitetip shark

pilot fish

remora

Wide-eyed 5 6
Sharks detect the electricity given off by other animals. The hammerhead has a wide head to make its electricity-detection system work better.

hammerhead

Deep waters 7 8
Many sharks never come to the coast. Blue sharks live in large groups in deep water far out at sea. They hunt for fish and squids.

dorsal fin

blue shark

squid

Wading birds

Shallow water is home to creatures such as worms and insects—food for wading birds. These birds catch the food with their long bills, or beaks.

1. What do spoonbills do with their beaks?

2. Where does a turnstone find food?

3. Why are a plover's eggs speckled?

4. An avocet's bill is short and flat. True or false?

5. Where does a heron stand while hunting?

6. Herons hunt for rats. True or false?

7. Unscramble ILBL to spell another word for beak.

8. A heron jumps on prey with its feet. True or false?

Waders ① ② ③ ④

A Spoonbills stir their beaks in the water to attract small fish.
B Redshank
C Turnstones look for insects under pebbles.
D Plovers lay speckled eggs, which are hard to see among the pebbles.
E Black-winged stilt
F Avocets skim the surface of the water with long, curved bills.

Fish hunter ⑤ ⑥ ⑦ ⑧

A heron stands at the edge of the water and waits for a fish to swim by. With lightning speed, the heron lunges forward with its long neck and snatches the fish in its bill.

Penguins

Penguins live near Antarctica, the icy land at the South Pole. These birds cannot fly. Instead, they hunt for food underwater.

1. Unscramble RICATACNAT.

2. Where do emperor penguins keep their eggs?

3. Penguins are fast runners. True or false?

4. Do penguins ever slide over ice?

5. How do penguins swim?

6. How long can a penguin stay underwater?

7. Penguins catch fish and what other creatures to eat?

8. Where do penguins find shellfish?

Hello, chick! 1 2
Emperor penguins spend the winter in Antarctica as they wait for their eggs to hatch. The eggs and chicks are kept warm in a pouch between the legs.

Ice slide ③ ④

Penguins can only waddle on land because their legs are short. They also slide on their bellies across the ice.

Water wings ⑤ ⑥

A penguin is at home in the water. The bird swims by flapping its wings as if it were flying through the water. It can dive underwater for 20 minutes.

Diving for food ⑦ ⑧

Penguins snatch fish and squids from the water and find shellfish on the seabed.

Albatross

The albatross has the longest wings in the world. The distance between its wingtips is 11.5 feet—more than the height of a basketball hoop!

1. How many eggs does an albatross lay?

2. Unscramble SAGRS to spell what albatross' nests are made from.

3. How long do albatross parents care for their chicks?

4. Where does an albatross find food?

5. What is an albatross's main food?

6. How does an albatross catch squids?

7. Why are an albatross's wings so long?

8. How do albatross fly high up in the sky?

Only chick   1 2 3

A female albatross lays a single egg on a nest made from a mound of grass. The mother and father raise the chick for nine months.

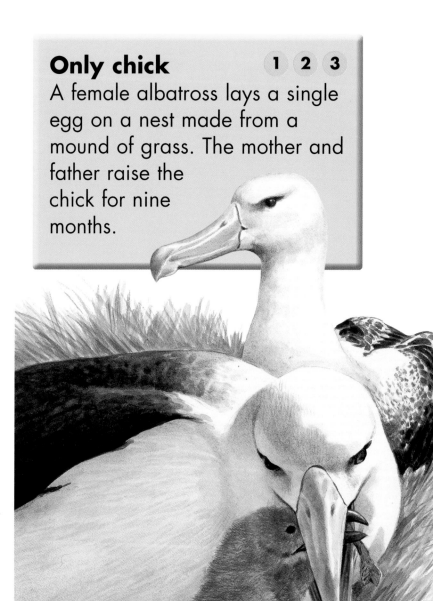

Scooping 4 5 6

The wandering albatross spends weeks far out at sea. It flies over the water, looking for food. Its main prey are squids, which it scoops from the water's surface with its strong, hooked beak.

Glider 7 8

An albatross's long wings are built for gliding. The bird rides warm winds that blow upward. The bird rises as high as possible and then glides along for several days.

SEA CREATURES
Record breakers

1. The largest animal ever to live on Earth is found in the sea. The blue whale can be almost 100 feet long.

2. Most of the animals that live in the oceans are tiny plankton. They are invisible to the naked eye.

3. The fastest animal in the ocean is the sailfish. It can swim at a speed of 68 miles per hour.

4. The world's largest fish is the whale shark, which can grow to 46 feet long.

5. The marine iguana is the only lizard that lives in the ocean.

6. The largest creature without a backbone lives in the ocean. The giant squid is 43 feet long.

7. The yellow-bellied sea snake has the most powerful venom of any snake.

8. The largest shell belongs to the giant clam. The shell is more than three feet tall and can weigh one fourth of a ton.

9. The Great Barrier Reef near Australia is the only living thing that can be seen from outer space.

10. Seahorse fathers, not mothers, give birth to young.

Chapter Four
PEOPLE AND PLACES

Savannas

Grassland with trees that are far apart, not close together like in a forest, is called a savanna. It is found between tropical rainforests and deserts and has both rainy and dry seasons.

1. Unscramble STEWLIEBED to spell a savanna animal.

2. Zebra stripes make them easy for lions to see. True or false?

3. Do meerkats hunt alone?

4. Is savanna grass good for grazing?

5. Are there many trees on a savanna?

6. What "N" is a person who moves around regularly?

7. Is the Maasai an African tribe?

8. Do the Maasai make mud houses?

Savanna survivors 1 2 3

A Wildebeests travel long distances as part of their annual migration.
B Zebra stripes look like shadows to lions, which are colorblind.
C Meerkats take turns looking for predators while other meerkats hunt.

Nomads ⑥ ⑦ ⑧

People who move from place to place, such as the Maasai tribe in Africa, are called nomads. They build homes out of cow dung and mud.

Good grazing ④ ⑤

D Gazelles can sprint at 50 miles per hour.
E Savanna grass is good for grazing.
F There are not many trees on a savanna, so the grass gets a lot of sun.

Grasslands

Also known as prairies, grasslands are large areas of land where grass and only a few trees grow. Around one fifth of Earth is covered by grasslands. They feed 800 million people.

1. Is grassland soil good for growing crops?

2. What is a dairy product starting with "C"?

3. Which two crops are grown on grasslands?

4. Name the famous grassland in Argentina.

5. The Pampas is endangered. True or false?

6. Name a bird with excellent eyesight.

7. Unscramble SINBO to name a grassland animal.

8. What does an omnivore eat?

A big farm ① ② ③

People use the rich, fertile grassland soil for grazing cattle, sheep, and goats to produce meat and dairy products such as milk and cheese. Wheat, grains, and other crops are also grown on grasslands.

Argentinian Pampas ④ ⑤

The Pampas of Argentina has a mild climate and rich soil. Horsemen called gauchos ride over the plain and tend their flocks. The Pampas is now endangered.

A

B

C

D

The grassland menu ⑥ ⑦ ⑧

A Eagles have excellent eyesight, so they can spot prey while flying.
B Bison eat a lot of grass.
C Coyotes are omnivores. They eat both plants and animals.
D Prairie grouse peck at seeds.

Jungles

A thick forest in a very hot, wet climate is called a jungle. Around one half of all of Earth's different types of plants and animals live in jungles.

1. Name an animal that works in some jungles.

2. Who cuts down trees in a jungle?

3. Tribes live in jungles. True or false?

4. What do some tribes make boats out of?

5. Unscramble WOPILPEB to name a tribal weapon.

6. Jungles cover how much of our planet?

7. Are jungles getting bigger or smaller?

8. What "D" is the word for many trees being cut down?

Logging
Vehicles can't get through dense jungles, but elephants can. This one is pulling a tree trunk cut down by loggers, who will sell the wood for money.

Tribes ③ ④ ⑤

Many tribes still live in jungles, although their numbers are falling. Some of them travel on boats made of hollowed-out trees and hunt using blowpipes or bows and arrows.

Shrinking jungles ⑥ ⑦ ⑧

Jungles cover around six percent of our planet, but 50 years ago it was more than twice that amount. Jungles are being cut down for trees and land. This is called deforestation.

Mountains

Mountains are parts of Earth that are much higher than the land around them. The world's highest mountain is Mount Everest, at 29,028 feet high.

1. Who climbs mountains?

2. Why do mountaineers breathe through masks?

3. What is the top of a mountain called?

4. What "G" is a river formed out of ice?

5. Layers of rock are called what word beginning with "S"?

6. Mountains are formed very fast. True or false?

7. Where is the forest zone?

8. Unscramble BERTIMENLI to name where the forest zone meets cold rocks.

Thin air ① ②
Mountaineers climb mountains for fun. The air is much thinner at a high altitude, so they carry oxygen, which they breathe in through masks.

Cool! 3 4

The air is cool high up, so the top (or peak) of a mountain is often cold and covered in snow. Ice rivers called glaciers can form there.

Crunch! 5 6 7 8

Mountains are made by layers of rock (strata) moving extremely slowly over time. The lower slopes are called the forest zone. Not much grows on the cold rocks above the timberline.

peak

snow line

layers of rock (strata)

8 timberline

forest zone

Volcanoes

There are around 1,500 active volcanoes in the world today. They look like mountains, and sometimes they erupt without any warnings, blasting out dangerous gases and hot lava.

1. What "L" gushes out of a volcano?

2. Lava is very cold. True or false?

3. Do volcanologists visit volcanoes?

4. What do volcanologists wear?

5. What forms as a cloud after a volcanic explosion?

6. Can volcanoes cause earthquakes?

7. Is a tsunami ice cream or a giant wave?

8. Unscramble GAMMA HARMBEC to find the name of part of a volcano.

volcano

lava

Lava ①②

When a volcano erupts, it spews out a very hot liquid called lava. Usually this lava flows slowly. Sometimes it pours out very fast, covering everything in its path.

Volcanologists ③ ④

Specially trained men and women called volcanologists visit active volcanoes to study them. They take samples of the lava and rocks. They always wear heatproof clothing.

ash and dust ⑤

Eruption ⑥ ⑦

Volcanic eruptions are caused by pressure deep below the ground. They can trigger earthquakes, floods, and tsunamis (giant waves).

vent, or pipe

Magma ⑧

Inside a volcano there is a pool of hot liquid called a magma chamber. During an eruption, magma is forced up a vent to the surface.

magma chamber

Earthquakes

An earthquake is a sudden movement of Earth's top layer, or crust. It makes the ground shake! Big quakes are rare, but small ones happen all the time—you can hardly feel them.

1. What "P" are the pieces of Earth that move very slowly over time?

2. What "P" builds up between Earth's plates?

3. Earth's crust is thick. True or false?

4. What can be cut off during a quake?

5. What might people do if their houses are unsafe?

6. When did the big Tokyo quake occur?

7. What "F" came after the Tokyo quake?

8. How many people became homeless in the Tokyo quake?

plate moves

earthquake happens here

plate moves

Buildup 1 2 3
Earth's surface has many plates that fit together. They move very slowly over time, but if they get stuck, the pressure builds up until our planet's thin crust cracks.

Destruction 4 5

When a big earthquake occurs, buildings can be destroyed. Water and electricity supplies can also be cut off. People might move away while their houses are rebuilt.

Japanese disaster 6 7 8

In 1923, a huge earthquake struck near Tokyo in Japan. The quake and the fires that followed killed 142,000 people and destroyed 570,000 houses. It left 1.9 million survivors homeless.

Villages

Small settlements that are not as big as towns are called villages. Many of today's cities began as villages, with houses, churches, and stores surrounded by farmland.

1. What are some houses built on?

2. Stilts protect houses from the sun. True or false?

3. Villages are often built close to where there is what?

4. Unscramble STEMNELTET, a word for a village.

5. Where are the Atlas Mountains?

6. Name a mountain range starting with the letter "C."

7. Name a country beginning with "R."

8. Can villages be home to many different people?

On stilts ①②
In some villages that are near rivers, houses are built on stilts. This stops them from flooding during the rainy seasons.

Moroccan village ③ ④ ⑤

Villages are often built where there is work to do. The people of this settlement in the Atlas Mountains of Morocco herd animals and grow crops.

Caucasus ⑥ ⑦ ⑧

Each village dotted along the Caucasus mountain range is home to people from Russia, Armenia, Georgia, and Azerbaijan. Many different languages are spoken there.

Cities

Cities are huge settlements. The biggest city by land size is New York City, at 93,463 square feet. The largest by population is Tokyo, Japan, where 33 million people live.

1. Unscramble AGICYEMT to find the word for a very large city.

2. How many people live in a megacity?

3. Name a megacity starting with "S."

4. Is land in cities cheap to buy?

5. City buildings are very tall. True or false?

6. How many floors does the Sears Tower have?

7. Where were many cities first settled?

8. Why did people settle next to rivers or by an ocean?

The megacity 1 2 3

Megacities have ten million or more inhabitants. Tokyo (Japan), below, is a megacity, and so are New York City, Mumbai (India), Mexico City (Mexico), and Shanghai (China).

Into the sky 4 5 6

Land is expensive in cities, so buildings are very tall to make the most use of the space available. This is the view across Chicago, Illinois, from the Sears Tower, which has 108 floors!

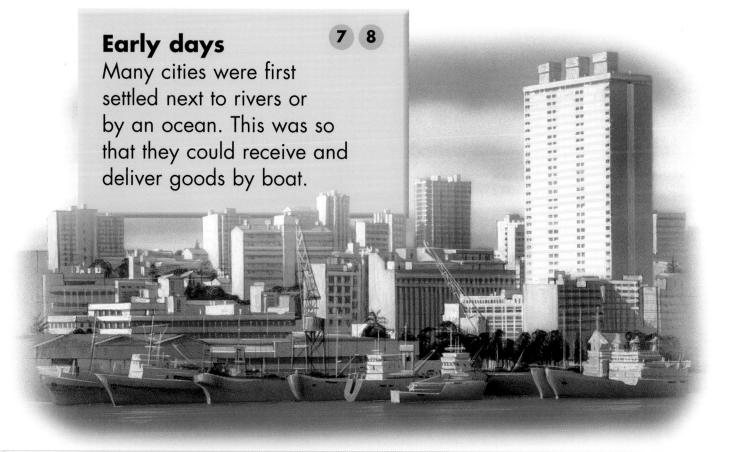

Early days 7 8

Many cities were first settled next to rivers or by an ocean. This was so that they could receive and deliver goods by boat.

On the farm

People began farming around 10,000 years ago in the Middle East. Farms are used to breed animals, grow plants, and harvest crops—we rely on them for almost all of our food.

1. Where are fruit trees planted?

2. Fruit has to be ripe before it is picked. True or false?

3. Unscramble BENMICO to name a farm machine.

4. When was the combine invented?

5. What do combines gather?

6. Is a plow used for watering?

7. Which animals starting with "O" pulled plows?

8. Which plowing machine replaced horses?

Fruit farming 1 2

Orchards have many fruit trees, often planted in rows. Crops such as apples, peaches, pears, and plums are picked when they are ripe.

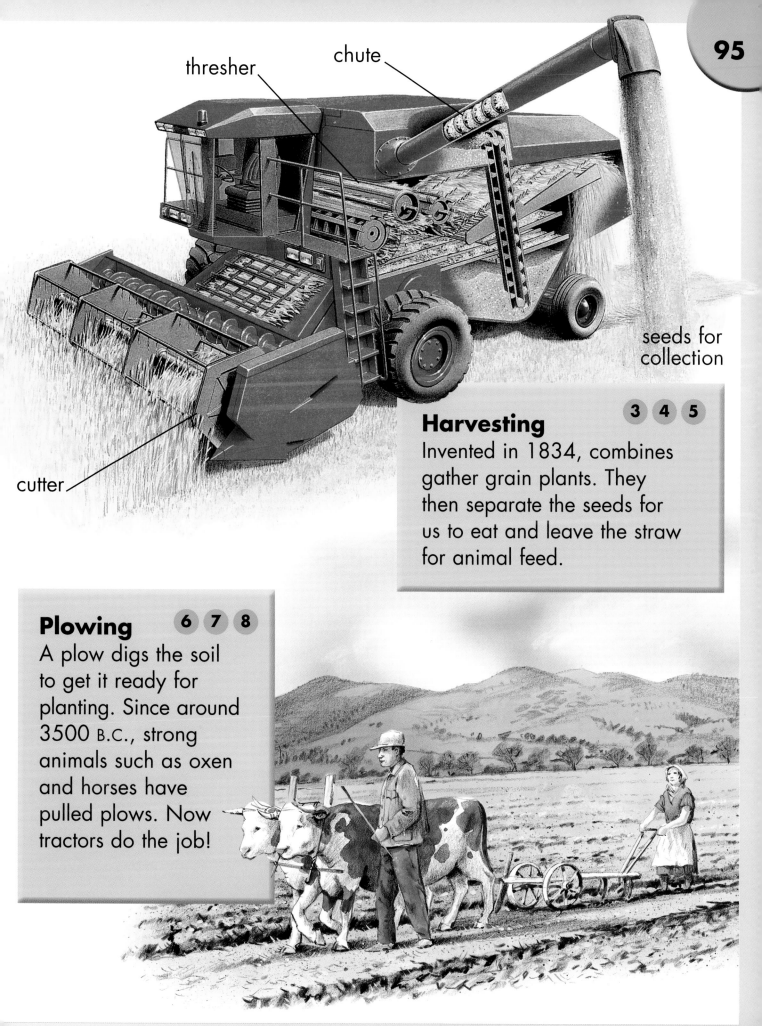

thresher

chute

seeds for
collection

cutter

Harvesting ③ ④ ⑤

Invented in 1834, combines
gather grain plants. They
then separate the seeds for
us to eat and leave the straw
for animal feed.

Plowing ⑥ ⑦ ⑧

A plow digs the soil
to get it ready for
planting. Since around
3500 B.C., strong
animals such as oxen
and horses have
pulled plows. Now
tractors do the job!

At the beach

The place where an ocean flows onto land is called a beach. Beaches can be made of sand, pebbles, or billions of small pieces of crushed shells. There are many things to discover on a beach!

1. What happens to rock pools when the tide is out?

2. Do rock-pool animals hide under umbrellas?

3. Name a beach bird that scavenges for food.

4. Some people eat seaweed. True or false?

5. Unscramble LESYJIFHL to reveal a sea creature that can sting you.

6. How many legs does a starfish have?

7. What can you build at the beach?

8. What should you wear at the beach?

On the rocks

A rock pool is a tiny world where plants and animals live. When the tide is out and the rock pools are no longer underwater, the animals hide under rocks and seaweeds.

Beach life 3 4 5 6

A Seagulls scavenge for food.
B Seaweed is a type of algae. Some people eat seaweed.
C Jellyfish can sting you—and some types are poisonous!
D Starfish have five legs but hundreds of tiny tube feet.

Vacations 7 8

People go to the beach for vacations. They can sunbathe, build sandcastles, swim, and play. It is important to wear sunscreen and swim in a safe place away from strong tides.

At home

1. Name a place where children can play outside.

2. Do yards need to be cared for?

3. Unscramble TARPADNRENG, a family member.

4. What "R" is the word for people in a family?

5. What is time away from work or school called?

6. Name a home leisure activity.

7. Name something beginning with "C" that you can do at home.

8. What can people make for friends?

A home is a building like a house or an apartment where people live, often with their families. Almost all of the 6.6 billion people in the world have homes, but some do not.

Outside the home ❶ ❷
Houses often have yards at the front and back. Children can play in the yard and exercise. There are also jobs to be done such as mowing the grass, raking fallen leaves, and looking after the plants.

Relatives

Many families are made up of different generations: children, parents, aunts, uncles, and grandparents. These relatives often meet to eat together.

Leisure time 5 6

Time away from school or work is called leisure time. This is when people can relax and watch television, use a computer, listen to music, or talk on the telephone.

Craft time 7 8

Making art and crafts at home is a great way to spend time. People can paint, draw, and cut and paste different things. They can make birthday cards for friends and photo albums of their favorite pictures.

At school

1. Are all schools the same?

2. What do some students have to help them learn?

3. Unscramble RICLUMURUC, the list of subjects taught at a school.

4. Do schools teach reading and writing?

5. Math helps you learn to use what?

6. What does science teach?

7. Why are students given tests?

8. Test scores can be very important. True or false?

Schools are places where children learn as part of their education. They have classrooms where teachers give lessons. Schools for adults are called colleges or universities.

Rich and poor ① ②

There are schools all around the world, but they are not all the same. In some schools, the classes are very big and there is very little equipment for the students. In others, every student has his or her own computer.

Learning 3 4 5 6

The set of subjects taught at a school is called the curriculum. This will include reading and writing, history, sports, math (how to use numbers), and science (how the world works).

Testing 7 8

Schools give tests, or exams, to check how much their students have learned. This is called assessment. Exam scores can be very important when children are older.

Bronze Age

This was a time when people began to use metal for tools and weapons. Its dates vary around the world, but in Europe it lasted from 2000 to 600 B.C., when bronze was replaced by iron.

1. People lived in bronze houses. True or false?

2. Did Bronze Age huts have fires?

3. Bronze Age hut walls were made of sticks, mud, and what else?

4. Unscramble RASPE to name a Bronze Age weapon.

5. Is bronze softer than gold?

6. Which two metals are mixed to make bronze?

7. What "A" is a mix of metals?

8. What "M" was bronze poured into while it cooled?

Smoky ① ② ③
People lived in round huts with fires in the middle. They covered the walls with sticks, mud, and dung.

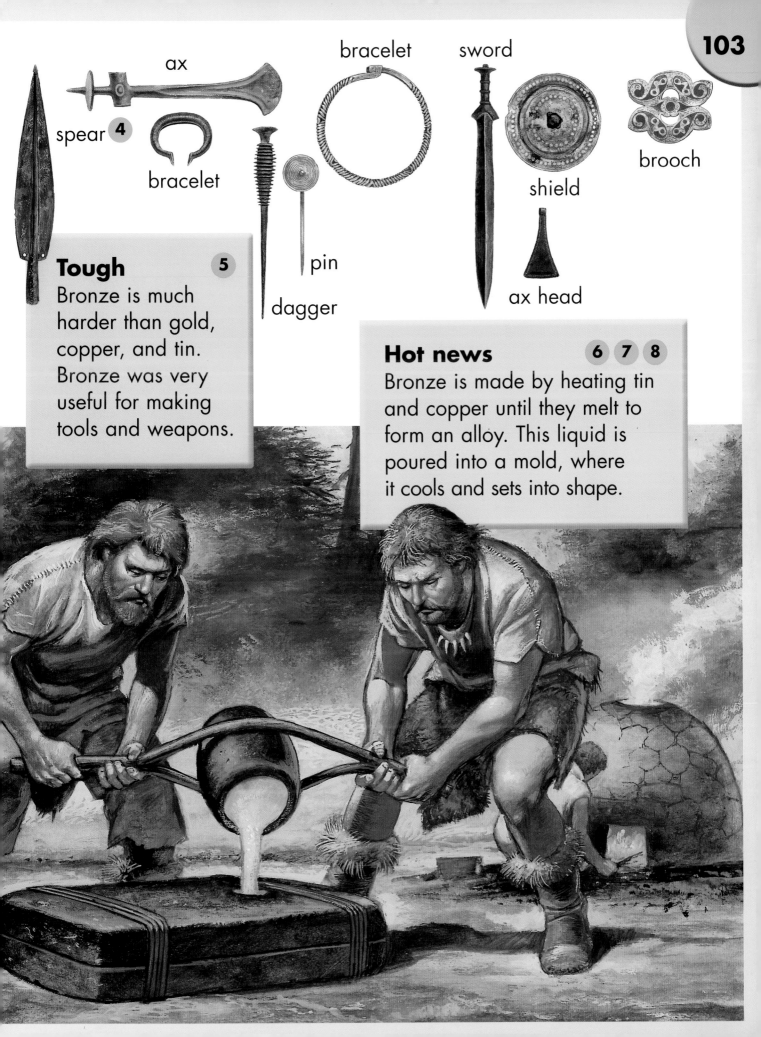

ax

spear **4**

bracelet

bracelet

sword

pin

dagger

shield

ax head

brooch

Tough **5**
Bronze is much harder than gold, copper, and tin. Bronze was very useful for making tools and weapons.

Hot news **6 7 8**
Bronze is made by heating tin and copper until they melt to form an alloy. This liquid is poured into a mold, where it cools and sets into shape.

Ancient Egypt

Ancient Egypt was a civilized kingdom for more than 3,000 years, from around 3100 B.C. to 30 B.C. It flourished on both sides of the Nile River.

1. Ancient Egyptians had only one god. True or false?

2. How did priests worship gods?

3. Most Egyptians were priests. True or false?

4. Name the Egyptians' important river.

5. Unscramble GIRIOTRAIN to find the word for managing water.

6. What "P" was the name for an Egyptian ruler?

7. Pharaohs were thought to be half man, half what?

8. Was magic part of Egyptian life?

Many gods ① ②
Ancient Egyptians had many gods, each with different roles. Priests worshiped them by offering food and drink.

Irrigation 3 4 5

Most people were farmers who planted and harvested crops in the rich soil by the Nile River. They dug ditches to bring water to the fields—this is called irrigation.

Pharaohs 6 7 8

Rulers were called pharaohs, and they were thought to be half human, half god. Religion and magic were woven into all aspects of everyday Egyptian life.

Mummies

Ancient Egyptians believed that they would go to the afterlife after death. Their bodies would be needed there, so they were preserved, or embalmed.

1. Unscramble LAMINBEMG, the word for preserving bodies.

2. Was embalming a fast process?

3. Was an embalmed body bandaged?

4. What happened to a mummy's brain?

5. Did all Egyptians have many coffins?

6. How was the death mask supposed to help the spirit?

7. Eygptian coffins were left undecorated. True or false?

8. What "S" is the name for the heavy stone outer coffin?

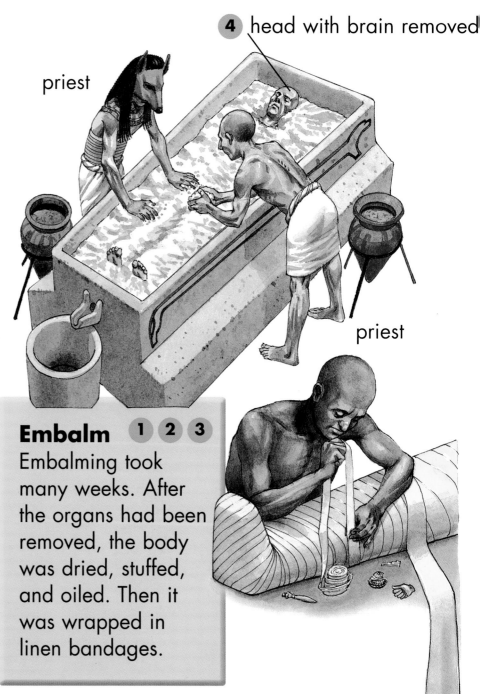

priest

4 head with brain removed

priest

Embalm ① ② ③
Embalming took many weeks. After the organs had been removed, the body was dried, stuffed, and oiled. Then it was wrapped in linen bandages.

Coffins 5 6

Only important dead people, such as pharaohs, were put inside many coffins. Some were fitted with a death mask to help the spirit recognize itself in the afterlife.

Jewels 7 8

The internal coffins were made of wood or gold and were painted and studded with jewels. The outer coffin was a heavy stone sarcophagus.

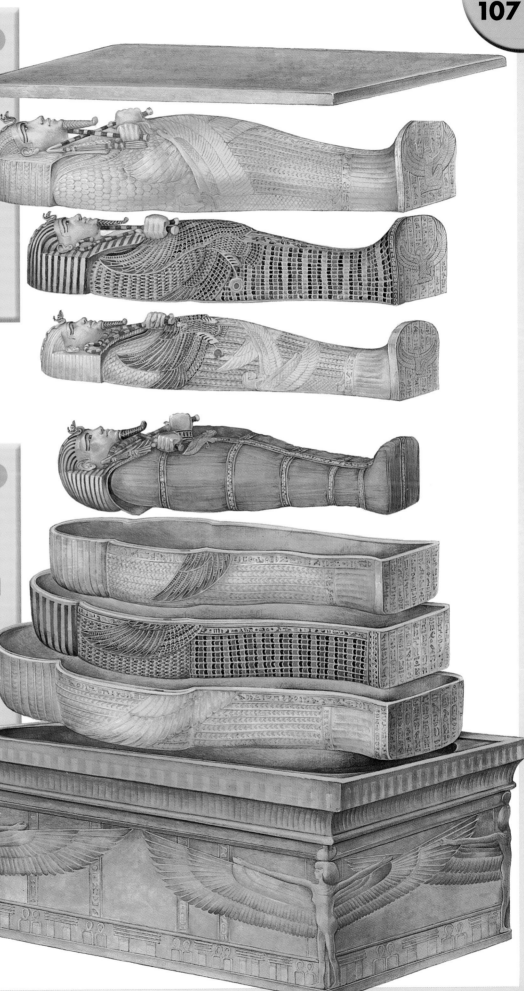

Buried treasures

Treasures are anything valuable that has been lost or hidden. In exciting movies like *Pirates of the Caribbean*, pirates look for treasures. There are many treasures around the world still to be found!

1. Unscramble STREEAUR PAM, which shows where treasures are buried.

2. Which letter "marks the spot"?

3. Which famous book did Robert Louis Stevenson write?

4. Who starting with "P" likes treasures?

5. What did pirates probably do with their treasures?

6. Which Spanish ship carried a lot of precious cargo?

7. What starting with "S" is a treasure?

8. Do treasure divers search on dry land?

Treasure maps 1 2

Treasure hunters often have treasure maps showing where the riches have been buried. The maps usually have an "X" to mark the spot where the treasures are hidden.

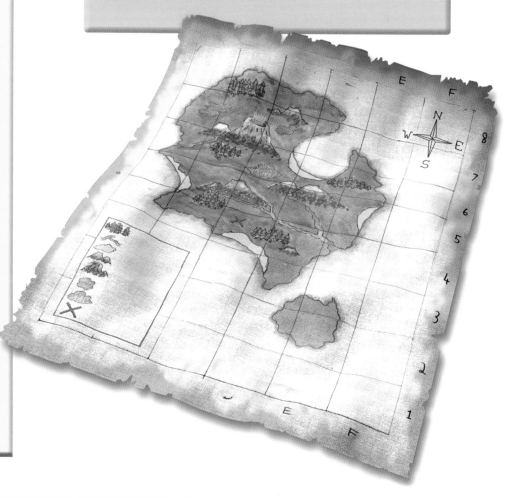

Yo, ho, ho! ③ ④ ⑤

Stories like Robert Louis Stevenson's *Treasure Island* suggest that pirates hid their loot in treasure chests. It is much more likely that they just spent it!

Sunken treasures ⑥ ⑦ ⑧

Over the years, countless ships, such as Spanish galleons, have sunk with their cargoes of gold, silver, and jewels. Divers swim down to the ocean floor hoping to find their fortunes.

PEOPLE AND PLACES
Record breakers

1. The Stromboli volcano in Italy has erupted frequently for more than 2,000 years!

2. The deadliest-ever earthquake killed 830,000 people in Shaanxi, China, on January 23, 1556.

3. In 1953, Edmund Hillary and Tenzing Norgay became the first people to climb Mount Everest.

4. The Praia do Cassino in Brazil is the longest beach in the world, stretching for 158 miles.

5. The Maasai people value cattle as a sign of wealth rather than the amount of land owned.

6. The oldest known city is Jericho on the West Bank, where people have lived since 9000 B.C.

7. The people of Africa did not have a Bronze Age—iron was the first metal to be used.

8. Hieroglyphic writing was developed by the ancient Egyptians in 3100 B.C.

9. The ancient Egyptians were the first people to use ramps and levers—invented for pyramid building.

10. The first record of a school was in ancient Greece; it was founded in around 385 B.C. in Akademia.

Chapter Five
TRANSPORTATION

Cars

Cars are four-wheeled vehicles used for carrying people. Most run on gasoline or diesel, but some run on electricity or even cooking oil!

1. Has the Mini been popular for more than 40 years?

2. Do some cars run on cooking oil?

3. Do Minis have four doors?

4. What does a driver use to change gears?

5. Unscramble HSELIDDWIN, the glass in front of a driver.

6. Do cars have only a few parts?

7. What helps control modern cars?

8. Which car was adapted from a U.S. Army vehicle?

A classic car ① ② ③
The Mini is a very famous car that has been popular for more than 40 years. Its shape has changed only a little bit; the modern Mini Cooper still has small wheels and two doors.

1960s

2007

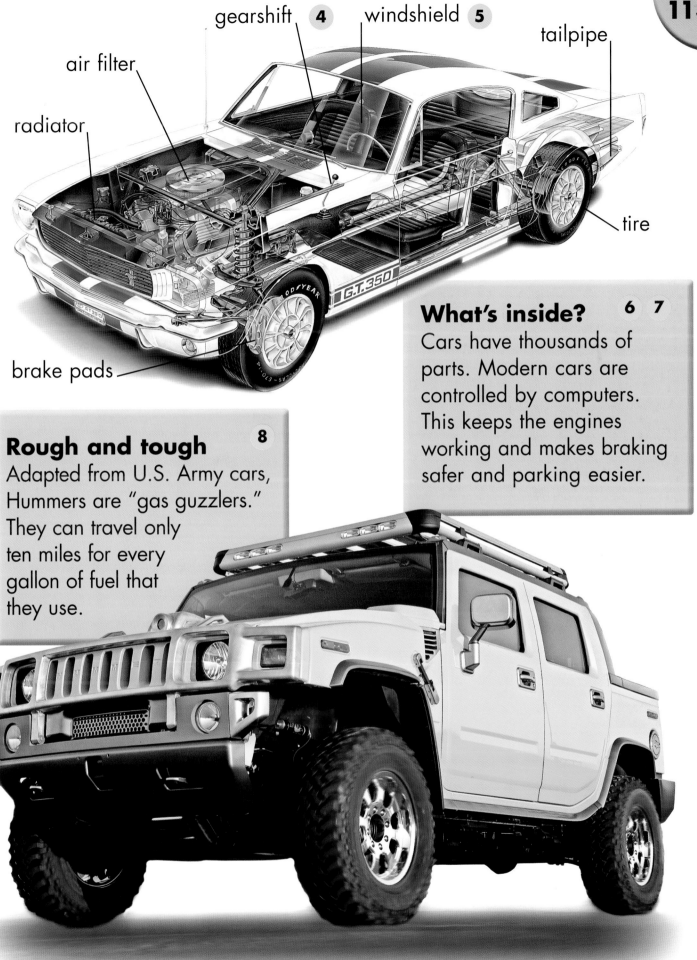

radiator

air filter

gearshift **4**

windshield **5**

tailpipe

tire

brake pads

What's inside? **6** **7**
Cars have thousands of parts. Modern cars are controlled by computers. This keeps the engines working and makes braking safer and parking easier.

Rough and tough **8**
Adapted from U.S. Army cars, Hummers are "gas guzzlers." They can travel only ten miles for every gallon of fuel that they use.

Racecars

Racecars are fast, light, single-seater cars with powerful engines mounted behind the drivers. They race at almost 190 miles per hour.

1. Unscramble TOCCPKI.

2. How many mechanics might be in a pit crew?

3. A quick tire change and refuel is known as what?

4. Is it hot in a racecar?

5. Racecar drivers brake often. True or false?

6. Where are the wings on racecars?

7. What might a racecar do without its wings to keep it close to the road?

8. Starting with "A," air pushing a car down is known as what?

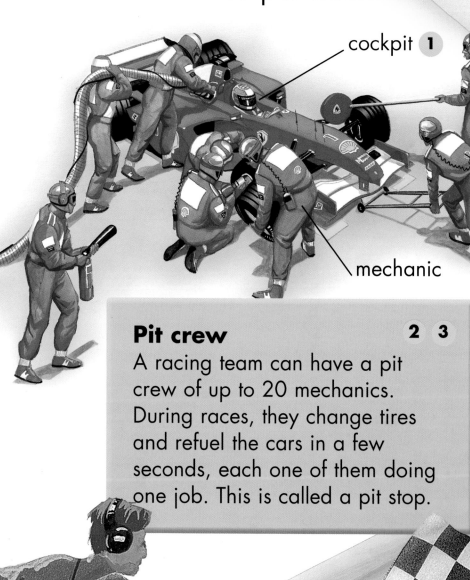

cockpit **1**

mechanic

Pit crew **2** **3**
A racing team can have a pit crew of up to 20 mechanics. During races, they change tires and refuel the cars in a few seconds, each one of them doing one job. This is called a pit stop.

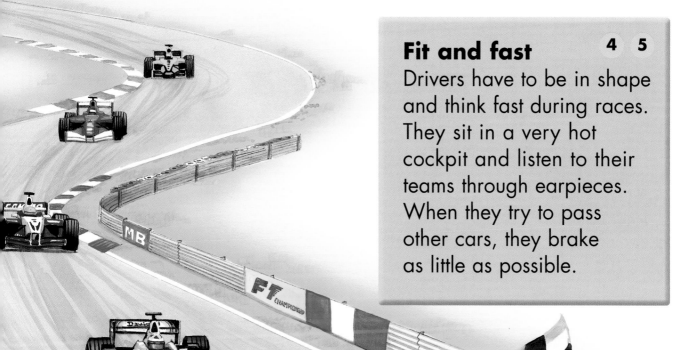

Fit and fast

4 5

Drivers have to be in shape and think fast during races. They sit in a very hot cockpit and listen to their teams through earpieces. When they try to pass other cars, they brake as little as possible.

Aerodynamics

6 7 8

The front and tail wings are sloped to push up air. This forces the car down, keeping it close to the road—otherwise it could crash. This is known as aerodynamics.

Trucks

Trucks deliver goods by road. Everything in your house probably came by truck. The biggest trucks can carry up to 360 tons!

1. Unscramble ROTCART to name a part of some trucks.

2. How many parts do tractor-trailers have?

3. Can tractor-trailers turn easily in small spaces?

4. Do some trucks have a bed?

5. What "C" is the rigid frame for trucks?

6. Does a truck have a single chassis?

7. What types of trucks carry sand?

8. Do dump trucks have telescopic rods?

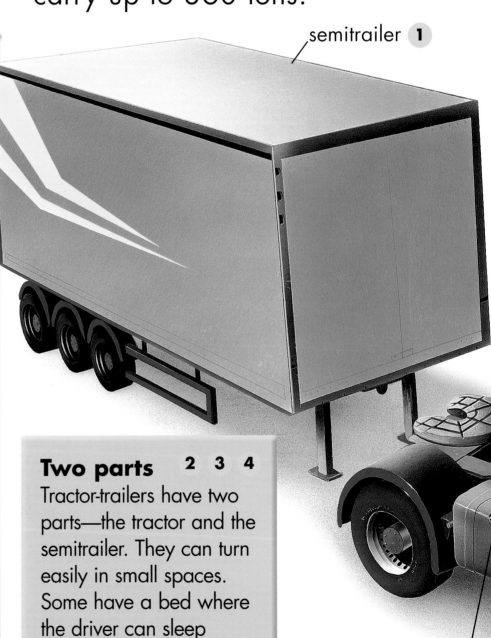

semitrailer **1**

tractor

Two parts **2** **3** **4**
Tractor-trailers have two parts—the tractor and the semitrailer. They can turn easily in small spaces. Some have a bed where the driver can sleep during long journeys.

van

truck

telescopic rod

trailer

dump truck

Rigid trucks

5 6

These smaller trucks have a rigid frame, called the chassis, to which the wheels and engine are attached. A truck, unlike a tractor-trailer, has a single chassis. A van is like a big, boxy car.

Pour me out!

7 8

Dump trucks carry loose loads such as sand or rubble. The trailer is pushed up by a telescopic rod, which is powered by oil under high pressure (this is called hydraulics). Then everything falls out and the job is done!

Diggers

Diggers are heavy-duty vehicles. They can dig up large amounts of earth such as soil or rocks. They can move tons of material very quickly.

1. How do diggers scoop up earth?

2. Where do digger drivers sit?

3. Unscramble BAEDL to give the name of part of a digger.

4. Are diggers used to build roads?

5. Do diggers make holes in the ground?

6. Diggers can move a lot of earth. True or false?

7. Diggers are sometimes called what?

8. What helps diggers grab a lot of earth at once?

crane

cables

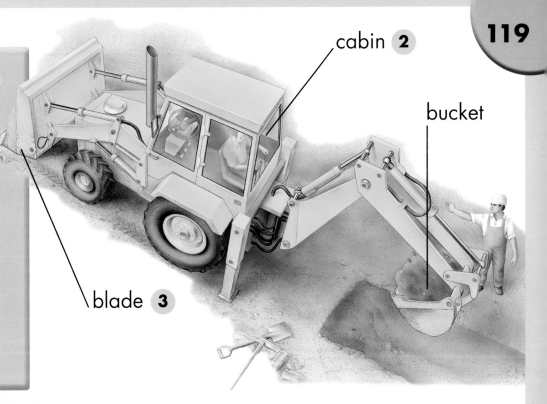

cabin **2**

bucket

Scooping up **1**

The driver operates the digger from inside the cabin. A bucket scoops up the earth. A blade at the front or back of the digger clears the path so that the driver can get on with the job!

blade **3**

Big dig **4 5**

Diggers are used in mining and the construction industry. They can make holes in the ground for roads, buildings, or canals.

Teeth! **6 7 8**

Buckets have teeth so that they can grab a lot of earth at once. Diggers are sometimes called earthmovers.

teeth **8**

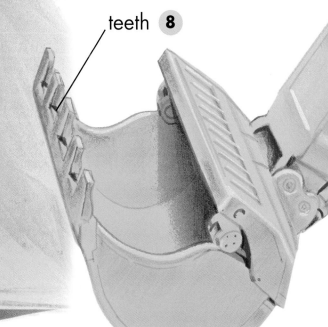

Trains

Trains have engines called locomotives that pull or push carriages along tracks made of steel rails. The first trains were invented around 200 years ago and were powered by steam.

1. How does a train driver see in the dark?

2. What "G" do freight trains carry?

3. How many wagons did the longest freight train have?

4. Do all trains have only one engine?

5. All trains are powered by diesel. True or false?

6. What comes from overhead wires?

7. Unscramble TNSOIAT to name where people get on and off trains.

8. How fast are the quickest trains?

driver's cab

1 headlights

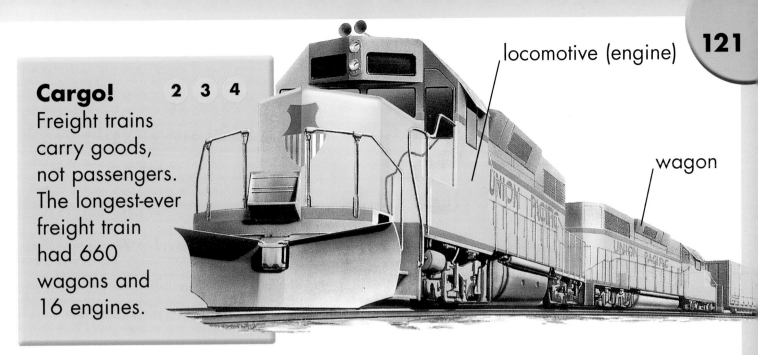

locomotive (engine)

wagon

Cargo! 2 3 4

Freight trains carry goods, not passengers. The longest-ever freight train had 660 wagons and 16 engines.

Bright spark 5 6

Many trains have diesel engines, but some are powered by electricity. They have special poles that touch overhead wires to collect the electric power.

overhead railroad

People carriers 7 8

Passenger trains carry people on journeys between stations. Some have carriages where you can eat or sleep. The fastest trains, in France, can travel at 356 miles per hour.

Ships

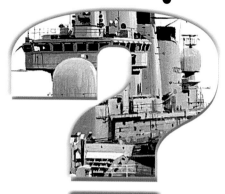

Ships carry passengers or goods across seas and oceans. Once made from wood and swept along by sails, ships are now built of steel and powered through the water by propellers.

1. What "W" do warships have?

2. What are warships usually part of?

3. Which types of ships carry goods?

4. Unscramble TONSERNAIC, which cranes lift onto a ship's deck.

5. Some tankers carry oil. True or false?

6. Where are ships controlled from?

7. Where would you sleep on an ocean liner?

8. How many passengers can the biggest cruise ship carry?

radar scanner

bridge

Warships 1 2
Warships are ships with weapons. They are usually part of a navy and carry fighting equipment such as guns, cannons, torpedoes, and missile launchers.

warship

Cargo ships 3 4 5 6

Cargo ships carry goods between countries. Cranes lift giant containers onto the deck. This tanker is carrying liquids such as oil and gasoline. Ships are controlled from the bridge.

bridge

tanker

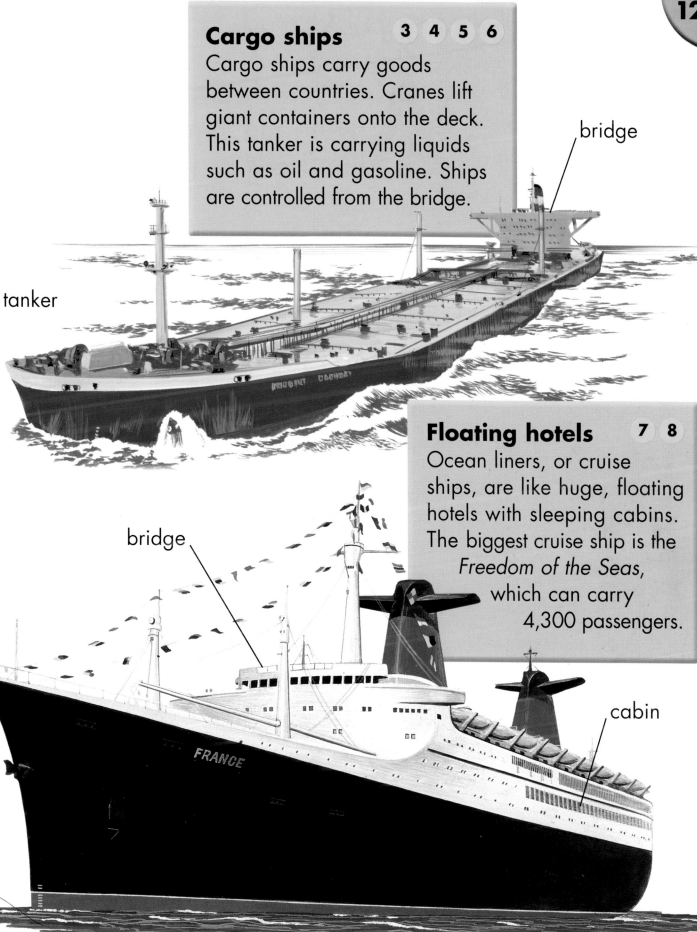

Floating hotels 7 8

Ocean liners, or cruise ships, are like huge, floating hotels with sleeping cabins. The biggest cruise ship is the *Freedom of the Seas*, which can carry 4,300 passengers.

bridge

cabin

FRANCE

ocean liner

Airplanes

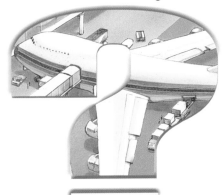

irplanes are big, heavy flying machines that carry hundreds of people and a lot of cargo over long distances. Only rockets can travel faster!

1. What does a jet engine suck in at the front?

2. What helps lift a plane up into the air?

3. Airplanes can cruise at what speed?

4. Unscramble YURWAN, where planes take off.

5. Who makes sure that planes land safely?

6. Who refuels planes?

7. There are different sections on a plane for people and what else?

8. How many passengers can big planes carry?

Fly high 1 2 3

Jet engines suck in air at the front and send out hot exhaust gases at the back, pushing the plane forward. The wings have flaps that help lift the plane up into the air. Airplanes cruise at 430 to 560 miles per hour.

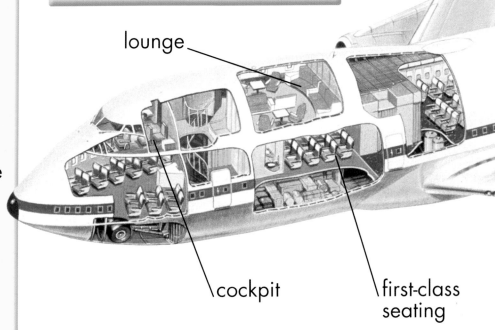

lounge

cockpit

first-class seating

Airport 4 5 6

Planes take off and land at an airport on a runway. Air-traffic controllers make sure that the planes land safely. The airport ground crew does safety checks and refuels the planes.

economy seating

luggage

Looking inside 7 8

There are different sections inside the body of a plane for people and luggage. The largest planes can carry more than 500 passengers.

jet engine

Rockets

Rockets blast spacecraft from Earth into space. They zoom into the sky at seven miles per second. They are used by the military and for exploring space.

1. Are some parts of rockets supposed to fall off?

2. Unscramble LOLOPA to name the craft that went to the Moon.

3. Are space shuttles reusable?

4. How many astronauts can an orbiter carry?

5. What are attached to a rocket's fuel tank for extra power?

6. Does the whole space shuttle go into space?

7. A rocket's fuel tank holds only two gallons of fuel. True or false?

8. What "P" bring a rocket's boosters back?

We have liftoff! ① ②

Rockets are held steady until they blast into the sky. Sections called "stages" fall off as their fuel burns up, leaving just the top part to enter space. *Saturn V* carried the *Apollo* Moon-landing craft.

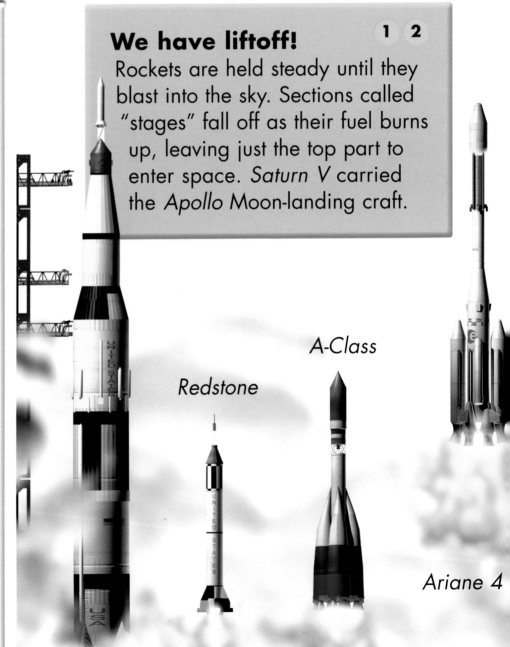

Redstone

A-Class

Ariane 4

Saturn V

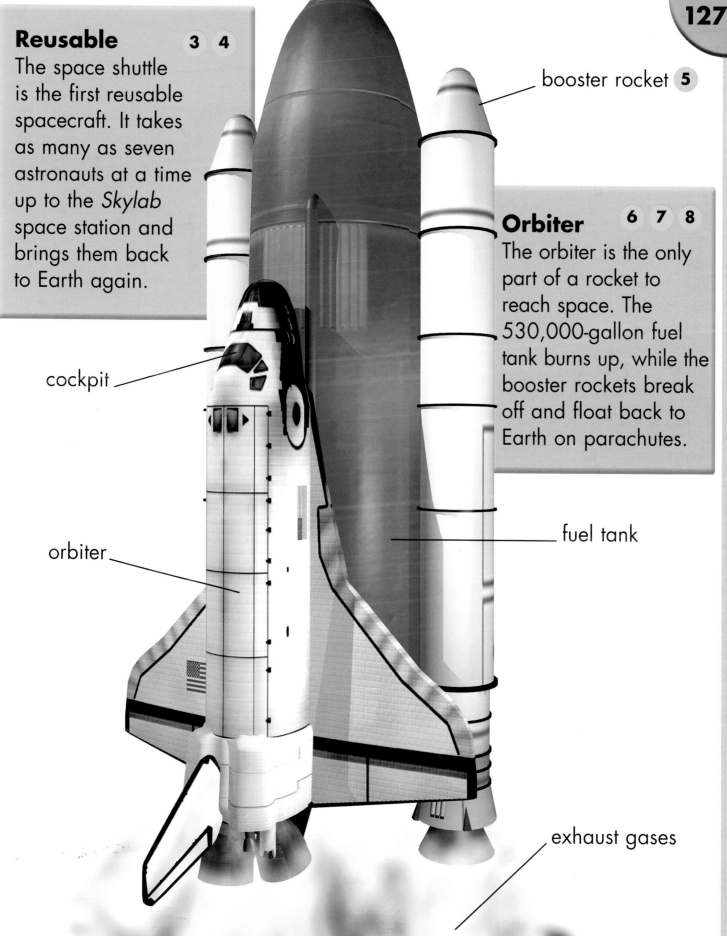

Reusable 3 4

The space shuttle is the first reusable spacecraft. It takes as many as seven astronauts at a time up to the *Skylab* space station and brings them back to Earth again.

booster rocket 5

Orbiter 6 7 8

The orbiter is the only part of a rocket to reach space. The 530,000-gallon fuel tank burns up, while the booster rockets break off and float back to Earth on parachutes.

cockpit

orbiter

fuel tank

exhaust gases

TRANSPORTATION
Record breakers

1. Ferdinand Magellan led the first expedition to sail around the entire world, from 1519 to 1522.

2. The first automobile was invented by Nicolas-Joseph Cugnot in 1769.

3. The first passenger train rolled along the track on March 25, 1807 in Swansea, Wales.

4. The biggest digger is the Bagger 288, a 984-foot-long mining monster.

5. The Liebherr T282, the world's biggest truck, can carry a 360-ton load at 40 miles per hour.

6. The jet-powered Thrust SSC car set a land speed record of 761 miles per hour in 1997.

7. The Lockheed SR-71A Blackbird set a record speed of 2,188 miles per hour for a manned plane.

8. In 1961, Yuri Gagarin became the first person to survive a trip into space and back.

9. The fastest aircraft was the pilotless Boeing X-43, which reached 7,529 miles per hour.

10. The longest airplane is the 276-foot AN-225 Mriya, with wings 289 feet across and 32 wheels.

ANSWERS

Did you get the answers right? Now it's time to check your answers and see how well you have done! Good luck . . .

Dinosaurs

Early dinosaurs

1. What does *dinosaur* mean?

Answer: Terrible lizard

2. All dinosaurs were small. True or false?

Answer: False. Many were large.

3. How many types of dinosaurs were there?

Answer: 10,000

4. Did dinosaurs lay eggs?

Answer: Yes

5. Unscramble DOOPRSAU to spell a type of dinosaur.

Answer: SAUROPOD

6. What were meat-eating dinosaurs called?

Answer: Theropods

7. Did crocodiles live at the same time as dinosaurs?

Answer: Yes

8. How did a *Coelophysis* move?

Answer: It ran on its back legs.

Meat eaters

1. Where did *Allosaurus* live?

Answer: North America

2. What did *Allosaurus* use to kill prey?

Answer: Jagged teeth

3. When did *Albertosaurus* live?

Answer: 70 million years ago

4. How did *Albertosaurus* kill its victims?

Answer: By biting the backs of their necks

5. *Deinonychus* moved slowly. True or false?

Answer: False. Deinonychus was a fast runner.

6. Did *Deinonychus* ever hunt in groups?

Answer: Yes, possibly

7. What does "*Deinonychus*" mean?

Answer: Terrible claw

8. Unscramble the word WALC.

Answer: CLAW

Tyrannosaurus rex

1. *Tyrannosaurus rex* ate dead bodies. True or false?

Answer: True

2. How did *T. rex* find dead bodies?

Answer: It sniffed them out.

3. Did *T. rex* stand on four legs?

Answer: No. It stood on two legs.

4. Was *T. rex* fast?

Answer: No. It was slow.

5. Unscramble GGEDAJ ETEHT to name something used by *T. rex* when hunting.

Answer: JAGGED TEETH

6. What does "Tyrannosaurus rex" mean?

Answer: King of the tyrant lizards

7. When did *T. rex* live?

Answer: 70 million years ago

8. Where have most *T. rex* fossils been found?

Answer: North America

Plant eaters

1. *Apatosaurus* was bigger than a blue whale. True or false?

Answer: False. It was almost as large as a blue whale.

2. What is another name for *Apatosaurus*?

Answer: Brontosaurus

3. Unscramble SUROTUESGAS.

Answer: STEGOSAURUS

4. What were the plates on a *Stegosaurus* used for?

Answer: For cooling down the animal

5. What was on a *Stegosaurus*'s tail?

Answer: Spikes

6. What does "Triceratops" mean?

Answer: Three horns

7. What were the horns of a *Triceratops* used for?

Answer: To fight off predators

8. What protected a *Triceratops*'s neck?

Answer: A thick shield

Brachiosaurus

1. Unscramble ELAESV to spell food eaten by a *Brachiosaurus*.

Answer: LEAVES

2. What made a *Brachiosaurus*'s teeth blunt?

Answer: Eating leaves and branches

3. Where were a *Brachiosaurus*'s nostrils?

Answer: On top of its head

4. Nostrils may have helped a *Brachiosaurus* smell. True or false?

Answer: True

5. What else may the nostrils have been used for?

Answer: Making loud calls

6. How heavy was a *Brachiosaurus*?

Answer: 77 tons

7. Which is taller, a *Brachiosaurus* or a telephone pole?

Answer: A Brachiosaurus

8. How long was a *Brachiosaurus*?

Answer: 72 feet

Ancient sea reptiles

1. When did *Archelon* live?

Answer: 220 million years ago

2. What did *Archelon* eat?

Answer: Shellfish

3. How long was *Archelon*?

Answer: As long as a car

4. Which sea reptile looked like a dolphin?

Answer: An ichthyosaur

5. Plesiosaurs had long necks. True or false?

Answer: True

6. What did *Placodus* eat?

Answer: Shellfish

7. What did *Globidens* crush?

Answer: Shells

8. Unscramble SAUROTHON to spell an ocean reptile with sharp teeth.

Answer: NOTHOSAUR

Flying reptiles

1. What does *pterosaur* mean?

Answer: Winged lizard

2. Was a pterosaur's wing made of skin?

Answer: Yes

3. A pterosaur's wing contained a long finger. True or false?

Answer: True

4. Were pterosaurs very good at flying?

Answer: No. They were not good fliers.

5. How did cliff-living pterosaurs catch their food?

Answer: By swooping over water and scooping up fish

6. Was *Dimorphodon* a fast runner?

Answer: Yes

7. Unscramble TCSNIE to spell a food eaten by *Dimorphodon*.

Answer: INSECT

8. Was the largest flying animal a pterosaur?

Answer: Yes

Early mammals

1. Unscramble SPARUMILAS.

Answer: MARSUPIALS

2. Where do marsupial babies stay after birth?

Answer: In their mother's pouch

3. Where do most marsupials live today?

Answer: Australia

4. Mammals lived at the same time as dinosaurs. True or false?

Answer: True

5. What happened when dinosaurs became extinct?

Answer: Mammals took over.

6. Did mammals eat dinosaur eggs?

Answer: Yes, possibly

7. Dinosaurs had hair. True or false?

Answer: False. Mammals have hair.

8. Does a mammal's hair keep it warm?

Answer: Yes

Land animals

Elephants

1. What is a group of elephants called?

Answer: A herd

2. Are male elephants in charge of a herd?

Answer: No. The females are in charge.

3. What is an elephant's tusk made of?

Answer: Ivory

4. Can you train an elephant to work?

Answer: Yes

5. Unscramble NALABINH to spell a famous general's name.

Answer: HANNIBAL

6. Do elephants eat leaves and grasses?

Answer: Yes

7. Elephants eat for 16 hours each day. True or false?

Answer: True

8. Are plants a high-energy food?

Answer: No. They are a low-energy food.

Lions

1. What is the thick hair on a lion's neck called?

Answer: A mane

2. Male and female lions are the same size. True or false?

Answer: False. Males are larger.

3. What is a group of lions called?

Answer: A pride

4. Who rules a group of lions?

Answer: A male lion

5. What are baby lions called?

Answer: Cubs

6. Which member of a pride always eats first?

Answer: The male leader

7. Unscramble SENOSIL to figure out who raises a baby lion.

Answer: LIONESS

8. What does a male lion do if he meets another male lion?

Answer: Fight

Tigers

1. Why do tigers have stripes?

Answer: To help them stay hidden

2. Do tigers make much noise when they walk?

Answer: No. They are quiet.

3. Unscramble RIGESTS to give the word for a female tiger.

Answer: TIGRESS

4. How long does a tiger cub stay with its mother?

Answer: Two years

5. Tigers live in large groups. True or false?

Answer: False. Tigers live alone.

6. How do tigers keep their claws sharp?

Answer: By scratching tree trunks

7. How does a tiger get close to its prey?

Answer: It hides in the undergrowth and creeps up.

8. How do tigers kill their prey?

Answer: They break their necks.

Wolves

1. Which small animal might a wolf catch?

Answer: A hare

2. When do wolves hunt as a team?

Answer: During the winter

3. Unscramble NURNGIN to name something wolves are very good at.

Answer: RUNNING

4. How far can a wolf run in one day?

Answer: 125 miles

5. A group of wolves is called a flock. True or false?

Answer: False. It is called a pack.

6. How many pack members have cubs each year?

Answer: Two

7. Why do wolves howl?

Answer: To warn other wolves to stay away

8. How far away can you hear a wolf howling?

Answer: Ten miles

Flightless birds

1. Cassowaries live in deserts.
True or false?

Answer: False. They live in forests.

2. Unscramble SQAECU to name the bone on a cassowary's head.

Answer: CASQUE

3. What is a cassowary's casque used for?

Answer: To push branches out of the way

4. What is the largest bird in the world?

Answer: The ostrich

5. Where do ostrich live?

Answer: Africa

6. How does an ostrich escape from danger?

Answer: By running away

7. How did the emu get its name?

Answer: From the call it makes

8. How does an emu find fresh food?

Answer: It follows the rain clouds.

Bears

1. How do bears climb trees?

Answer: By gripping with their claws

2. How long are the claws of a brown bear?

Answer: Four inches long

3. Unscramble EVEEBIH to find the place where bears get honey.

Answer: BEEHIVE

4. Bears never eat fish. True or false?

Answer: False. They eat salmon and trout.

5. Where do bears often gather to catch fish?

Answer: Waterfalls

6. Bears can catch fish with their teeth. True or false?

Answer: True

7. Do bears like to eat nuts and berries?

Answer: Yes

8. How do bears eat honey?

Answer: They lick it out from beehives with their tongues.

Pandas

1. Why do pandas have white faces with black eyes and ears?

Answer: To make it easier to see one another in forests

2. Unscramble OBAMOB to find the plant that pandas eat.

Answer: BAMBOO

3. Where do pandas sleep?

Answer: Out in the open

4. What sticks out of a panda's wrist?

Answer: A sixth "finger"

5. How long does it take for a panda cub to grow up?

Answer: Four years

6. Which country do pandas live in?

Answer: China

7. How many pandas live in the wild?

Answer: 1,000

8. Do pandas live on mountains?

Answer: Yes

Polar bears

1. Is a polar bear's fur white?

Answer: No. It is see-through.

2. Why do polar bears have a layer of fat under their skin?

Answer: So that they can survive if they cannot find food

3. Unscramble END to name the place where cubs are born.

Answer: DEN

4. How long do cubs stay in a den?

Answer: Three months

5. What does a polar-bear mother eat when she is in a den with her cubs?

Answer: Nothing

6. What do polar bears hunt?

Answer: Seals

7. Where do polar bears wait for their prey?

Answer: Next to holes in the ice

8. Polar bears catch seals with fishing rods. True or false?

Answer: False. They use their paws.

Jungle animals

1. Why are jungles being cut down?

Answer: To make room for farms

2. Why are some jungle animals rare?

Answer: They have few places left to live.

3. Unscramble VAJNA to spell the name of a rare rhino.

Answer: JAVAN

4. How many horns does a Javan rhino have?

Answer: One

5. How do toucans crack nuts?

Answer: With their big beaks

6. How long is a quetzal's tail?

Answer: Four times longer than the rest of its body

7. What would happen if someone touched a red frog?

Answer: He or she might die.

8. Where does an ocelot hunt?

Answer: In the undergrowth

Apes and monkeys

1. Where could you find a wild gorilla?

Answer: Africa

2. Which ape lives in Southeast Asia?

Answer: The orangutan

3. What is the most common type of ape in the world?

Answer: The human

4. When do howler monkeys call?

Answer: In the morning

5. How far away can a howler monkey's call be heard?

Answer: Almost two miles

6. Where is a howler monkey's voice box?

Answer: In its throat

7. Unscramble DRIMLALN to spell the name of the largest monkey.

Answer: MANDRILL

8. Where do mandrills live?

Answer: In the jungles of Africa

Bugs and beetles

1. What do bugs have instead of bones?

Answer: Hard skin

2. How do bugs breathe?

Answer: Through holes in their skin

3. A water bug has hairy legs to stay warm. True or false?

Answer: False. Its hairy legs help it swim.

4. How do water bugs catch fish?

Answer: With their long claws

5. What do stag beetles use their pincers for?

Answer: Fighting

6. Unscramble NATENANE to give another word for insect feelers.

Answer: ANTENNAE

7. How many legs does a bug have?

Answer: Six

8. Where do beetles keep their wings?

Answer: Underneath a hard wing case

Ants

1. Where do weaver ants live?

Answer: In nests of leaves

2. Baby ants are called larvae. True or false?

Answer: True

3. What do larvae make to glue leaves together?

Answer: Sticky silk

4. Which ants defend a nest?

Answer: Soldier ants

5. Soldier ants are armed with sharp jaws and what other weapons?

Answer: Stingers in their tails

6. Where might you find an ant's nest?

Answer: Underground

7. Which types of ants gather food?

Answer: Worker ants

8. Unscramble UPAPE to find the name for ant cocoons.

Answer: PUPAE

Butterflies and moths

1. What hatches from a butterfly egg?

Answer: A caterpillar

2. What do caterpillars eat?

Answer: Leaves and fruit

3. What is the name of the silk bag that a caterpillar spins?

Answer: A cocoon

4. Unscramble CRAMNOH to spell the name of a common butterfly.

Answer: MONARCH

5. Moths fly at night. True or false?

Answer: True

6. Which are more colorful, moths or butterflies?

Answer: Butterflies

7. How many wings do butterflies have?

Answer: Four (two pairs)

8. What is the mouthpart of a butterfly called?

Answer: A proboscis

Farm animals

1. Roosters lay eggs. True or false?

Answer: False. Hens lay eggs.

2. What is a female chicken called?

Answer: A hen

3. Where does wool come from?

Answer: Sheep

4. Which breed of cattle is best for producing milk?

Answer: Jersey

5. Unscramble FROHEERD to spell the name of a cattle breed.

Answer: HEREFORD

6. What is special about Highland cattle?

Answer: Their thick hair

7. Ham, pork, and what other meat comes from a pig?

Answer: Bacon

8. What is a female pig called?

Answer: A sow

Dogs

1. What does *carnivore* mean?
Answer: Meat eater

2. What does a dog use its teeth for?

Answer: Chewing

3. Dogs have no sense of smell. True or false?

Answer: False. Dogs have a very good sense of smell.

4. How many puppies can a female dog produce?

Answer: Up to 12

5. How long does it take puppies to become adults?

Answer: Two or three years

6. When did dogs start to live with people?

Answer: 15,000 years ago

7. What is a mongrel?

Answer: A mixed-breed dog

8. Unscramble GOBDULL to spell a breed of dog.

Answer: BULLDOG

Cats

1. Cats hunt for birds. True or false?
Answer: True

2. Where are a cat's claws stored?

Answer: Inside a sheath on its toes

3. How does a mother cat clean her kittens?

Answer: By licking them

4. What does a happy cat do?

Answer: It purrs.

5. Which wild animals are pet cats closely related to?

Answer: African wildcats

6. Some cats are black and white. True or false?

Answer: True

7. What are cats with spots and blotches called?

Answer: Tabbies

8. Unscramble SNAPIER to spell the name of a cat breed.

Answer: PERSIAN

Sea creatures

Blue whales

1. Blue whales are a type of fish. True or false?

Answer: False. They live in the ocean, but they are not a type of fish.

2. What is the flat part of a whale's tail called?

Answer: A fluke

3. What is a blue whale as long as?

Answer: A tennis court

4. How much can a blue whale eat in one day?

Answer: Four tons of food

5. What does a blue whale eat?

Answer: Krill

6. Unscramble LENABE TALSEP to name the bristles in a blue whale's mouth.

Answer: BALEEN PLATES

7. What is a baby whale called?

Answer: A calf

8. Name the word for a whale's nostril.

Answer: Blowhole

Dolphins

1. Where is a dolphin's "melon"?

Answer: Inside its head

2. A dolphin's melon contains oil. True or false?

Answer: True

3. What does a dolphin use its melon for?

Answer: To pick up sounds underwater

4. What is another name for a dolphin's snout?

Answer: Beak

5. What do dolphins have instead of legs?

Answer: Flippers

6. Unscramble SOLRAD INF to give the name of part of a dolphin.

Answer: DORSAL FIN

7. Dolphins breathe air. True or false?

Answer: True

8. Dolphins never catch fish to eat. True or false?

Answer: False. They do catch fish to eat.

Killer whales

1. Do killer whales hunt for other types of whales?

Answer: Yes

2. What is the name of a group of whales?

Answer: A pod

3. Whale pods never contain females. True or false?

Answer: False. Females do live in pods.

4. Which type of killer whale has a curved dorsal fin?

Answer: A female killer whale

5. What shape is the dorsal fin of a male killer whale?

Answer: Tall and pointed

6. What happens if a whale's fin is very tall?

Answer: It can flop over to one side.

7. How does a whale look around?

Answer: By poking its head out of the water

8. Unscramble PSY PHPOGIN.

Answer: SPY HOPPING

Seals

1. Can baby seals swim?

Answer: No. They cannot swim.

2. Why is a baby seal's fur white?

Answer: So it can hide in the snow

3. Name the world's largest type of seal.

Answer: Elephant seal

4. What is the word for a male seal?

Answer: Bull

5. Elephant-seal cows are larger than the bulls. True or false?

Answer: False. Elephant-seal bulls are larger than the cows.

6. Where do harp seals hunt?

Answer: Under the ice in the Arctic Ocean

7. Unscramble LESHIFLSH to name something that harp seals eat.

Answer: SHELLFISH

8. What do seals use to sense water currents made by their prey?

Answer: Their whiskers

Sharks

1. What do killer sharks have in their mouths?

Answer: Large, pointed teeth

2. What is the largest killer shark called?

Answer: The great white shark

3. What does a remora use to stick itself to a shark?

Answer: A sucker

4. What do pilot fish eat?

Answer: A shark's leftovers

5. Can sharks detect electricity?

Answer: Yes

6. Hammerheads have pointed snouts. True or false?

Answer: False. They have wide heads.

7. Where do blue sharks live?

Answer: Far out at sea

8. Unscramble DQISU to spell something eaten by a shark.

Answer: SQUID

Wading birds

1. What do spoonbills do with their beaks?

Answer: Stir the water to attract fish

2. Where does a turnstone find food?

Answer: Under pebbles

3. Why are a plover's eggs speckled?

Answer: So the eggs are hard to see among pebbles

4. An avocet's bill is short and flat. True or false?

Answer: False. Its bill is long and curved.

5. Where does a heron stand while hunting?

Answer: At the edge of the water

6. Herons hunt for rats. True or false?

Answer: False. Herons hunt for fish.

7. Unscramble ILBL to spell another word for beak.

Answer: BILL

8. A heron jumps on prey with its feet. True or false?

Answer: False. It catches fish in its bill.

Penguins

1. Unscramble RICATACNAT.

Answer: ANTARCTICA

2. Where do emperor penguins keep their eggs?

Answer: In a pouch between their legs

3. Penguins are fast runners.
True or false?

Answer: False. They can only waddle because their legs are short.

4. Do penguins ever slide over ice?

Answer: Yes

5. How do penguins swim?

Answer: By flapping their wings as if they were flying

6. How long can a penguin stay underwater?

Answer: 20 minutes

7. Penguins catch fish and what other creatures to eat?

Answer: Squids

8. Where do penguins find shellfish?

Answer: On the seabed

Albatross

1. How many eggs does an albatross lay?

Answer: One

2. Unscramble SAGRS to spell what albatross' nests are made from.

Answer: GRASS

3. How long do albatross parents care for their chicks?

Answer: Nine months

4. Where does an albatross find food?

Answer: Far out at sea

5. What is an albatross's main food?

Answer: Squids

6. How does an albatross catch squids?

Answer: It scoops them from the surface of the water with its beak.

7. Why are an albatross's wings so long?

Answer: So that it can glide

8. How do albatross fly high up in the sky?

Answer: By riding warm winds that blow upward

People and places

Savannas

1. Unscramble STEWLIEBED to spell a savanna animal.

Answer: WILDEBEEST

2. Zebra stripes make them easy for lions to see. True or false?

Answer: False. It makes them look like shadows to the colorblind lions.

3. Do meerkats hunt alone?

Answer: No. They hunt in groups.

4. Is savanna grass good for grazing?

Answer: Yes

5. Are there many trees on a savanna?

Answer: No. There are few trees.

6. What "N" is a person who moves around regularly?

Answer: Nomad

7. Is the Maasai an African tribe?

Answer: Yes

8. Do the Maasai make mud houses?

Answer: Yes

Grasslands

1. Is grassland soil good for growing crops?

Answer: Yes

2. What is a dairy product starting with "C"?

Answer: Cheese

3. Which two crops are grown on grasslands?

Answer: Wheat and grains

4. Name the famous grassland in Argentina.

Answer: The Pampas

5. The Pampas is endangered. True or false?

Answer: True

6. Name a bird with excellent eyesight.

Answer: Eagle

7. Unscramble SINBO to name a grassland animal.

Answer: BISON

8. What does an omnivore eat?

Answer: Both plants and animals

Jungles

1. Name an animal that works in some jungles.

Answer: Elephant

2. Who cuts down trees in a jungle?

Answer: Loggers

3. Tribes live in jungles. True or false?

Answer: True

4. What do some tribes make boats out of?

Answer: Hollowed-out trees

5. Unscramble WOPILPEB to name a tribal weapon.

Answer: BLOWPIPE

6. Jungles cover how much of our planet?

Answer: Six percent

7. Are jungles getting bigger or smaller?

Answer: Smaller

8. What "D" is the word for many trees being cut down?

Answer: Deforestation

Mountains

1. Who climbs mountains?

Answer: Mountaineers

2. Why do mountaineers breathe through masks?

Answer: They need oxygen because the air is thinner at a high altitude.

3. What is the top of a mountain called?

Answer: Peak

4. What "G" is a river formed out of ice?

Answer: Glacier

5. Layers of rock are called what word beginning with "S"?

Answer: Strata

6. Mountains are formed very fast. True or false?

Answer: False. They are made by layers of rock moving slowly over time.

7. Where is the forest zone?

Answer: On the lower slopes of a mountain

8. Unscramble BERTIMENLI to name where the forest zone meets cold rocks.

Answer: TIMBERLINE

Volcanoes

1. What "L" gushes out of a volcano?

Answer: Lava

2. Lava is very cold. True or false?

Answer: False. It is a very hot liquid.

3. Do volcanologists visit volcanoes?

Answer: Yes

4. What do volcanologists wear?

Answer: Heatproof clothing

5. What forms as a cloud after a volcanic explosion?

Answer: Ash and dust

6. Can volcanoes cause earthquakes?

Answer: Yes

7. Is a tsunami ice cream or a giant wave?

Answer: A giant wave

8. Unscramble GAMMA HARMBEC to find the name of part of a volcano.

Answer: MAGMA CHAMBER

Earthquakes

1. What "P" are the pieces of Earth that move very slowly over time?

Answer: Plates

2. What "P" builds up between Earth's plates?

Answer: Pressure

3. Earth's crust is thick. True or false?

Answer: False. It is thin.

4. What can be cut off during a quake?

Answer: Water and electricity

5. What might people do if their houses are unsafe?

Answer: Move away while their houses are rebuilt

6. When did the big Tokyo quake occur?

Answer: 1923

7. What "F" came after the Tokyo quake?

Answer: Fires

8. How many people became homeless in the Tokyo quake?

Answer: 1.9 million

Villages

1. What are some houses built on?

Answer: Stilts

2. Stilts protect houses from the sun. True or false?

Answer: False. Stilts protect houses when rivers flood.

3. Villages are often built close to where there is what?

Answer: Work

4. Unscramble STEMNELTET, a word for a village.

Answer: SETTLEMENT

5. Where are the Atlas Mountains?

Answer: Morocco

6. Name a mountain range starting with the letter "C."

Answer: Caucasus

7. Name a country beginning with "R."

Answer: Russia

8. Can villages be home to many different people?

Answer: Yes

Cities

1. Unscramble AGICYEMT to find the word for a very large city.

Answer: MEGACITY

2. How many people live in a megacity?

Answer: Ten million or more

3. Name a megacity starting with "S."

Answer: Shanghai

4. Is land in cities cheap to buy?

Answer: No. It is expensive.

5. City buildings are very tall. True or false?

Answer: True

6. How many floors does the Sears Tower have?

Answer: 108

7. Where were many cities first settled?

Answer: Next to rivers or by an ocean

8. Why did people settle next to rivers or by an ocean?

Answer: So that they could receive and deliver goods by boat

On the farm

1. Where are fruit trees planted?

Answer: Orchards

2. Fruit has to be ripe before it is picked. True or false?

Answer: True

3. Unscramble BENMICO to name a farm machine.

Answer: COMBINE

4. When was the combine invented?

Answer: 1834

5. What do combines gather?

Answer: Grain plants

6. Is a plow used for watering?

Answer: No. It digs the soil.

7. Which animals starting with "O" pulled plows?

Answer: Oxen

8. Which plowing machine replaced horses?

Answer: Tractor

At the beach

1. What happens to rock pools when the tide is out?

Answer: They are no longer underwater.

2. Do rock-pool animals hide under umbrellas?

Answer: No. They hide under rocks and seaweeds.

3. Name a beach bird that scavenges for food.

Answer: Seagull

4. Some people eat seaweed. True or false?

Answer: True

5. Unscramble LESYJIFHL to reveal a sea creature that can sting you.

Answer: JELLYFISH

6. How many legs does a starfish have?

Answer: Five

7. What can you build at the beach?

Answer: Sandcastles

8. What should you wear at the beach?

Answer: Sunscreen

At home

1. Name a place where children can play outside.

Answer: Yard

2. Do yards need to be cared for?

Answer: Yes

3. Unscramble TARPADNRENG, a family member.

Answer: GRANDPARENT

4. What "R" is the word for people in a family?

Answer: Relatives

5. What is time away from work or school called?

Answer: Leisure time

6. Name a home leisure activity.

Answer: Watching television, listening to music, or talking on the telephone

7. Name something beginning with "C" that you can do at home.

Answer: Crafts

8. What can people make for friends?

Answer: Birthday cards and photo albums

At school

1. Are all schools the same?

Answer: No. Schools are different.

2. What do some students have to help them learn?

Answer: Computers

3. Unscramble RICLUMURUC, the list of subjects taught at a school.

Answer: CURRICULUM

4. Do schools teach reading and writing?

Answer: Yes

5. Math helps you learn to use what?

Answer: Numbers

6. What does science teach?

Answer: How the world works

7. Why are students given tests?

Answer: To find out how much they have learned

8. Test scores can be very important. True or false?

Answer: True

Bronze Age

1. People lived in bronze houses.
True or false?

Answer: False. They lived in huts.

2. Did Bronze Age huts have fires?

Answer: Yes

3. Bronze Age hut walls were made
of sticks, mud, and what else?

Answer: Dung

4. Unscramble RASPE to name a Bronze
Age weapon.

Answer: SPEAR

5. Is bronze softer than gold?

Answer: No. It is harder.

6. Which two metals are mixed to
make bronze?

Answer: Copper and tin

7. What "A" is a mix of metals?

Answer: Alloy

8. What "M" was bronze poured
into while it cooled?

Answer: Mold

Ancient Egypt

1. Ancient Egyptians had only one god.
True or false?

Answer: False. They had many gods.

2. How did priests worship gods?

*Answer: By offering them food
and drink*

3. Most Egyptians were priests.
True or false?

Answer: False. Most were farmers.

4. Name the Egyptians' important river.

Answer: The Nile River

5. Unscramble GIRIOTRAIN to find the
word for managing water.

Answer: IRRIGATION

6. What "P" was the name for an
Egyptian ruler?

Answer: Pharaoh

7. Pharaohs were thought to be half
man, half what?

Answer: God

8. Was magic part of Egyptian life?

Answer: Yes

Mummies

1. Unscramble LAMINBEMG, the word for preserving bodies.

Answer: EMBALMING

2. Was embalming a fast process?

Answer: No. It was slow.

3. Was an embalmed body bandaged?

Answer: Yes

4. What happened to a mummy's brain?

Answer: It was removed.

5. Did all Egyptians have many coffins?

Answer: No. Only important people did.

6. How was the death mask supposed to help the spirit?

Answer: It helped the spirit recognize the body in the afterlife.

7. Egyptian coffins were left undecorated. True or false?

Answer: False. They were painted and decorated with jewels.

8. What "S" is the name for the heavy stone outer coffin?

Answer: Sarcophagus

Buried treasures

1. Unscramble STREEAUR PAM, which shows where treasures are buried.

Answer: TREASURE MAP

2. Which letter "marks the spot"?

Answer: X

3. Which famous book did Robert Louis Stevenson write?

Answer: Treasure Island

4. Who starting with "P" likes treasures?

Answer: Pirates

5. What did pirates probably do with their treasures?

Answer: Spent them

6. Which Spanish ship carried a lot of precious cargo?

Answer: A Spanish galleon

7. What starting with "S" is a treasure?

Answer: Silver

8. Do treasure divers search on dry land?

Answer: No. They search in oceans.

Transportation

Cars

1. Has the Mini been popular for more than 40 years?

Answer: Yes

2. Do some cars runs on cooking oil?

Answer: Yes

3. Do Minis have four doors?

Answer: No. They have only two.

4. What does a driver use to change gears?

Answer: A gearshift

5. Unscramble HSELIDDWIN, the glass in front of a driver.

Answer: WINDSHIELD

6. Do cars have only a few parts?

Answer: No. They have many parts.

7. What helps control modern cars?

Answer: Computers

8. Which car was adapted from a U.S. Army vehicle?

Answer: The Hummer

Racecars

1. Unscramble TOCCPKI.

Answer: COCKPIT

2. How many mechanics might be in a pit crew?

Answer: Up to 20

3. A quick tire change and refuel is known as what?

Answer: A pit stop

4. Is it hot in a racecar?

Answer: Yes

5. Racecar drivers brake often. True or false?

Answer: False. They brake as little as possible.

6. Where are the wings on racecars?

Answer: On the fronts and tails of the cars

7. What might a racecar do without its wings to keep it close to the road?

Answer: Crash

8. Starting with "A," air pushing a car down is known as what?

Answer: Aerodynamics

Trucks

1. Unscramble ROTCART to name a part of some trucks.

Answer: TRACTOR

2. How many parts do tractor-trailers have?

Answer: Two

3. Can tractor-trailers turn easily in small spaces?

Answer: Yes

4. Do some trucks have a bed?

Answer: Yes

5. What "C" is the rigid frame for trucks?

Answer: Chassis

6. Does a truck have a single chassis?

Answer: Yes

7. What types of trucks carry sand?

Answer: Dump trucks

8. Do dump trucks have telescopic rods?

Answer: Yes

Diggers

1. How do diggers scoop up earth?

Answer: With buckets

2. Where do digger drivers sit?

Answer: In the cabin

3. Unscramble BAEDL to give the name of part of a digger.

Answer: BLADE

4. Are diggers used to build roads?

Answer: Yes

5. Do diggers make holes in the ground?

Answer: Yes

6. Diggers can move a lot of earth. True or false?

Answer: True

7. Diggers are sometimes called what?

Answer: Earthmovers

8. What helps diggers grab a lot of earth at once?

Answer: Teeth

Trains

1. How does a train driver see in the dark?

Answer: With headlights

2. What "G" do freight trains carry?

Answer: Goods

3. How many wagons did the longest freight train have?

Answer: 660

4. Do all trains have only one engine?

Answer: No. The longest-ever train had 16 engines.

5. All trains are powered by diesel. True or false?

Answer: False. They are also powered by electricity.

6. What comes from overhead wires?

Answer: Electric power

7. Unscramble TNSOIAT to name where people get on and off trains.

Answer: STATION

8. How fast are the quickest trains?

Answer: The fastest trains can travel at 356 miles per hour.

Ships

1. What "W" do warships have?

Answer: Weapons

2. What are warships usually part of?

Answer: A navy

3. Which types of ships carry goods?

Answer: Cargo ships

4. Unscramble TONSERNAIC, which cranes lift onto a ship's deck.

Answer: CONTAINERS

5. Some tankers carry oil. True or false?

Answer: True

6. Where are ships controlled from?

Answer: The bridge

7. Where would you sleep on an ocean liner?

Answer: In a cabin

8. How many passengers can the biggest cruise ship carry?

Answer: 4,300

Airplanes

1. What does a jet engine suck in at the front?

Answer: Air

2. What helps lift a plane up into the air?

Answer: Flaps on the wings

3. Airplanes can cruise at what speed?

Answer: 430 to 560 miles per hour

4. Unscramble YURWAN, where planes take off.

Answer: RUNWAY

5. Who makes sure that planes land safely?

Answer: Air-traffic controllers

6. Who refuels planes?

Answer: Airport ground crew

7. There are different sections on a plane for people and what else?

Answer: Luggage

8. How many passengers can big planes carry?

Answer: More than 500

Rockets

1. Are some parts of rockets supposed to fall off?

Answer: Yes

2. Unscramble LOLOPA to name the craft that went to the Moon.

Answer: APOLLO

3. Are space shuttles reusable?

Answer: Yes

4. How many astronauts can an orbiter carry?

Answer: As many as seven

5. What are attached to a rocket's fuel tank for extra power?

Answer: Booster rockets

6. Does the whole space shuttle go into space?

Answer: No. Only the orbiter does.

7. A rocket's fuel tank holds only two gallons of fuel. True or false?

Answer: False. It holds 530,000 gallons of fuel.

8. What "P" bring a rocket's boosters back?

Answer: Parachutes

INDEX

Progress Chart

This chart lists all the topics in the book.
Once you have completed each page, stick a star
in the correct box below.

Page	Topic	Star	Page	Topic	Star	Page	Topic	Star
8	I know why I have a skeleton	☆	15	I know what my different teeth do	☆	22	I know about the viscosity of liquids	☆
9	I know that some other animals have bones	☆	16	I know what is in my food	☆	23	I can recognize liquids	☆
10	I know what my muscles do	☆	17	I know about balanced diets	☆	24	I know which materials will mix	☆
11	I know about how the heart works	☆	18	I know that matter is either a solid, a liquid, or a gas	☆	25	I know about water cooling down	☆
12	I know about blood	☆	19	I know which gas flows the quickest	☆	26	I know how quickly different liquids evaporate	☆
13	I have felt my pulse	☆	20	I can tell solids, liquids, and gases apart	☆	27	I know how to separate salt from sand	☆
14	I know what happens when I exercise	☆	21	I know the properties of different gases	☆	28	I know how to filter mixtures	★

 When you see this symbol you need to take extra care -
ask an adult to supervise you.

Page	Topic	Star	Page	Topic	Star	Page	Topic	Star
29	I know that some changes are reversible	☆	41	I know which materials conduct heat	☆	53	I know that some microbes are harmful	☆
30	I know how to separate mixtures	☆	42	I can use a key to identify different metals	☆	54	I know what vertebrates are	☆
31	I know that some changes are irreversible	☆	43	I know what makes things fall	☆	55	I know the key features of invertebrates	☆
32	I know what happens when matter burns	☆	44	I know that a force acts in one direction	☆	56	I know what yeast is and what it eats	☆
33	I know how the water cycle works	☆	45	I know what effect friction has	☆	57	I can use a key to identify animals	☆
34	I know how a condenser works	☆	46	I know what makes boats float	☆	58	I know the key features of arthropods	☆
35	I know that some substances are soluble	☆	47	I know what a Newton is	☆	59	I know how long different life cycles are	☆
36	I know that all substances are not equally soluble	☆	48	I know that some woods are stronger than others	☆	60	I know about growth patterns	☆
37	I know about water purity	☆	49	I know which fabric will stretch the most	☆	61	I know the similarities between plants and animals	☆
38	I know that temperature affects solubility	☆	50	I know that some matter is elastic	☆	62	I know how plants make food	☆
39	I know that adding salt changes water	☆	51	I know that some matter is crushable	☆	63	I can make up a key for identifying birds	☆
40	I know when different liquids freeze	☆	52	I know that some microbes are useful	☆	64	I can make up a key for identifying plants	☆

Page	Topic	Star	Page	Topic	Star	Page	Topic	Star
65	I can use a key to identify plants	☆	77	I can read and label the symbols on a circuit diagram	☆	89	I know which star is the brightest	☆
66	I know how microbes can be helpful	☆	78	I can draw a circuit diagram	☆	90	I know that shadows from the Sun move during the day	☆
67	I know how microbes can be harmful	☆	79	I know about switches	☆	91	I know why the Sun appears to move	☆
68	I know how friction affects moving objects	☆	80	I know what batteries do	☆	92	I know how gravity affects the weight of objects	☆
69	I know how parachutes work	☆	81	I know that the length of a wire affects a circuit	☆	93	I know what causes night and day	☆
70	I know the four forces involved in flight	☆	82	I know how bulbs affect a circuit	☆	94	I can describe the phases of the Moon	☆
71	I know about Bernoulli's Principle	☆	83	I know how a lever works	☆	95	I know that the Moon travels around Earth	☆
72	I know what affects the way a plane flies	☆	84	I know about the different classes of lever	☆	96	I know that sound cannot travel through space	☆
73	I know how a jet engine works	☆	85	I know how the gears on a bicycle work	☆	97	I know how sound is affected by distance	☆
74	I know how to design a parachute	☆	86	I know what a machine does	☆	98	I know why the Moon appears to change shape	☆
75	I know about electrical conductors	☆	87	I know how pulleys and cranes work	☆	99	I know why I would weigh less on the Moon	☆
76	I know which materials conduct electricity	☆	88	I know how a wheelbarrow helps us move things	☆	Once you have completed this book, you've earned the certificate overleaf!		

3

Certificate

Grades 5-6

Congratulations to

.....................................(Name)

for successfully finishing this book.

Well done!

Age.................Date.................

Science

Science made Easy

Grades 5–6
Ages 10–12

Canadian Editor
Marilyn Wilson

EDITOR Julia Roles
PROJECT EDITORS Ian Whitelaw, Ankush Saikia
DTP CO-ORDINATOR Pankaj Sharma
DTP DESIGNERS Harish Aggarwal, Pushpak Tyagi
PRODUCTION Erica Rosen

First Canadian Edition, 2007

Dorling Kindersley is represented in Canada by Tourmaline Editions Inc.,
662 King Street West, Suite 304, Toronto, Ontario M5V 1M7

ISBN: 978-1-55363-081-4

Colour reproduction by Colourscan
Printed and bound in China by L. Rex Printing Co., Ltd.
07 08 09 10 6 5 4 3 2 1

Discover more at
www.dk.com

An Invitation to *Science made Easy*

Learning science is a major component of the knowledge base needed to live and work in today's world. There is an old adage, "I hear and I forget; I see and I remember; I do and I understand." *Doing* is the basis of inquiry science, which uses a constructivist approach to learning, whereby knowledge is constructed from the experiences of the learner. The caveat here is that these experiences must both minimize and address misconceptions about the natural world. For example, we do not catch a cold from the cold, but from a virus. And heavier objects do not fall faster! All objects will fall at the same exact rate if there is no air resistance.

The three workbooks in this series stress an inquiry approach to learning the key ideas in science, while developing the skills needed to do this science. They support how science should be taught as described in the Pan-Canadian Science Curriculum and the Provincial Ministry of Education Science Curriculum Guidelines, and are meant to provide additional support to the learning of science whether at home or at school.

There are three learning levels for *Science made Easy*:
- Grades K–2
- Grades 3–4
- Grades 5–6

On every work sheet, the relevant grade is indicated in a star at the top.

Each lesson in these workbooks has the following sections:
- *Background information:* A key idea in science is described and new science terms are explained.

- *Science activity:* These are all guided activities to explore science and develop the skills for doing science.

- *Science investigation:* These inquiry investigations are learner directed. They provide the learner with the opportunity to elaborate or extend upon a key idea in science. **Investigations involving chemicals, electricity, sharp tools, human subjects, or an open flame must be monitored by an adult. Look for the safety icon ⓘ shown here for these types of investigations.**

Two support templates follow the work sheets:
- *Concept map graphic organizer:* This is used to develop the language of science and to evaluate the learning of new concepts. It should be used in every activity in which a new science term is introduced–these terms are italicized in the text.
- *Inquiry template:* The young investigator should use this as a guide for carrying out the *science investigation* described on each page.

At the end of the book you will find the:
- *Answer Section with Notes for Adults:* This section provides answers and explanatory notes for the science activities and investigations.

Why do you have a skeleton?

Background information

Your skeleton provides you with support so you have a form and shape. Otherwise you would be a blob of jelly! This support allows you to move. The skeleton also provides protection for the organs of your body. The skeleton is composed of bones. When you were born, you had about 350 bones. As you grew, some of these bones fused together. When you become an adult you will have 206 bones. The bones of your body make up your *skeletal system*.

Science activity

Draw an arrow from each label to the correct part of the skeleton.

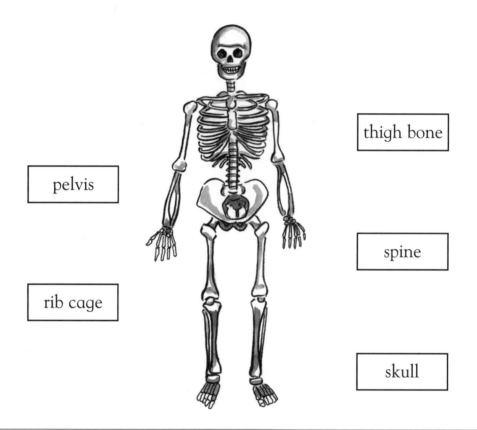

thigh bone

pelvis

spine

rib cage

skull

Science investigation

Use the Internet to learn about the skeletons of other types of living things. Make a scrapbook showing the skeletons of 5–10 different animals. Include animals that have exoskeletons. Compare and contrast the skeletons. Now use what you have learned to make your own cardboard model of a movable skeleton using round head paper fasteners to create movable parts.

Can you feel your bones?

Background information

Not all animals have bones. Animals with bony skeletons inside of them are called *vertebrates*. All vertebrates have a backbone. Vertebrates include humans, dogs, snakes, fish, and birds. Skeletons give protection and support to the body, and help it to move. Animals such as worms, insects, snails, and jellyfish do not have bony skeletons; they are called *invertebrates*.

Science activity

Here are the skeletons of a fish, a bird, and a frog. On each of the drawings, color in the part that protects the brain, and colour in the backbone.

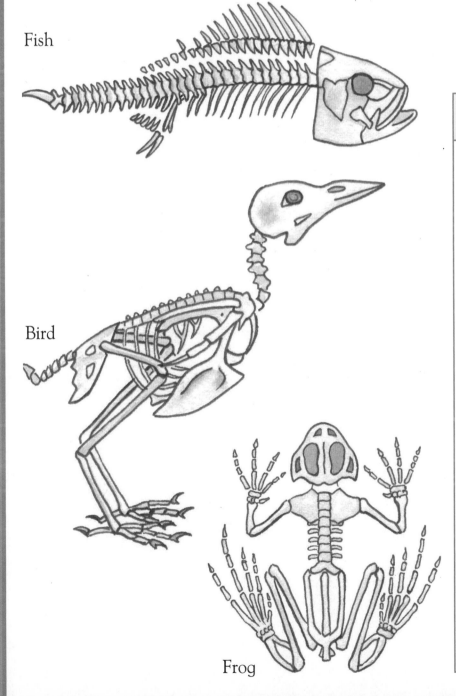

Fish

Bird

Frog

Science investigation

⚠ Ask an adult to remove the meat from a cooked beef bone and the wing, leg, and neck of a chicken. Trace the bones onto a piece of paper and label them. Draw an arrow to a joint on the chicken wing. How does a beef bone compare to a chicken bone? Is one harder than the other?

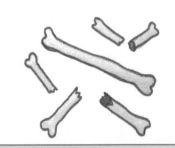

Where are your muscles?

Background information

The muscles all over your body move your skeleton. When muscles work, they get thicker and shorter. We say that muscles *contract*. When a person "makes a muscle," you see their muscle contract. A contracting muscle pulls on a bone, making it move. Muscles need energy to work. They get their energy from sugars in your blood. Most muscles rest or relax after they have been used. They get longer and flatter. The heart is a muscle that works very hard—every time you feel a pulse, your heart muscle has contracted!

Science activity

When you move your legs, feet, hands, or arms, the muscles that move them get thicker and shorter.

On picture A, draw arrows pointing to where you think the muscles moving the foot will get thicker.

On picture B, draw an arrow pointing to where you think the muscle raising the forearm will get thicker.

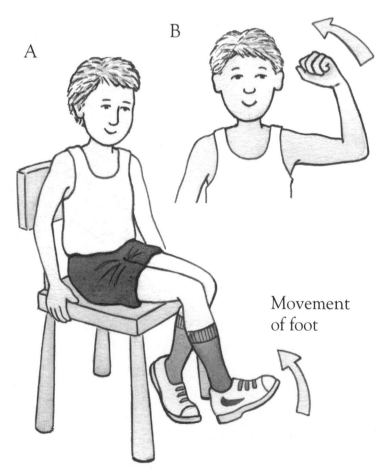

Movement of arm

Movement of foot

A

B

Science investigation

Design and conduct an experiment to see how your muscles move your arms and legs. Which muscles thicken and shorten when you move different parts of your body? Use the Internet to learn more about muscles and bones.

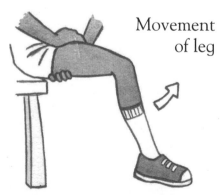

Movement of leg

How does the heart work?

Background information

The human heart is a powerful, muscular organ located near the centre of the chest, protected by the ribcage. The heart's main job is to pump blood throughout your body. It pumps the blood through blood vessels, which branch out to all parts of your body. In order to do this, it has very muscular walls that contract and squeeze the blood into the blood vessels. You can feel a throbbing sensation when you place your fingers on the side of your neck or on your wrist where the blood surges through blood vessels close to the surface of the skin. The throbbing is called your *pulse*. Your heart is the strongest muscle of your body. It beats from 60 to 100 times per minute, but can go much faster when necessary. It beats about 100000 times a day, which is more than 30 million times per year. A 70-year-old person's heart will have beaten about 2.5 billion times!

Science activity

The picture of the body has four empty circles. Colour the circle that represents the position of the heart. Place an X where you can locate a pulse on the body shown.

Science investigation

Fill a balloon with a small amount of air so that it can fit into your hand. Squeeze it 80 times in 1 minute. What did you learn about your heart by doing this? Now find your pulse by placing your forefinger and middle finger on your wrist. Count how many times you feel a throb in 1 minute.

What carries the blood?

Background information

Every time the heart beats, blood is sent throughout the body, carrying oxygen and nutrients to all of the cells. Each day, the average adult heart pumps more than 7570 litres of blood many times through about 96560 km of blood vessels. The blood that leaves the heart and goes to the body is rich in oxygen. After the oxygen is delivered to the cells, the blood returns to the heart to be sent to the lungs to pick up more oxygen. Blood vessels that carry blood away from the heart are called *arteries*. They have thick, muscular walls to help move the blood to your cells. Veins are the thin-walled blood vessels that carry blood back to the heart. Your heart, veins, and arteries are part of your circulatory system. This system delivers important substances to your cells and removes waste. You can think of your circulatory system as your blood highway.

Science activity

Fill in the missing letters in the labels for this diagram.

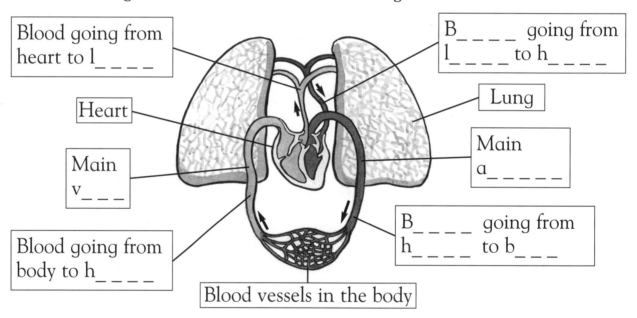

Blood going from heart to l_ _ _ _

B_ _ _ _ going from l_ _ _ _ to h_ _ _ _

Heart

Lung

Main v_ _ _

Main a_ _ _ _ _ _

Blood going from body to h_ _ _ _

B_ _ _ _ going from h_ _ _ _ to b_ _ _

Blood vessels in the body

Science investigation

A *stethoscope* is a device that can listen to your heart. Obtain 30 cm of rubber tubing, some masking tape, and two small funnels. Attach a funnel to each end of the tubing with some tape. The funnel end should fit into the tube. Place one funnel over your heart and the other over your ear. How many times does your heart beat per minute? How does this compare to your pulse? Explain any similarities or differences.

Can you feel the pulse?

Background information

When your heart beats, it pumps blood to parts of your body through vessels called *arteries* and *veins*. Arteries carry blood away from your heart to the rest of your body, while veins return blood to your heart. Where an artery crosses a bone, you can press a finger against your skin to feel the blood pumping. This is called your pulse. It is a measure of how fast your heart is beating. A child's pulse is usually about 70 to 80 beats per minute.

Science activity

A doctor found that a girl's pulse was 80 beats per minute. After running slowly for 1 minute, her pulse went up to 120 beats per minute. After skipping for another minute, her pulse was 170 beats. After resting for 2 minutes, her pulse was 140 beats.

Using the chart below, draw a bar graph of the results. What effect does exercise have on the girl's pulse?

....

Pulse (number of beats per minute)

170				
160				
150				
140				
130				
120				
110				
100				
90				
80				
70				
60				
50				
40				
30				
20				
10				
0	Resting	Running slowly	Skipping	Resting

Science investigation

Find your pulse by pressing your first two fingers against the underside of your wrist, below the thumb. Take and measure your pulse before and after exercise. Design and conduct an experiment to see how your pulse rate changes after exercise.

What happens when you exercise?

Background information

Your heart contracts to push blood through your body. The contractions are called heartbeats. You can feel your *heartbeat*, or pulse, by placing a finger across blood vessels close to the surface of your skin. Your pulse rate is a measure of how many times your heart beats in 1 minute. When you exercise, your muscles work harder and need more oxygen. Exercise makes the pulse rate go up so that the blood can deliver more oxygen to the muscles.

Science activity

Angela measured her pulse rate after 1 minute, 2 minutes, 3 minutes, and 4 minutes of exercise. She plotted her results on this graph.

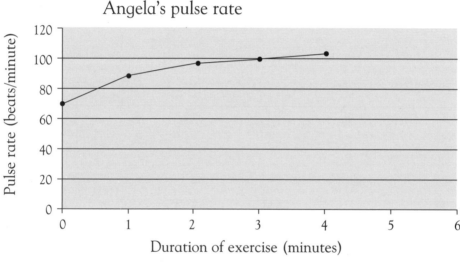

Describe the relationship between exercise and pulse rate. ....

....

Can Angela's pulse rate go on increasing? Give reasons for your answer. What would her pulse rate be after six minutes of exercise? Plot this on the graph.

....

Science investigation

(!) Mark where your pulse is with an X on your wrist so you can easily find it again. Use washable ink. Take your pulse for 15 seconds and then multiply by 4. This will give you your pulse rate for 1 minute. Try this 2–3 times for accuracy. Next, run in place for 3 minutes. Quickly take your pulse. Continue to take it until it is back to your resting pulse rate. Graph your data.

What do our teeth do?

Background information

Humans have four different types of teeth. Young children have about 20 teeth called *milk teeth*. They have eight teeth called *incisors* at the front of the mouth (four above and four below). These are used for cutting food. The next four sharp, pointed teeth are *canines*, which are used for tearing food. Next to these are the *premolars*, used for grinding and chewing. Between the ages of 5 and 10, these milk teeth are replaced by adult teeth, which include another 12 teeth called *molars*. These are also used for chewing.

Science activity

Animals that eat meat have canines and incisors to cut and tear meat. Animals that eat plants have large, flat teeth called molars for grinding and chewing. Humans eat both meat and plants. What sort of teeth do humans have? Label each type of tooth in the diagram below.

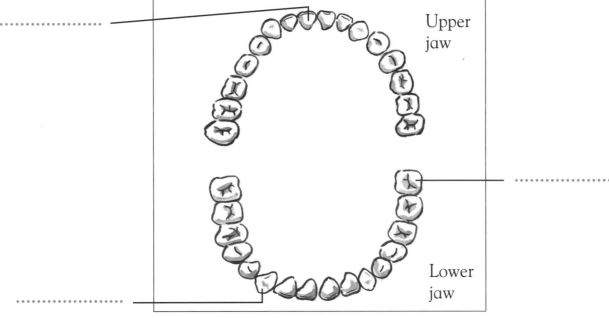

A set of adult human teeth

Science investigation

Use a mirror to look inside your mouth. Then colour in all the teeth that you have of each kind in the diagram above. You may not have all of the teeth in the diagram, as it shows an adult's teeth. Check with friends and some adults to see if they have the same number of teeth as you. Use disposable rubber gloves when you check inside someone else's mouth.

What is in our food?

Background information

You should think about what you eat, as your health depends on it. The food groups that provide you with the most energy are *carbohydrates* (sugars and starches) and *fats,* although fats do not provide energy as quickly as carbohydrates do. Examples of foods high in carbohydrates are cereals, breads, cookies, crackers, potatoes, and rice. Oils and butter are high in fat. Foods that provides you with the raw materials you need for growth and repair are rich in a substance called *protein*. Meat, poultry, fish, eggs, and beans are all high in protein. Living things also need *vitamins* and *minerals* to remain healthy. Fruits and vegetables are foods naturally rich in vitamins and minerals.

Science activity

Classify each of the foods shown in the picture below according to what your body needs them for.

 Fish   Cake   Egg   Apple

 Bread   Cabbage   Butter   Beans

Growth and repair	Energy	Health
....	....	....
....	....	....
....	....	....

Science investigation

Keep a record of what you eat over two days and ask a friend to do the same. When classifying what you eat, remember that some meals you eat may have a number of foods combined into one dish. For example, pizza may have meat (growth and repair), tomato sauce (vitamins and minerals) and the crust (energy). Compare your diets. What did you learn?

Is your diet balanced?

Background information

A healthy diet is a balanced combination of food for growth and repair, energy-giving food, and vitamins and minerals. You also need food that contains fibre. You cannot digest fibre, but it helps move food through your digestive tract. The amount of food you need depends on how active you are and how much you are growing. If you eat too little, you can suffer from *malnutrition* because your body is not getting the nutrients it needs. If you eat too much, you can become overweight, which can lead to health problems such as diabetes.

Science activity

Here are some meals with an item missing form each one. Decide what food item you would add to make each meal part of a balanced diet. Write the name of the item and which food group it is from.

1
- Boiled potato
- Cabbage
- Carrot

  ....

2
- Pizza (cheese and tomato topping)

  ....

  ....

3
- Boiled rice
- Grilled lamb chop
- Bacon

  ....

  ....

4
- Chicken drumsticks
- Peas

  ....

5
- Lettuce
- Spring onions
- Grated carrots
- Bread

  ....

6
- Fried egg
- Bacon
- Toast
- Pudding

  ....

  ....

Science investigation

Collect pictures of food and make a collage of a healthy dinner, by sticking them on paper plates. Label each food group. Use the Internet to learn about Health Canada's *Food Guide to Healthy Eating.*

Is it a solid, liquid, or gas?

Background information

Three *phases* of matter exist naturally on Earth: solids, liquids, and gases. Generally, solids are substances that retain their shape and do not flow. Liquids flow and take the shape of the container they are in. Gases also flow and fill all of the space available. Some types of matter can exist in all phases on our planet.

Science activity

Which of these materials are solids (S), which are gases (G), and which are liquids (L)? Circle the ones that exist in all three phases on Earth. Write **S**, **G,** or **L** in each box.

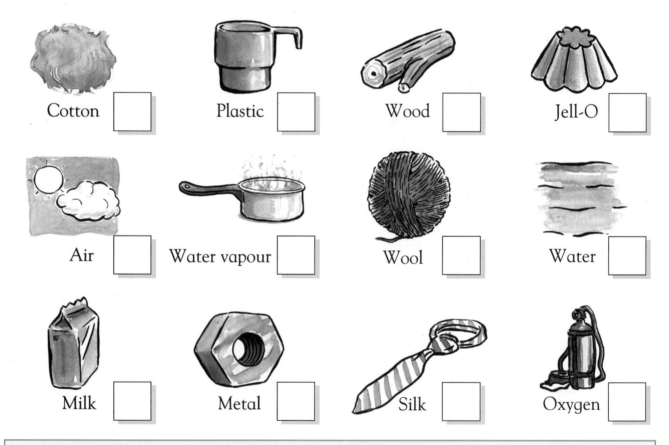

Cotton ☐   Plastic ☐   Wood ☐   Jell-O ☐

Air ☐   Water vapour ☐   Wool ☐   Water ☐

Milk ☐   Metal ☐   Silk ☐   Oxygen ☐

Science investigation

Obtain a plastic zipper bag, borax, and glue. In a bowl, mix 125 mL of glue with 125 mL of water until thoroughly combined. Pour the mixture into the zipper bag. Then measure 25 mL of borax and mix it into another 125 mL of water. Pour 50 mL of the dissolved borax into the zipper bag with the other mixture. Close the bag and knead the mixtures together for 2–3 minutes, until thoroughly combined. Remove your mixture and test whether it is a liquid or solid. Also test for other properties.

What is a gas?

Background information

Some types of matter easily change into a gas. Gasoline and perfumes are examples of this type of matter. Dry ice, which is solid, can change phase directly into a gas, but it has no odour. This property of matter is called its *volatility*. Some gases flow more rapidly than others because of differences in their density. Denser gases sink under less dense gases. Less dense gases spread out faster than denser gases. You can smell dinner cooking in the kitchen because heat from the stove changes some of the food into volatile gases, which spread through your home.

Science activity

Name of gas	Density in grams per mL
hydrogen	0.00009
carbon dioxide	0.00198
helium	0.00018
nitrogen	0.00126
oxygen	0.00143

The information in the above data tables lists the density of some common gases. The density of air is 0.0013 grams per mL. According to this data table, why do helium balloons float in air?

....

....

Place the gases in order from least dense to densest. Which gas would flow the fastest? Explain.

....

....

Science investigation

Do grapes float? You will need some soda water and grapes. Fill a glass three quarters full with soda water. Drop some grapes in the water and record what happens. Next, peel the skin off a few of the grapes and drop them into the soda water. Record what happens. Explain your observations. Make sure to include your understanding of density in your explanation.

What kind of material is it?

Background information

Materials can exist as solids, liquids, and gases. Liquids and gases can easily be poured to fill a space. Liquids can make a surface feel wet. You cannot easily pass your hand through a solid. Many gases have no colour. Knowing some of these things can help you identify materials.

Science activity

The table below tells you the properties of four different materials–chlorine, paraffin, mica, and margarine. Use this table to answer the questions.

Material	Chlorine	Paraffin	Mica	Margarine
Can it fill a space?	Yes	Yes	No	No
What colour is it?	Yellow	No colour	White and silvery	Yellow
Can it be poured?	Yes	Yes	No	No
Can you put your finger through it?	Yes	Yes	No	Yes
Can it make a piece of paper wet?	No	Yes	No	Yes

Which materials are solids? ....

Which materials are liquids? ....

Which materials are gases? ....

Science investigation

Using a medicine dropper, place one drop of each of the following liquids onto wax paper: soapy water, fresh water, oil, rubbing alcohol. Have an adult help you. Can the shape of a drop of the liquid be used to identify the liquid? Explain.

Which gas is it?

Background information

Air is a mixture of gases. The main gases in air are nitrogen and oxygen. There are also small amounts of other gases, including carbon dioxide, helium, and argon. Each of these gases has different properties that are useful to us in different ways. They can be separated from each other by cooling because each one condenses at a different temperature. *Condensation* is the phase change by which matter changes from a gas to a liquid.

Science activity

The properties of some of the gases in air are listed below. A chemically reactive gas can react with other substances to form new substances. For example, oxygen is chemically reactive; it causes iron to rust.

Gas	Properties
oxygen	chemically reactive; necessary for burning, and for living things to respire (use food for energy)
carbon dioxide	chemically reactive; extinguishes flames; quite a dense (heavy) gas; needed by plants for photosynthesis
argon	not chemically reactive (inert)

Decide which gas should be used in each of the following cases.

Filling cylinders to help people with lung disease breathe more easily

....

Filling fire extinguishers

....

Filling light bulbs so that the filament does not react chemically

....

Helium is an inert gas. It is used to fill balloons to make them buoyant. What happens when you let go of a balloon? What does this tell you about helium?

....

Science investigation

Fill three separate balloons with helium, air, and carbon dioxide. You can fill a balloon with carbon dioxide by placing it over a freshly opened bottle of soda (carbonated) water and letting it sit a few minutes until it inflates. Design and conduct an experiment to test differences in the density of these gases.

5 Do all liquids flow equally well?

Background information

Liquids flow and take the shape of the container into which they are poured. Some liquids feel "thin" and flow quickly, while others feel "thick" and flow slowly. This property of resistance to flow is called *viscosity.*

Science activity

Hunter tested the viscosity of different liquids by pouring each one into a tall jar and timing how long it took for a small lump of modelling clay to drop to the bottom.

Using the chart below, number the liquids in order of their viscosity. Write **1** for the least viscous liquid and **7** for the most viscous.

Liquid	Time taken (for modelling clay to fall)	Order
water	2 seconds	
vegetable oil	4.5 seconds	
olive oil	6 seconds	
nail polish remover	1 second	
golden syrup	90 seconds	
motor oil	10 seconds	
dishwashing liquid	7 seconds	

How long do you think the modelling clay would take to fall through apple juice? Explain.

....

....

Science investigation

Collect different liquids in your home such as liquid soap, molasses, or one of the liquids noted in the above chart. Design and conduct an experiment to see which liquid has the greatest viscosity.

How runny is it?

Background information

Liquids are materials that make things wet. All liquids flow. This means that they are runny and you can pour them. If you spill liquids, they spread out. If you pour a liquid into a container, it takes the shape of the container. If you leave a liquid to stand, its surface will flatten, with the edges a bit higher than the centre. You can easily push your finger through a liquid.

Science activity

Lauren and Tai did an experiment to find out which of the five liquids below was the runniest. The same amount of each liquid was poured from a pitcher into a glass. Each pitcher was held in the same position over the glass. The time it took to fill each glass was written down.

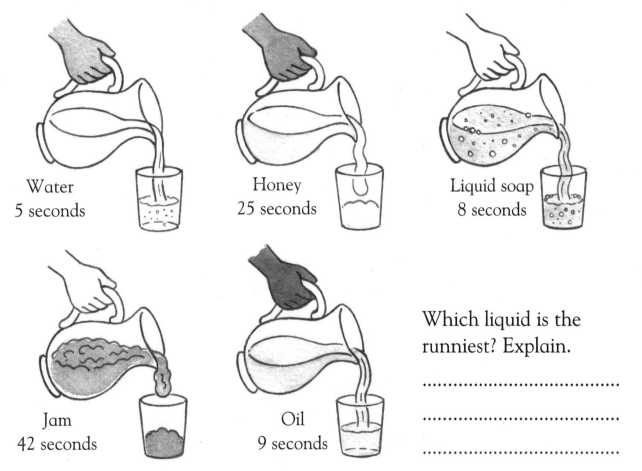

Water
5 seconds

Honey
25 seconds

Liquid soap
8 seconds

Jam
42 seconds

Oil
9 seconds

Which liquid is the runniest? Explain.

....

....

....

Science investigation

Design and conduct an experiment to see which of the following liquids is runniest: water, juice, maple syrup, soda, and liquid soap. Drop a small object, such as a marble, into each liquid to help you determine this.

Will they mix?

Background information

When solids are added to some liquids, the solid dissolves into very tiny particles and seems to disappear. A mixture in which one material dissolves in another is called a *solution*. When you add sugar to a cup of tea, the sugar dissolves in the tea to form a solution. Some solids will not dissolve in liquids. For example, flour will not dissolve in water. Materials that dissolve in liquids are called *soluble*. Materials that do not dissolve in liquids are called *insoluble*. Water is a liquid that can dissolve many types of materials.

Science activity

Read the sentences below and decide which ones are true and which ones are false. Circle the right answers.

Sand dissolves in boiling water.	True	False
Sugar dissolves in lemon juice.	True	False
Soil dissolves in water.	True	False
Salt dissolves in tomato soup.	True	False
Sugar dissolves in sand.	True	False
Oil is soluble in vinegar.	True	False

Boiling water

Sand

Science investigation

Design and conduct an experiment to see if a sugar cube dissolves faster in hot water or cold water.

How fast do things cool down?

Background information
Hot water will cool down until it reaches the temperature of its surroundings. There is a pattern in the way things cool down.

Science activity
Look at the axes on the graph below. Estimate the shape of a line showing how hot water cools down. Draw this line on the graph. Francesca did an experiment to see what really happens. Her results are shown in the table on the right. Plot the results on the graph using a different colour pencil. Do a line graph and connect all of the points. Does it match the drawing you made? Explain.

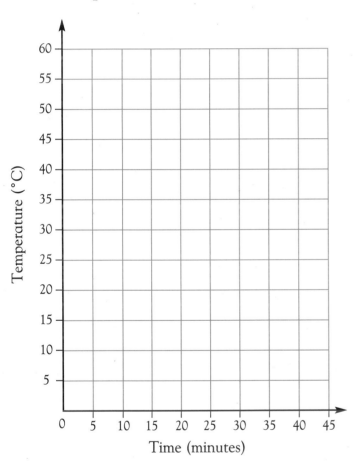

Cooling time	Temperature of water
0 minutes	60°C
5 minutes	40°C
10 minutes	28°C
15 minutes	24°C
20 minutes	23°C
25 minutes	22°C
30 minutes	22°C
35 minutes	22°C

Predict the temperature after 45 minutes. Explain. ....

Science investigation

Design and conduct your own experiment to measure the change in the temperature of refrigerated water that is placed in room temperature. Create a data table and graph your results.

How quickly does it evaporate?

Background information
Water left in a bowl will slowly disappear. The water evaporates into water vapour, the gas phase of water. The water vapour mixes with the air. *Evaporation* is a type of phase change in which matter changes from a liquid to a gas. Some liquids evaporate more quickly than others. Liquids with high boiling points (those that boil at very high temperatures) tend to evaporate more slowly than those with lower boiling points.

Science activity
Number the liquids listed below in order of how fast you would expect them to evaporate at room temperature. Explain why you think this is so.

☐ water   ☐ rubbing alcohol   ☐ vegetable oil

....

....

....

How do you think you can make the water evaporate more quickly?

....

....

Science investigation

(!) What happens when a liquid evaporates from your skin? Gently rub some water on your upper arm. Wait a few minutes and describe what you feel on your arm. Repeat this experiment, but this time apply some rubbing alcohol on your upper arm. Wait a minute and describe what you feel. You can try this with other liquids.

Can you separate salt from sand?

Background information

Filtering removes *insoluble* particles from water (particles that do not dissolve). Salt is *soluble* in water, but sand is insoluble (it is not soluble). The water in a salt solution will evaporate if it is left uncovered. Rock salt is a mixture of salt and sand.

Science activity

Using the information above and the equipment shown below, explain how you would separate the salt in rock salt from its insoluble parts. You may add other equipment that is not shown here. You may want to draw a flow chart to show the steps in your procedure.

Draw your flow chart here.

Science investigation

A lot more matter would be recycled if it could be separated from a mixture. Try out your skills. Mix together some sand, aluminum paper clips, and pennies in a bowl (and anything else you want to add). Design a procedure to separate the mixture. Test out your procedure to see if it works.

Can we filter it?

Background information

Sometimes it is necessary to separate a mixture. For example, coffee filters are used to keep the coffee grinds out of the coffee. When you pour coffee into a filter, the holes in the filter are large enough for the water to drain away, but too small for the grinds to pass through. The coffee grinds are trapped by the filter. When the materials in a mixture are *insoluble* in water, you can use a filter to separate them.

Science activity

Here are some lentils, peas, and marbles all mixed up in a pot. Pictures A and B show the bottom of the pot. On A, draw the sizes of the holes you must make to separate the lentils from the peas and marbles. On B, draw the holes you would need to make to separate the lentils and peas from the marbles.

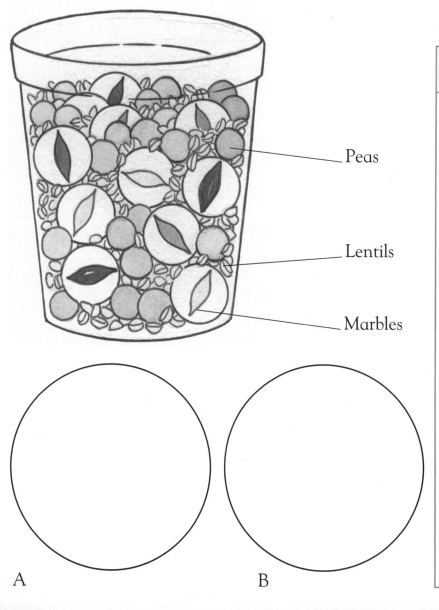

Peas

Lentils

Marbles

A

B

Science investigation

Mix together sand, potting soil, and aquarium gravel. Design a filtering method to separate this mixture. Use your knowledge about the properties of each material in the mixture. Test out your filtering method. Did it work? What are some of the problems you had in your design?

Are some changes reversible?

Background information

When ice is warmed, it melts to form water. When water is heated further, it boils to form *water vapour*, a colourless, odourless gas. These changes from solid to liquid to gas can be reversed by cooling water vapour. The water vapour will condense to form liquid water, and if cooling continues the water will eventually freeze.

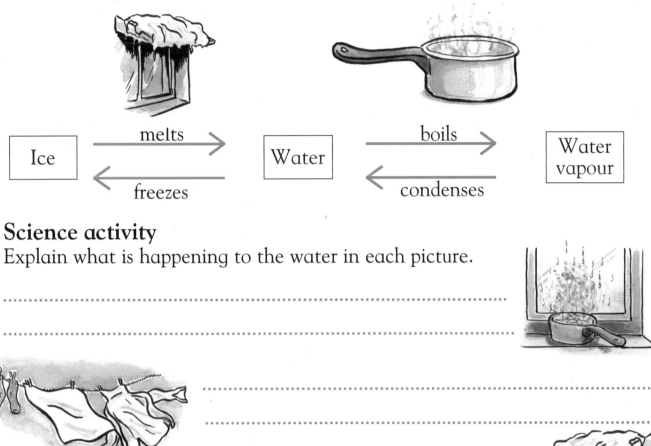

| Ice | melts → ← freezes | Water | boils → ← condenses | Water vapour |

Science activity

Explain what is happening to the water in each picture.

....

....

....

....

....

....

Science investigation

Look at weather maps in different parts of the country. Find some cities in which it is snowing. What is the temperature in these cities? Find some cities in which it is raining. What is the temperature in these cities? Create a data table to summarize the data you collected. What is the relationship between temperature and weather?

⭐ How can we separate mixtures?

Background information

Mixtures are two or more materials combined together. They can be separated in many different ways. To find out which is the best way to separate a mixture, you must first ask yourself some important questions. For example, are the materials in the mixture soluble? Are the materials attracted to a magnet? Do the materials change when they are heated? What size are the particles in the mixture?

Science activity

On the left, you can see four mixtures. On the right are four different methods for separating mixtures. Draw a line between each mixture and the best separation method. On a separate piece of paper, explain your choice.

Steel nails and copper nails

Dissolve in water and then use a filter.

Use a colander.

Rice and beans

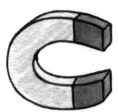

Use a magnet.

Soil containing mud and sand

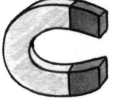

Shake in a bottle with some water and leave to settle.

Sand and salt

Science investigation

⚠️ Suppose somebody mixed together sand, paper clips, and sugar. Design and conduct an experiment that will separate the three materials from one another. How could you get the sugar back if you dissolved it in water?

Are some changes irreversible?

Background information

When you mix substances together, they may change to form a new substance. Sometimes the change is *reversible*, while at other times it is *irreversible*. For example, when vinegar is mixed with baking soda, the two fizz and a new substance is formed. This change is irreversible. A change is more likely to be irreversible if there is a reaction such as a fizz, colour change, or a change in temperature.

Science activity

Are the following mixing processes reversible or irreversible?

1. Dissolving sugar in water ....

2. Shaking together vinegar and oil ....

3. Mixing sand and sugar ....

4. Adding lemon juice to red cabbage juice
(the colour changes from bluish-purple to red) ....

Science investigation

Try mixing the following substances together, and decide whether the change is reversible or irreversible. Do any mixtures result in a temperature change? Explain.
1. Lemon juice added to baking powder
2. Vinegar added to chalk
3. Vinegar added to salt
4. Lemon juice added to sugar

What happens when it burns?

Background information

Oxygen from the air is needed for something to burn. *Burning* is an irreversible process that forms new substances. Some of these substances are solids, such as ash or soot, and some are gases, such as water vapour and carbon dioxide. When paper burns, it produces soot (mostly carbon), water vapour, carbon dioxide, a small amount of other gases, and ash (minerals that do not burn).

Science activity

Look at the drawing. It shows a candle burning inside an upturned jam jar.

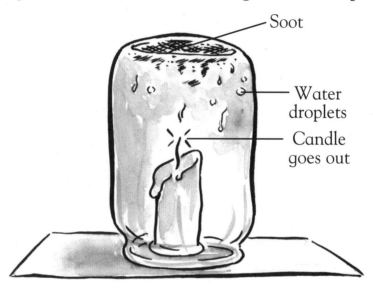

Soot

Water droplets

Candle goes out

What is produced when a candle burns? What is a possible explanation as to why the candle went out?

....

....

....

Science investigation

(!) Light a candle and place a jar over it. Time how long it takes for the candle to go out. When the flame goes out, let the jar cool down a bit. Carefully lift the jar, keeping the open end facing downward and placing it quickly on a table. Relight the candle. Place the jar over the candle. Does the candle burn now? If so, time how long it burns. Explain your observations.

How does the water cycle work?

Background information

The process by which water changes from one phase to another is called the *water cycle*. *Evaporation* is when water (a liquid) turns into water vapour (a gas). *Condensation* is when water vapour turns back into liquid water. Evaporation increases with heating while condensation increases with cooling. The Sun causes water to evaporate into the atmosphere. Cooling of the atmosphere results in the formation of clouds (water droplets). Rain occurs when the droplets become too heavy for the clouds. Rainwater then soaks into the ground and eventually ends up back in the rivers and oceans.

Science activity

Place a check mark (✔) by the correct statements and a cross (✘) by the incorrect ones. Then decide whether or not statement 1 happens because of statement 2.

Statement 1	(✔) or (✘)	Statement 1 happens because of Statement 2 – True or False	Statement 2	(✔) or (✘)
Rain falls when clouds are formed.			Water vapour condenses to form water when cooled.	
Water only evaporates from oceans.			Water vapour is formed faster when water is warmed.	
Water vapour condenses faster in the higher regions of the atmosphere.			It is colder in the higher regions of the atmosphere.	

Science investigation

⚠ Make your own cloud chamber with a 250 mL glass jar filled 2 cm high with tap water, a large rubber balloon with the mouth end cut off, a match, a rubber band, and a flashlight. Add water to jar. Light match over the jar and blow it out. Place balloon over jar and secure in place with rubber band. Wait 2 minutes. Darken the room. Push down on balloon while shining flashlight on jar. Observe and record what you see when you let go of the rubber balloon. Do this a number of times. Explain your observations.

How does a condenser work?

Background information

Condensers are devices that turn gases into liquids by cooling the gas quickly. You can find condensers in many places, such as air conditioners, power stations, and laboratories. A condenser can change water vapour to a liquid. The water vapour comes in contact with a cold surface and condenses back into liquid water. It is important to keep the surface cold. The surface normally gets heated by the vapour and so becomes less efficient. In a laboratory condenser, this warming up is prevented by placing the cold surface inside a jacket of cold, flowing water.

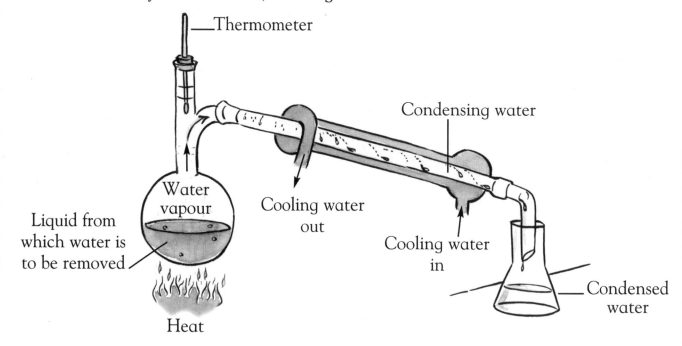

Science activity

When Juan gets out of the shower, he notices that the mirror is all "steamed up." He also notices that when he drinks iced tea, there is moisture on the outside of the glass. Explain Juan's observations.

....

....

Science investigation

Design and conduct an experiment to determine the best surface for condensing water vapour. Predict which surface you think will be best and explain why you think so. One suggestion is to place water in paper cups and place a cover made of a different type of matter over each cup.

How soluble are materials?

Background information

Substances that can be dissolved in a liquid are said to be *soluble*. Substances that do not dissolve are *insoluble*. The liquid in which a substance dissolves is called the *solvent*. The substance that dissolves is called the *solute*. When mixed together, they make a solution. Water is an excellent solvent. It dissolves many substances. Sugar and salt are very soluble in water, while substances such as sand and chalk are insoluble.

Science activity

Rosa collected two different plant fertilizers from a garden centre. The directions said to mix each fertilizer with water and to sprinkle the solution on her plants. When she mixed the first fertilizer in the water, it seemed to disappear. However, when she mixed the second fertilizer, she noticed it sank to the bottom of the watering can.

Which fertilizer should Rosa use for her plants? Explain.

....

....

Science investigation

(!) Design and conduct an experiment to test which common household substances are soluble in water. Always add the substance to water and not the water to the substance, as there could be a strong reaction. Wear safety glasses. You might try flour, baking soda, alcohol, or cooking oil.

Are all substances equally soluble?

Background information

All soluble substances do not dissolve equally well. Sugar dissolves very easily, while other substances, such as salt, dissolve less easily. The amount of solute that will dissolve in a solvent is a measure of its *solubility*.

Science activity

Below is a graph showing the solubility of different substances.

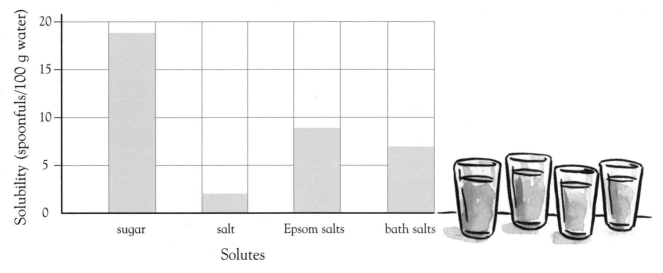

About how many spoonfuls of salt dissolve in the water? ....

About how many spoonfuls of bath salts dissolve in the water? ....

Another substance is more soluble than bath salts but less soluble than Epsom salts. What range of spoonfuls would you expect to dissolve? ....

List the solutes in the bar graph in order of their solubility.
Write the name of the most soluble substance first.

....

Science investigation

Does the size of a sugar particle affect its solubility? Obtain sugar cubes, powdered sugar, and granulated sugar. Design and conduct an experiment to see which type of sugar is most soluble.

Is water really pure?

Background information

Tap water contains substances (solutes) already dissolved in it. The amount and type of dissolved substances depend on where you live. This is one of the reasons that tap water tastes different in different areas. You can find out how much solute is dissolved in water by pouring a small amount into a glass and allowing it to evaporate. The white ring or scale left behind in the glass contains minerals that were dissolved in the water. Water that contains a lot of dissolved substances is called *hard water*, while water that contains very few dissolved substances is called *soft water*.

Science activity

Tiah had a fish tank. As the water evaporated, she would add more water. She noticed a line of white scale on the inside of the fish tank where the water had evaporated. Explain Tiah's observation.

....

....

Science investigation

Obtain a black, water-soluble marker. Cut a white paper coffee filter into a circle just a bit larger than the opening of a glass. Draw a circle 2 cm wide in the middle of the filter. Now place the filter on top of a glass. With an eyedropper, place one small drop of water in the centre of the marker circle, making sure not to get any water on the marker. Observe what happens as the water moves across the paper. Explain your observations.

5 Does temperature affect solubility?

Background information
It is easier to dissolve soluble substances in warm water than in cold water. However, heat increases the solubility of some substances more than of others.

Science activity
Make a line graph to plot the data from the table. Be sure to connect all the points after they are plotted. The data shows the solubility of table salt and of Epsom salts as temperature increases.

Temperature (°C)	Amount dissolved per jug (in grams)	
	Salt	Epsom salts
20	10	20
30	12	30
40	14	40
50	16	50
60	18	55

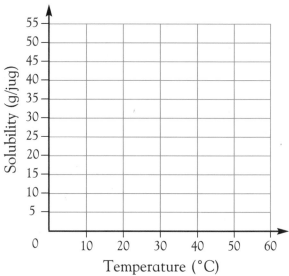

1   Do you see a relationship between temperature and the solubility of table salt? Explain.

....

2   Is this relationship the same for Epsom salts? Explain.

....

3   Describe any differences temperature has on the solubility of Epsom salts as compared to table salt.

....

Science investigation

(!) You can make rock candy by dissolving 2 cups of sugar in a cup of boiling water. Let the solution cool and pour it into plastic cups, filling each half way. Tie 12 cm of plain dental floss in the center of a pencil. Place the pencil over a cup and let the floss drop into the solution. Repeat for the other cups. Observe what happens over two weeks. Draw diagrams and explain your observations.

Does adding salt change water?

Background information

Mixing substances together can cause their properties to change. Adding salt to water makes the water salty. Salt water boils at a higher temperature than fresh water and freezes at a lower temperature. *Buoyancy* is the upward pushing force of a fluid. Objects float more easily in salt water than in fresh water, because salt water is more buoyant. This is also why it is easier to swim in salt water than in fresh water.

Science activity

Look at the pairs of pictures. Which picture in each pair shows sea water and which shows fresh water?

....

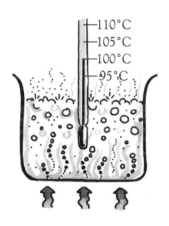

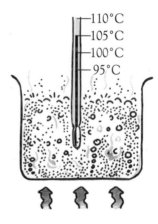

....

If you added sand to water, would it boil at a higher temperature? Explain.

....

Science investigation

Obtain a small toy boat. Design and conduct an experiment to see the effect of different concentrations of salt on the buoyancy of the boat.

When do liquids freeze?

Background information

Pure water freezes at 0°C. Water with substances dissolved in it (a solution) freezes at a lower temperature. Some substances, such as candle wax, freeze (solidify) at temperatures above 0°C. Other substances, such as vegetable oil, freeze at a temperature below 0°C. The temperature at which a substance freezes is called its *freezing point*.

Science activity

The freezing points of different liquids are shown in the bar graph below.

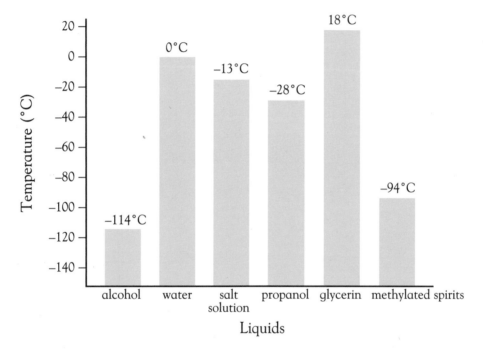

Looking at the bar graph, which substances will be solid on a winter's day but liquid on a summer's day? The rhyme below will help you.

"Minus 5, plus 10 and 21 – winter, spring, and summer sun."

....

Science investigation

Design and conduct an experiment to determine the effect of different concentrations of salt on the freezing of water. Note down the temperature of the salt water when it begins to freeze. *Hint:* Slush or ice crystals will begin to form.

Is it a thermal insulator?

Background information

Matter that allows heat to pass through it is a *thermal conductor*. Metals are excellent thermal conductors, though the best thermal conductor is diamond. Diamonds are crystals made of carbon. Glass, water, wood, and air are poor thermal conductors. Matter that is a poor conductor of heat is called a *thermal insulator*. Some types of matter are better thermal insulators than others.

Science activity

Five glasses containing water at 60°C were each wrapped in different types of matter. After 10 minutes, the water temperature in each glass was recorded. The results are shown in the table below.

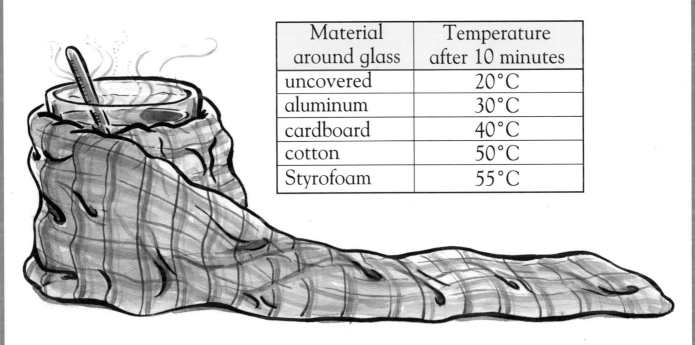

Material around glass	Temperature after 10 minutes
uncovered	20°C
aluminum	30°C
cardboard	40°C
cotton	50°C
Styrofoam	55°C

Which type of matter is the best insulator? Explain. Why was one glass uncovered?

....

....

....

Science investigation

Animals that live in cold climates have thick layers of fat. Fats and oils have similar properties. Using vegetable oil, design and conduct an experiment to test the purpose of the fatty layers.

Which metal is it?

Background information

A metal is a type of matter. Most metals are shiny and *malleable* (can be hammered into shapes), *ductile* (can be pulled into wires), and can conduct heat and electricity. There are different types of metals like iron, copper, gold, lead, and tin. Each metal has a set of additional properties that make it unique. These properties can be used to identify the type of metal. For example, some metals are denser than other metals. *Density* has to do with how much matter can occupy a given amount of space.

Science activity

Use the branching key below to identify each of the five metals in this chart. Write the correct letter for each metal below its name.

Metal	Properties
A	hard; brown in colour; good conductor of electricity
B	relatively soft; yellow colour; does not rust; very good conductor of electricity
C	soft; silver colour; tarnishes quickly; very heavy; weak conductor of electricity
D	hard; silver colour; magnetic; tarnishes easily (rusts)
E	hard; silver colour; not magnetic; does not tarnish easily

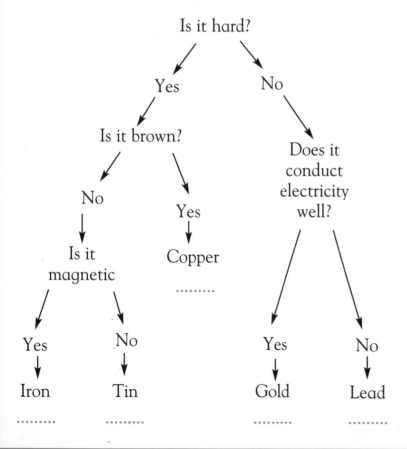

Science investigation

1. Collect 10 small pieces of metal.
2. Create a poster chart to show the properties of each metal and some of their possible uses. You may have to design an experiment to determine some properties.
3. Use a magnet to determine which metals are magnetic.

What makes things fall?

Background information

Gravity is a pull or force of attraction between two objects, and is a property of all matter. The more mass an object has, the bigger its attraction to another object. Earth is a huge object with a lot of mass. Everything on Earth is pulled towards its centre. Our weight is caused by the pull of gravity. The more mass we have, the greater our response to the pull of gravity. Our weight is a force that is measured in units called *Newtons* (N). The force of gravity on one kilogram of mass equals about 10 Newtons. The force of gravity does not change on Earth. What changes is an object's response to the force. Prove this by dropping a heavy book and a light book from the same height. Since the force of gravity is the same on both objects, they will hit the ground at the same time.

Science activity

Draw an arrow to show the direction of the force extending the spring.

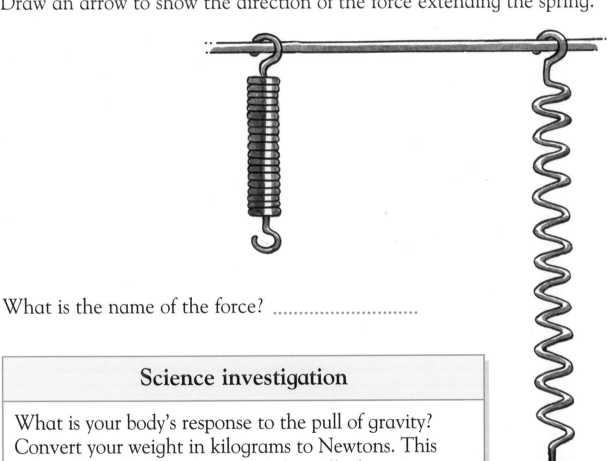

What is the name of the force? ....

Science investigation

What is your body's response to the pull of gravity? Convert your weight in kilograms to Newtons. This value is your body's response to the pull of gravity. Who in your family has the greatest response to the pull of gravity? Use the following conversion: 1 kg = 10 N.

Does a force have a direction?

Background information

A *force* is a push or pull. Forces can start or stop an object from moving. They can increase or decrease the speed of a moving object. The force that opposes motion is called *friction*. Forces can also make things change their direction of motion. For example, the force of the wind can blow a boat off course. A force acts in one direction. This direction is shown in the diagrams by using arrows. A longer arrow is used to show a bigger force.

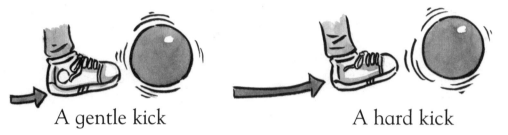

A gentle kick   A hard kick

Science activity

Examine the diagrams below. On each diagram, draw an arrow to show the direction of each force mentioned.

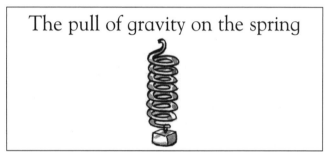

The pull of gravity on the spring

The force of friction slowing the rolling can

The force of the hammer

The force exerted by each team (two arrows)

Science investigation

Using the spring balance that you made in the last investigation or a store-purchased spring balance, investigate the amount of force needed to: lift a cookie, lift a cup, brush your teeth, write with a pen or pencil, or another activity of your choice.

What effect does friction have?

Background information

Friction is a force that slows things down. When two surfaces come in contact with one another, there is a frictional force. The amount of friction depends on a number of factors. Rougher surfaces create more friction than smooth surfaces. It is a lot easier to ride a bike on a newly paved road than on a dirt trail. The weight of an object pushing on the surface causes friction. The amount of surface in contact with another surface also affects the amount of friction. For example, wheels reduce the amount of surface contact.

Science activity

Gail covered a ramp with different materials and measured how far a wooden block slid on each surface before coming to a halt. Here are her results.

Type of surface	How far the block slid after being pushed
sandpaper	50 cm
glass	500 cm
wood	100 cm
plastic	300 cm
cardboard	90 cm

Which is the smoothest surface, and which is the roughest surface?

....

Explain how you worked out the answers to the question above.

....

....

Science investigation

Using a spring balance, test out the friction of various objects on a wooden ramp. Keep in mind that if you want to test the effect of different surfaces, the same object must be tested each time. Make sure to explain how you will use the spring balance to measure friction.

What makes boats float?

Background information

Boats are built so they can float on water. A boat builder must consider both the shape and weight of the boat. Remember, weight is an object's response to the pull of gravity. When an object is placed in water, the water pushes upward against it. This upthrust is known as *buoyancy*. The force of gravity pulls the boat down. In order for the boat to float above water, the buoyant force must be greater than the force of gravity.

Upthrust   Gravity

Science activity

Objects weigh less in water than in air because of the buoyant force. Marcos used a spring balance to measure and compare the weights of different objects in air and in water. His results are given in the table below.

Object	Weight in air (N)	Weight in water (N)
stone	130 N	6 N
wood block	20 N	0 N
plastic hair clip	5 N	1 N
metal pan	500 N	0 N

Use the table above to work out which objects will float. Explain your conclusions.

....

....

Science investigation

Build a boat out of about 30 square centimetres of aluminum foil. Obtain about 200–300 pennies. Predict how many pennies your boat can hold before sinking. Explain your design. If you don't have pennies, substitute with something like rice, beans, or macaroni.

How much does it weigh?

Background information

Scientists measure the weight of objects using its metric weight. The unit is called a Newton (N). All matter has weight due to the force of gravity. Since a 1 kg (1000 g) mass weighs 10 N, a 100 g mass is 1 N. A metric spring balance or scale can be used to measure force.

Science activity

What is the weight in Newtons of each objects in the pictures below?

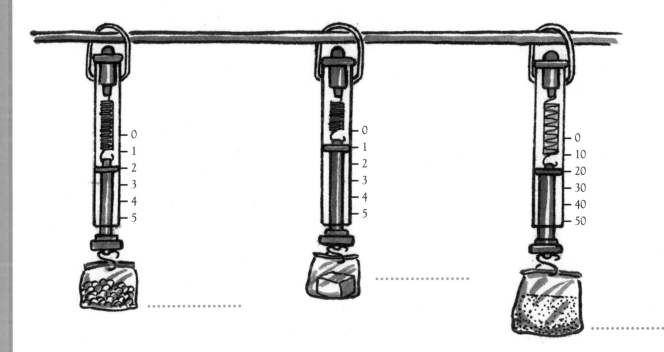

Science investigation

Build and calibrate your own spring balance. Use white heavy board, a large adhesive hook, a large rubber band, and a paper clip bent into a hook. Attach the hook to the heavy board near the top. Hang the rubber band off the hook. Hang the paper clip from the rubber band to create another hook. Attach a sandwich-size plastic bag or cup to this hook so you can add objects for calibration. Instead of Newtons, create your own unit: pennies, marbles, etc. Every time you add one of these objects, draw a line for calibration. Make sure to decide where the 0 unit will be. Once completed, try measuring different objects in this unit. Can you use your unit to tell which object weighs more?

Which is the strongest wood?

Background information

Tensile strength is an important property of matter. It measures the amount of force a type of matter can withstand before breaking. Since wood is a material often used in construction, it is important to know its tensile strength. One simple way to compare the strength of different materials is by hanging increasingly heavier weights from them until they break.

Science activity

Dylan hung weights on strips of wood until the wood broke in the middle.

Type of wood	Weight needed to break wood (in Newtons)
beech	2000 N
oak	3000 N
walnut	2600 N
ash	2500 N
pine	500 N
sycamore	2500 N

Based on the data you have collected, which wood would you choose for constructing a bridge? Explain your choice.

....

....

Science investigation

Thread can be made of different type of materials such as nylon, rayon, or silk. Design an experiment to test the strength of different types of thread. If Spiderman had to purchase thread to climb buildings, what type of thread would he choose based on your data? Explain.

Which fabric will stretch the most?

Background information

There are many properties that can be used to describe matter. Fabrics are a type of matter. Some fabrics stretch more than others. A property of matter in which it can stretch and return to its original shape is called *elasticity*. Some fabrics are more elastic than others. You can compare the elasticity of two types of fabric by hanging equal weights off each and measuring how much they stretch.

Science activity

Lauren tried to compare the stretch in five different fabrics. All of the fabrics were the same length at the beginning of the experiment. Her data table of results is shown below. A Newton (N) is a metric measurement of weight.

Fabric	Weight hung from fabric	Amount of stretch
cotton	10 N	3 cm
wool	100 N	40 cm
nylon	100 N	55 cm
polyester	500 N	200 cm
denim	10 N	3 cm

According to this data table, which fabric stretched the most?
(Hint: Consider both the weight hung and the amount of stretch for each fabric.) Explain.

....

How could Lauren have improved this experiment?

....

....

Science investigation

Design and conduct an experiment to test which pair of your socks stretches the most. Use the results of the science activity to guide your investigation. Incorporate your suggested improvements for Lauren's experiment.

Is it elastic?

Background information

One of the properties of matter is *elasticity*. This is its ability to stretch and then go back to its original shape. Rubber is elastic. Metals can be made into springs that behave as if they were elastic. When you pull a spring to stretch it, you can feel a force pulling in the opposite direction. When you push a spring together, you can feel a force pushing against you.

Science activity

Rubber bands stretch when they are pulled. The graph shows how much a rubber band stretched when different forces were applied.

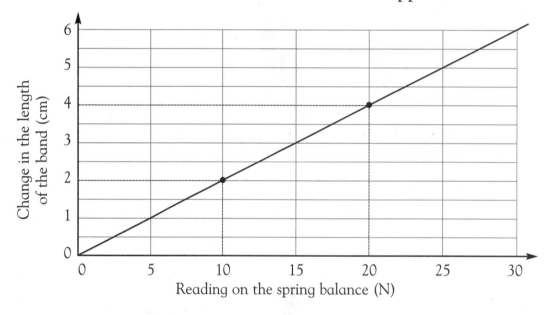

By how much is the rubber band
stretched when pulled by a force of 20 N? ....

By how much do you think the band
would stretch if the spring balance read 30 N? ....

The rubber band was 15 cm long to start with.
How long was it when the spring balance read 10 N? ....

Science investigation

Make a spring by coiling some thin, bare copper wire around a pencil, and then removing the pencil. Use a ruler to measure how long the spring stretches when first 5, then 10, and finally 15 paper clips are hung on it. How much would you expect it to stretch with the weight of 30 clips?

Is it crushable?

Background information

Force can change the shape of an object as it pushes or pulls on it. Some shapes can withstand greater forces than others. For example, you can easily crush a Styrofoam cup by squeezing its sides, but it is more difficult to crush the cup by squeezing it from top to bottom.

Science activity

A scientist tested how much force differently shaped pillars could withstand before they collapsed. Here are her results.

Shape of pillar base	Weight supported before collapsing
triangular	550 N
square	450 N
circular	900 N
rectangular	430 N

Which shape of pillar would best support the roof of a building?

....

Explain how you worked out the answer to the question.

....

....

Science investigation

Use three pieces of paper and 30 cm of clear tape to build a support for a cup filled with rice, beans, or pebbles. How many of the objects can your support take before it collapses? Describe the design you used.

Are all microbes harmful?

Background information

Not all microbes are harmful; some are extremely useful. Microbes help the remains of plants and animals to decay. This returns important nutrients to the soil that plants will use to grow. Some microbes are used to make foods such as yogurt and cheese. A microbe called yeast is used to make bread. Yeast is also used to make alcohol. Bacteria convert sugars in some fruit juices to vinegar that is used in salad dressing.

Science activity

Put a check mark (✔) beside the drinks that are made with the help of useful microbes.

Wine ☐

Orange juice ☐

Beer ☐

Mineral water ☐

Yogurt drink ☐

Cola ☐

Science investigation

Make your own yogurt! Place a teaspoon of plain yogurt into a cup of milk. Cover the container and keep it in a warm place overnight. What is the evidence that yogurt formed? What causes yogurt to form? Always wash your hands after handling food.

What are the causes of disease?

5

Background information

Microbes such as viruses, bacteria, and fungi can infect living things and make them sick. They can cause illness and disease in humans. In some cases, the illness can kill people. Our bodies have special cells that fight microbes and help us get better. Medical doctors can give us medicines called *antibiotics* to help our bodies fight some harmful microbes. Antibiotics cannot treat viral infections.

Science activity

Write the letter **M** in the box beside each person infected with a microbe.

Cold ☐

Toothache ☐

Sprained ankle ☐

Chicken pox ☐

Broken arm ☐

Science investigation

Make a poster for your room that informs your friends and family about the importance of washing your hands.

What are vertebrates?

Background information

The animal kingdom is divided into two types: animals with backbones are called vertebrates; animals without backbones are called invertebrates. People are vertebrates. So are snakes, goldfish, ducks, cats, and frogs. Scientists divide vertebrates into different classes—reptiles, fish, birds, mammals, and amphibians.

Science activity

Using the Internet and other resources, look for the key features of each vertebrate class. Some features of each class are given below. Add the results of your research to this information.

Vertebrates	Key features
Reptiles	Are cold blooded; breathe air using lungs; may be found in water but live on land
Fish	Are cold blooded; live in water; breathe by means of gills
Birds	Have hollow, light bones; bodies are covered with feathers; develop from eggs
Mammals	Are warm blooded; breathe air using lungs; have body hair or fur
Amphibians	Are cold blooded; have smooth, loose wet skin; return to water to breed

Science investigation

What is the main difference between warm-blooded and cold-blooded animals?

What are invertebrates?

Background information
All animals that are not vertebrates are called invertebrates. Invertebrates do not have a backbone. All invertebrates are cold blooded. Like vertebrates, invertebrates are divided into classes.

Science activity
Using the Internet and other resources, look for the key features of each invertebrate class. See how many features you can add to the ones below.

Invertebrates	Key features
Porifera	Simplest of animals; stiff bodies; filter feed through their bodies
Cnidaria	Soft and jelly-like; have hollow, sack-like bodies with one opening
Nemertea	Flat worm; very long, up to 27m
Platyhelminthes	Simple animals with only one opening—the mouth; most are no more that 1 mm wide
Nematoda	Many are parasites in humans; more complex than flatworms
Annelida	Round worms (segmented worms); have a mouth and an anus
Echinidermata	Have tough spiny skin; body parts are arranged in fives or multiples of five
Arthropoda	Jointed legs; hard skin or shell (cuticle); have an outer skeleton (exoskeleton)
Mollusca	Soft body surrounded by a hard shell; most are marine animals, some live on a land

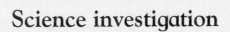

Science investigation

What kind of animals are crabs and lobsters? How many legs do they have?

What is yeast?

Background information

Scientists place yeasts, mushrooms, moulds, and other fungi together in their own kingdom. Yeast is a one-celled, microscopic member of the fungi kingdom. Fungi cannot make food for themselves like plants can.

Science activity

Below is a table to show how yeast cells were grown over a period of 12 hours. Show this same data using the bar graph below. If you have access to a computer, enter the data into a spreadsheet or graphing program. Explain what your graph tells you.

Time	Number of yeast cells
2 hours	50 yeast cells
4 hours	95 yeast cells
6 hours	190 yeast cells
8 hours	360 yeast cells
10 hours	500 yeast cells
12 hours	700 yeast cells

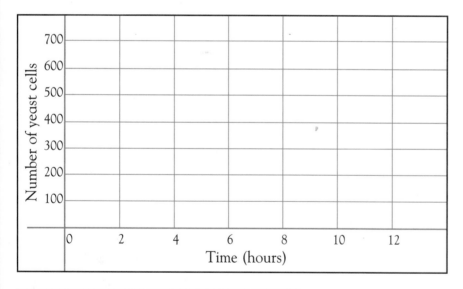

Science investigation

Try feeding some yeast with sugar. Pour a small amount of warm water into a small plastic ziplock bag. Then add a teaspoon of yeast. In another ziplock bag, put the same amount of warm water and yeast but add 3 teaspoons of sugar. Squeeze the air out of the bags and zip them up. Place them in a pail of warm water and observe. Discuss your findings.

What kind of animal is this?

Background information

There are many different animals that make up the animal kingdom. Scientists often use keys to help identify an unknown animal. Being able to use keys is an important skill. One type of key is called a *dichotomous key*. This is a branching key in which there are two choices in each branch. The last choice in the key will identify what the scientist is trying to determine. A dichotomous key can be used to identify animals.

Science activity

Arthropods are small animals with jointed legs and other appendages to their body. The word arthropod actually means "jointed feet."

Use the dichotomous key to identify the arthropods shown above.

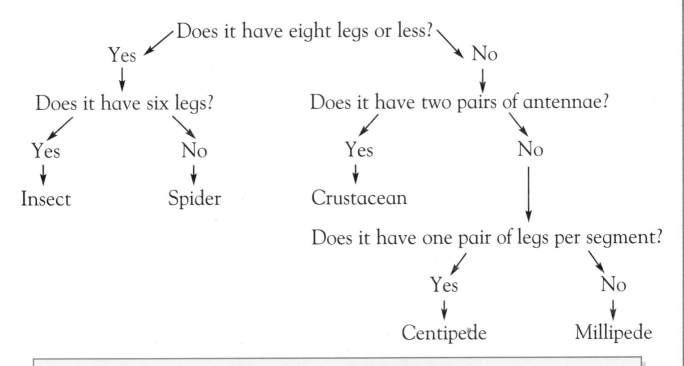

Science investigation

⚠ Create your own dichotomous key to identify eating utensils (knives, forks, spoons, soup spoons, salad forks, steak knives, etc.). Try this key out on your friends and/or members of your family. How well does it work? Did you have to make any changes? Explain.

How do you describe an arthropod?

Background information

Arachnids, crustaceans, and insects are part of the arthropod class of invertebrates. Insects are by far the largest of these three groups. All arthropods have a jointed body with a tough body case. The case is shed as the animal grows.

Science activity

Creative people, such as computer designers and moviemakers, often invent lifelike creatures that don't really exist. Your challenge is to create a realistic arthropod for a science fiction movie. Plan your design and draw your creature in its own habitat. Label all of its features. Now, create your arthropod from your design using household materials, such as empty plastic containers, packaging, paper, and cardboard.

My arthropod

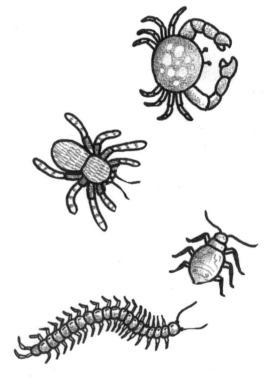

Science investigation

Write a description of your arthropod including all its features. Include a name for it and explain how it adapts to its surroundings. What does it eat? How does it protect itself and survive in the environment? Get creative and write a storyline for a movie based on your creature.

How long is a life cycle?

Background information

Animals and plants have life cycles. The period of development before birth is called *gestation*. It is followed by a period of growth leading to adulthood. Adults can then reproduce and repeat the cycle. In humans, the gestation period and the time taken to reach maturity are very long. The growth phase can be divided into: infancy (birth to age 2); childhood (age 2 to before puberty); adolescence (puberty to adulthood); and adulthood (after puberty to old age).

Science activity

Animal	Gestation period (days)	Average age of maturity
human	270 days	14 years
bear	230 days	4 years
horse	336 days	2 years
dog	63 days	15 months
cat	60 days	9 months
elephant	624 days	14 years
mouse	20 days	6 weeks

Which animal has the longest gestation period? ....

Which animal reaches maturity in the shortest time? ....

Is there a relationship between the age of maturity and the size of the animal?

....

....

Science investigation

Make a booklet that shows the life cycle of a human. Make four sections for each life stage: *infancy, childhood, adolescence,* and *adulthood.* Under each section, describe the major characteristics of that stage of life. Find pictures of people from magazines or your own family and friends and include them in each section. Note down any similarities or differences among people who are the same age. What do you conclude?

How quickly do we grow?

Background information

Most animals have similar patterns of growth—they grow when they are young and stop at adulthood. Girls and boys grow at different rates. Rates of growth and size at maturity are also affected by things such as diet and heredity. For example, tall parents are more likely to have offspring who grow into tall adults.

Science activity

These charts show the heights of some girls and boys. They are measured in Year 1, then in Year 3 and in Year 5. Find out how much each child has grown by working out the difference between their heights in Year 1 and Year 5. Fill in each growth chart.

Girls	Height in cm			
Name	Year 1	Year 3	Year 5	Growth
Susan	110	116	128	
Dela	109	116	130	
Rachel	102	110	121	
Jasmine	112	118	126	

Boys	Height in cm			
Name	Year 1	Year 3	Year 5	Growth
Jack	110	115	126	
John	112	119	126	
Dave	112	120	131	
Peter	100	105	111	

Which child grew the most in four years? ....

What was the average growth of the girls? ....

What was the average growth of the boys? ....

Did all the girls grow at the same rate? ....

Did all the boys grow at the same rate? ....

Did the girls or the boys grow faster? ....

Science investigation

(!) Soak 10 lima beans in water overnight. Obtain five paper cups filled with soil and plant two beans in each cup about 3 cm apart. Repeat this set up for 10 pea seeds. Measure the growth of each plant after it sprouts. Create data tables to record your information. Make a bar graph to compare the growth of the bean plant with the growth of the pea plant.

Are plants and animals similar?

Background information

Animals and plants need water, air, and nutrients. They also live best under certain temperatures. For example, while an iguana and a rubber tree prefer warm climates, polar bears and certain pines prefer very cold climates. Plants and animals grow, reproduce, move and/or respond to things in the environment, such as sunlight and water. However, while animals are dependent on other living things for their food, plants make their own food. Plants have a green substance (mostly in their leaves) that helps them use the energy from the sun to make food. Plants have roots that anchor them into the soil. Plants reproduce by producing seeds. Animals reproduce by laying eggs that hatch into their young or by giving birth to live offspring.

Science activity

These numbered words and phrases are features of plants and animals. Write the numbers under the correct heading in the chart below (some phrases are true for both plants and animals).

1 Move	2 Respond	3 Grow
4 Make food	5 Form seeds	6 Reproduce
7 Need air	8 Lay eggs or have live young	9 Need nutrients
10 Need sunlight	11 Contain chlorophyll	12 Eat

Animals		Plants	
....	....	....	....
....	....	....	....
....	....	....	....
....	....	....	....
....	....	....	....

Science investigation

(!) Obtain a large paper cup and add soil. Plant one or two sunflower seeds in the cup. Try to begin this experiment in the spring. Describe and do what is needed to keep the plant healthy. Sketch the plant to keep a record of its growth, or if you have a camera take regular pictures. Measure your plant's growth. Record it in a data table and graph it. Which characteristics of plant life did you observe? Explain.

How do plants get food?

Background information

A plant needs sunlight, carbon dioxide, and water to make food. A green substance in plants called *chlorophyll* traps the energy from the Sun needed to make food. Chlorophyll is mostly found in the leaves of a plant. The leaf can be thought of as a food factory. Leaves of plants vary in shape and size, but they are always the plant organ best suited to capture solar energy. Once the food is made in the leaf, it is transported to the other parts of the plant such as the stem and roots.

Food moving to rest of plant

Carbon dioxide

Sunlight

Water from roots

Science activity

Kenny found a plant that had been put in a cabinet by accident. It looked very unhealthy. Some of its leaves were yellow and drooping, and others had fallen off. Kenny decided to put the plant on the windowsill to see if it would revive.

What else will Kenny need to do to help the plant recover?

....

....

What do you predict would happen after several days? Give reasons for your ideas.

....

Science investigation

Obtain a geranium plant. Design and conduct an experiment to see what happens to a leaf when it does not get sunlight. One suggestion is to fold some black paper over one of the leaves. Make sure to place the plant near the sunlight and water it when the soil becomes dry. Predict what you think will happen.

Can you make a bird key?

Background information

Dichotomous keys work best when they are divided into groups and then further divided into smaller groups. When putting birds into groups, you could first divide them into wading birds (those with webbed feet) and non-wading birds, then think of some subsets, such as size, shape, or colour of the beak. Charles Darwin, who developed the present-day theory of evolution, studied the many types of beaks found on the finch, each adapted to eating different types of food.

Science activity

Swan

Blackbird

Duck

Coot

Magpie

On another piece of paper, make your own dichotomous key for the birds pictured above. Make sure the questions are based on clear differences. For example, "Does the bird have webbed feet?" A poor question would be, "Does the bird have large wings?"

Science investigation

Identify birds in your yard, nearby park, or school. Use the Internet and reference books for help. Make a bird feeder out of recycled material to attract birds to your garden or school. Create a booklet of birds in your area. Include their names and the types of bird feeder that should be used to attract them.

Can you make a plant key?

Background information

Some *dichotomous keys* used to identify plants and animals ask *yes or no* questions. They also rely on looking for clear differences. Questions are numbered and answered in order. Look at the three pictures. A simple key would be:

1   Is the plant over 200 cm tall?
    If yes, go to 2; if no, go to 3.
2   It is an oak tree.
3   Does the plant have a flower?
    If yes, go to 4; if no, go to 5.
4   It is a daffodil.
5   It is moss.

Science activity

Make a yes/no key to distinguish between the different flowers shown below.

Iris

Rose

Daffodil

....
....
....
....
....
....
....
....

Science investigation

Collect some flowers and create your own yes/no key. Ask an adult to help you. If there are no flowers available, then use pictures of flowers. Books and the Internet can help you identify some common garden flowers.

What sort of plant is this?

Background information

Trees are plants. There are many different types of trees. A *dichotomous key* can be used to identify different species of trees.

Science activity

Look at the pictures of the four twigs below. Use the dichotomous key to identify each one. Write your answer on the dotted line.

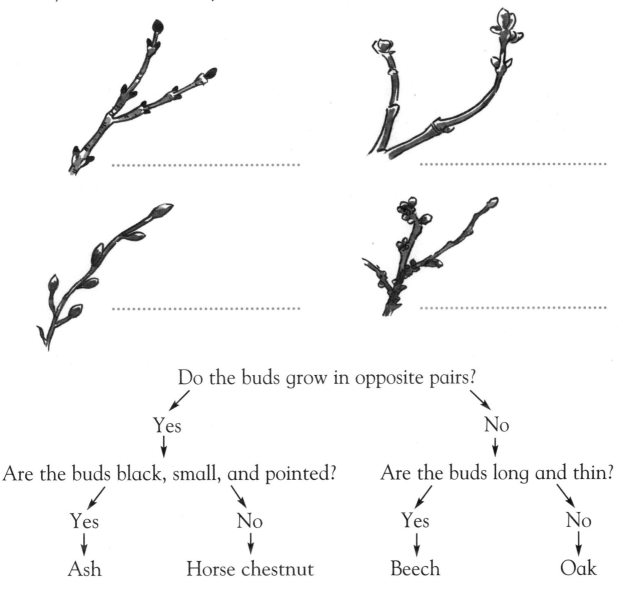

Do the buds grow in opposite pairs?

Yes → No

Are the buds black, small, and pointed?   Are the buds long and thin?

Yes → No   Yes → No

Ash   Horse chestnut   Beech   Oak

Science investigation

During spring, collect some twigs and create your own key to identify the twigs. During fall, collect and identify tree leaves. Make a booklet. Use the Internet and reference books for more information on tree identification.

How do microbes help?

Background information

Microbes, or micro-organisms, are living things that are often too small to be seen. Common types of microbes are bacteria, viruses, and some fungi. These organisms need food, warmth, and moisture to grow and reproduce. Some microbes feed on things that were once living, such as fallen leaves and dead animals, causing them to breakdown or decay. The decayed materials mix with soil, providing essential nutrients for plants to use. Without this process, the nutrients in the soil would run out. These types of organisms are called *decomposers*. They are the natural recyclers of living things on our planet. Microbes also help us make some of our foods, such as bread, cheese, yogurt, beer, and wine. They feed on the sugar in grain, fruit, or milk, giving these foods a special texture and taste.

Science activity

Donna put the following items into a large plastic bag. She took them out again after two weeks. In the boxes below, write **D** for the items that would have decayed and **U** for those that would be unchanged.

☐ Grass ☐ Tangerine

☐ Plastic spoon ☐ Bread

☐ Apple peel ☐ Leaves

☐ Pop can ☐ Nylon tights

Why have some of the items not decayed?

....

....

Science investigation

Take a large coffee can and obtain some soil, food samples, and non-food items. Bury the food and non-food items in different layers of soil placed in the coffee can. Add about 60 mL of water. Place a cover with punched holes on top of the can so air can get in. After 2–3 months, determine what has decayed.

How are microbes harmful?

Background information

Some microbes, often called germs, can cause illness or disease. Chickenpox, mumps, and measles are caused by microbes. They are infectious diseases. Some microbes can cause food to decay. Moldy bread or fruit, sour milk, and rotten meat are examples of decayed food. If eaten, this rotten food and drink can cause stomach upsets. Other microbes cause tooth decay. You can protect yourself from harmful microbes by storing and preparing food properly, cleaning your teeth, washing your hands, and by avoiding close contact with ill people.

Science activity

Look at the picture above. It shows a number of unhygienic ways in which germs can travel into food and cause illness. List all of the ways this could happen in the picture.

....

....

Science investigation

(!) Design and conduct an experiment to see what type of bread grows mould the best. Obtain different samples of bread. Make sure to wash your hands before and after each time you experiment or use rubber gloves. Explain why mould grows better on some bread than on others.

What is friction?

Background information

When an object travels across a surface, there is friction between the object and the surface. Friction is the force that resists the movement of one surface over the other. It's much easier to slide on something smooth, such as ice, than on a rough surface. This is because rough surfaces create more friction than smooth ones, and friction slows things down.

Science activity

Test for friction. Lean a piece of wood against two books so that it makes a ramp. Roll a marble down the ramp. Keep adding books to increase the angle and make the slope steeper. What difference does this make to the way the marble rolls down the ramp?

Replace the marbles with a small block of wood or a toy car and compare. If you have to make the ramp steeper to make the object slide, what does this tell you about the friction? How does putting a little oil or water on the ramp affect what happens? Record your findings.

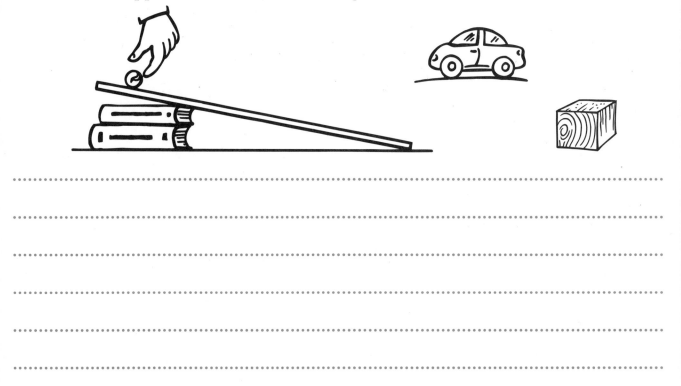

....

....

....

....

....

Science investigation

Investigate friction. Describe two ways of reducing friction. How can friction help you complete tasks? List at least three situations in which friction works against what you are trying to do. What can you do to reduce the friction in each case?

How do parachutes work?

Background information

Gravity is a pulling force. It pulls objects toward Earth. *Air resistance* is a pushing force. It is a source of friction because it opposes motion. When parachutes fall to Earth, air resistance pushes against them. The fabric of a parachute has a lot of surface on which air can push. The effect of this force is to slow the parachute down. The larger the parachute, the slower it will fall, because there is more air resistance.

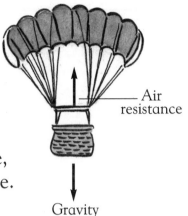

Air resistance

Gravity

Science activity

Examine the drawing of two people jumping with parachutes.

Which person will fall to Earth faster? Explain your answer.

....

....

Describe all of the forces acting on the parachute. Make sure to state the direction of the force.

....

Science investigation

Obtain five pieces of paper of the same size. Leave one piece of paper unfolded. Fold one in half and tape it closed. Repeat this, but fold and tape two pieces of paper together. Fold one piece of paper in half two times and then tape it closed. Design and conduct an experiment to see which paper falls first when they are dropped from the same height.

What are the four forces of flight?

Background information

Gravity is the force that acts on all objects and pulls them toward the centre of the Earth. The greater the mass of an airplane, the more it is affected by gravity. *Thrust* is the force that moves a plane forward. Experiment with a toy airplane or glider. When you throw the plane, you provide the thrust. In a real airplane, the thrust comes from the propellers or the jet engine.

The forward movement produced by the thrust causes air to move across the surface of the wing, and this creates *lift*, an upward force that keeps the plane in the air. This is how an airplane can fly.

As the airplane moves forward, the air creates *drag* on the plane and slows it down. A disadvantage of drag is that it is a force that tries to prevent motion. A plane needs more thrust than drag if it is to fly.

Drag can be used by the pilot to control the plane. An airplane has flaps on the wings and the tail, and the pilot turns these to increase the drag on one side of the plane or the other in order to steer it. When it comes in to land at an airport, the flaps are used to deliberately slow the airplane down. Planes that must land in a short distance, such as on an aircraft carrier, use parachutes to increase the drag on the plane and slow it down suddenly.

Science activity

On the drawing of the airplane, draw arrows that show the direction in which each of the forces—gravity, thrust, lift, and drag—is acting. Describe the effect of each force on an airplane.

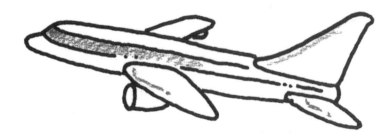

Science investigation

Like planes, birds and insects make use of the four forces of flight. List the similarities and differences between an airplane and a bird or insect.

What is Bernoulli's Principle?

Background information

Aero means "air" and dynamics means "motion." Aerodynamics is the study of gases (particularly air) in motion and of objects moving through them. The work of Daniel Bernoulli was instrumental in the study of aerodynamics. In 1738, he published his first article explaining that moving fluids exert less pressure than do stationary fluids. This was found to be true for moving air as well, and today this discovery is called Bernoulli's Principle. It means that the faster the air moves over an object, the lower the pressure it exerts.

Science activity

Take a hairdryer set to cool, and hold it pointing upward. Place the ping-pong ball in the middle of the air stream and observe and describe what happens. Draw a picture of the experiment. Use Bernoulli's Principle to explain how we are able to make a ping-pong ball hover in the air.

My drawing

....

....

....

....

....

....

....

....

Science investigation

To make a mini hovercraft, wash a glass in hot soapy water and place it upside down on a wet, smooth surface. Now give the glass a little push, and it will slide easily as the expanding warm air escapes. How is this like a mini hovercraft? Investigate hovercrafts on the Internet.

How do you fly a plane?

Background information

When birds and aircraft fly, moving air around their wings helps carry them high into the sky. Building and flying a model plane will help show you how moving air lifts up a wing and keeps it airborne.

Science activity

Fold a sheet of paper to make a simple paper dart or model plane. If you don't know how to do this, ask an adult or look on the Internet for folding instructions. Experiment with throwing your plane and see how it flies. Record your findings.

Now make adjustments to its shape and balance to see how these affect the way it flies. Start by bending up the back edge of both wings. What effect does this have? Now bend up the back of just one wing. Does it still fly straight? What happens if you bend one flap or both flaps downward?

To change the balance of the plane, attach a paper clip to the front of it. How does this affect the flight pattern? Attach the paper clip to the tail of the plane instead and see what difference this makes. Can you make your plane loop the loop or fly in a circle?

After your investigation, write a report summarizing your results. Add flying tips that would make the plane fly better.

....

....

....

....

....

....

Science investigation

Tape cotton threads to two lightweight balls and hang them about 15 cm apart. Try blowing air through the space between the balls. Describe what happens.

How does a jet engine work?

Background information

Airplanes fly around the world at high speed. They have large jet engines that produce a powerful stream of air to push the airplane through the sky. The engine that powers a space rocket works on the same principle.

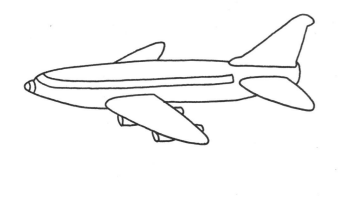

Science activity

Make your own simple jet engine to show how it produces a force that propels an object through the air. You will need the following materials:
1. A piece of thread long enough to stretch across your room.
2. Two pieces of sticky tape.
3. A drinking straw.
4. A balloon.

Feed one end of your thread through the drinking straw. Attach one end of the thread to one side of the room, and the other end to the other side of the room at the same height from the ground. Make sure that the thread is stretched tight. Slide the straw to one end of the thread, and stick the two pieces of tape across the straw so that they stick out on both sides of it. Now blow up the balloon and hold onto the neck of it tightly so that no air escapes. Position the balloon under the straw with the neck pointing at the wall, and attach the balloon to the straw with the tape. Now let go of the balloon. What happens?

Science investigation

Do you think a jet engine could be used to propel an object across the land or over water? Describe how this would work. Search the Internet to find out whether jet engines have been used to power cars or boats.

How do you design a parachute?

Background information

When a moving object travels through air, the air causes friction. This is called air resistance. If people want to travel *faster* through the air, they must **reduce** air resistance. **Increasing** the air resistance *slows* moving objects down. This can be done by increasing the area of the moving object that pushes against the air. A parachute is a good example of increasing air resistance. Parachutes have many uses such as for the sport of skydiving; dropping supplies for people; slowing down space capsules and racing cars.

Science activity

Design your own parachute. Think about what important factors you should consider when designing your parachute. What material would you use? The top of a parachute resembles that of an umbrella and is usually made from nylon or silk. They must be light weight but strong enough to prevent tearing while catching the air and supporting the person's body mass. Using materials that you already have, create your own parachute from your design. Experiment with your parachute by dropping it from various heights to hit a target. Can you improve your design? Draw your final design and label the materials used.

My parachute design

Science investigation

Do you think there is friction when an object travels through a liquid? Make a variety of paper boats with differently shaped bottoms. Test the theory that there is friction between the surface of a moving object and a liquid by pushing your boats across water in the sink or bathtub.

Is it an electrical conductor?

Background information

Matter that allows electricity to pass through it easily is called an *electrical conductor*. Electricity passes through a conductor to turn on a TV or computer, for example. Metals can conduct electricity, but some are better conductors than others. Solutions that have dissolved charged particles in them can also conduct electricity.

Science activity

An electrical circuit was set up to test the conductivity of different types of matter. A bulb was placed in the circuit. If the matter conducted electricity, the bulb lit up.

Material tested	Status of bulb
gold	very bright
copper	bright
plastic	not lit
wood	not lit
graphite	fairly bright
lead	fairly bright
paper	not lit
salt water	bright
distilled water	not lit

What factor was used to determine the conductivity of the matter?

....

Which sample(s) of matter are the best conductors? ....

What types of matter are the best conductors of electricity?

....

Why do you think salt water can light the bulb but distilled water cannot?

....

Science investigation

(!) Build your own circuit using a 6-volt battery as your source of electricity and a LED light bulb. Test other types of matter for conductivity. Create a data table to record your observations.

Will it conduct electricity?

Background information

When you build an *electric circuit*, all of the parts of the circuit must be connected. Each part must also let electricity flow through it before the circuit will work. A working circuit can light a bulb or ring a bell, for example. Materials that allow electricity to flow through it are called *electrical conductors*. Materials that block the flow of electricity are called *electrical insulators*.

Science activity

Which of the following objects will make the buzzer sound when they are connected to the alligator clips in the circuit? Place a check mark (✔) beside each one that makes the buzzer sound.

☐ PVC-coated wire not stripped at the end
☐ PVC-coated wire stripped at the end
☐ Spaghetti
☐ String
☐ Nylon fishing line
☐ Iron wire
☐ Paper drinking straw
☐ Wooden rod

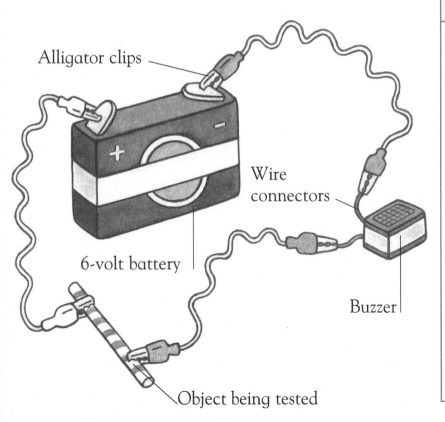

Alligator clips

Wire connectors

6-volt battery

Buzzer

Object being tested

Science investigation

⚠ Build your own circuit with alligator clip wires, a 6-volt battery, a switch, and an object that will use electricity, such as a bulb, buzzer, or bell.

What does a circuit diagram show?

Background information

Electricity always flows in a circuit from the negative pole of a battery to its positive pole. The flow of electricity creates an electric current. Electrical circuits can be represented by special diagrams. There is a symbol for each electrical component in a circuit.

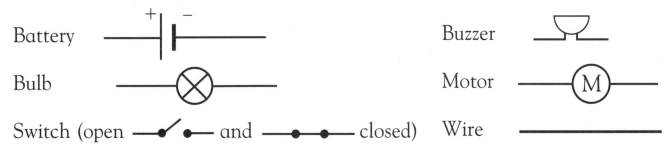

Battery

Bulb

Switch (open —✓— and —•—•— closed)

Buzzer

Motor

Wire

Science activity

Look at the circuit diagram shown below.

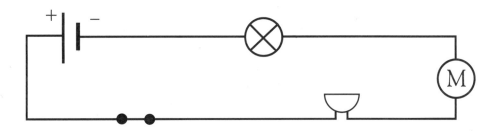

Label each of the five components shown in the circuit.

Complete the following sentences about the circuit shown above.

The electric current leaves the battery and passes through the ....

It then travels through the .... , next through the .... ,

and finally passes through the .... , before returning to the battery.

Science investigation

Create a model of a parallel circuit that contains two bulbs, one motor, and one buzzer. You might draw the symbols on small cards and then arrange them into the circuit. Connect the circuit with wires.

Can you draw a circuit diagram?

Background information

A simple circuit diagram often looks like a rectangle. It shows how the loads, batteries, wires, and switches are linked together, and how the circuit is organized.

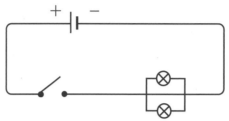

Science activity

Look at the two pictures of circuits.

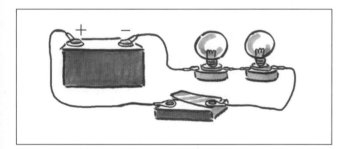
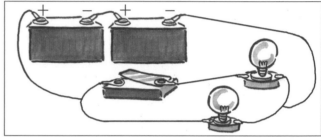

Draw a circuit diagram for each of the circuits shown.

What will happen in the second circuit when the switch is off and when it is on?

....

....

Science investigation

⚠ Using small cards, create a game to teach your friends about circuits. Draw different parts of the circuit on each card. One card can be a lamp and another can be a connecting wire. Players can pick cards and the first player with enough cards to make a complete circuit wins. Try the game out with your family and friends.

Will it switch on or off?

Background information

Electricity will only flow through a circuit that has no gaps in it. A switch is a useful device because it allows you to open or close a circuit. When a circuit is open, electricity cannot flow through the circuit to run a load in it. When a switch is turned on, it closes the circuit so that loads in the circuit can operate. Loads such as light bulbs and appliances in your home are turned on and off with switches.

This is the symbol for an open switch. ——• •—— It is off.

This is the symbol for a closed switch. ——•——•—— It is is on.

There are different types of switches.

This switch is closed by pressing down the metal bar

This one is closed by turning the lever and slotting it into the clip.

Science activity

Look at this circuit diagram.

Battery
+ | −

Switch 4
Switch 3
Bulb ⊗
Switch 1
Switch 2

What is the least number of switches you would need to light up the bulb ? ....

Identify the switches you would need ....

Science investigation

One type of switch is called a *pressure switch*. You have to press the switch to close it. Design and build your own pressure switch and then connect it to a circuit with a load on it, such as a buzzer or light bulb. Some pressure switches work by stepping on them. Can you name any common pressure switches in your home?

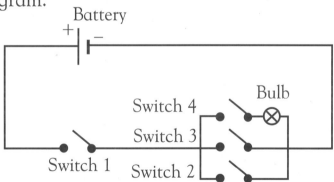

What do batteries do?

Background information

Batteries are a source of electricity because they contain charged particles that can flow. The amount of energy provided by a battery depends on its *voltage* and is measured in units called *volts*. For example, a 1.5-volt (V) battery has less energy than a 6-V battery. If a lower voltage battery is used in a flashlight, the bulb will be less bright than in a flashlight using a battery with higher voltage. A battery has two ends called *poles*. One end is called the positive (+) pole and the other, the negative (–) pole. When wires connect the poles, an electric circuit is created. *Current electricity* is produced, which lights up the light bulb. This flowing electricity can be turned on or off by a *switch*. When more batteries are added to a circuit, the current is also increased. The circuit has more electrical power.

Science activity

The drawings below show two electric circuits.

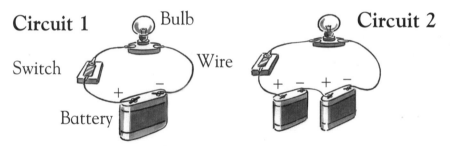

What will happen to the flow of electricity when the switch is opened in circuit 1 and circuit 2?

....

In which circuit is the bulb brighter when the switch is closed? Explain.

....

....

Science investigation

(!) Roll a lemon to release its juices. Cut two slits in the lemon about 5 cm apart. Stick half of a shiny penny (the + pole) into one slit and half of a shiny dime (the – pole) in the other slit. Create a circuit. Use wires with alligator clips to connect the coins and bulb. If the bulb does not light up, add more lemons to the circuit. Why can a lemon light a bulb?

Why change the length of wire?

Background information

Conductors are a type of matter through which electricity can flow. Most metals are good conductors of electricity. Copper is used to make wires because it is a very good conductor. When current flows through a conductor, friction can reduce its flow. Some metals cause less friction than others. It is friction that makes wires feel hot. The type of wire conductor and its length and thickness affect current. Longer wires offer more resistance to flow than shorter wires, while thicker ones offer less resistance. This knowledge can be used to control the speed of a motor. For example, speed controllers on electric car tracks and dimmer switches on lights work by varying the length of wire in a circuit.

Science activity

Susan made a model electric windmill by attaching toy windmill blades to a motor in a homemade circuit. She wanted to change the speed at which the blades turn, to show what happens when the wind blows in the blades of a real windmill. She found that she could do this by changing the length of wire in the circuit. Here are her results. Can you fill in the missing values?

Length of wire in the circuit	Number of turns in 5 seconds
25 cm	80
50 cm	70
100 cm	....
150 cm	30
200 cm	....

Science investigation

(!) Use the Internet to provide you with a materials list and directions to build a motor. You can experiment with how the length of the wire affects the speed of the motor by varying the number of coils in the copper wire.

Do more bulbs mean more light?

Background information

A light bulb is a fairly simple device that has not changed much since its invention by Thomas Edison in 1879. Inside a bulb is a filament. When current flows through the filament, some of the electrical energy is converted into light energy. The devices on a circuit using the electricity are called *loads*. The more loads added to the same circuit, the slower the flow of electricity. If the load is a light, as more lights are added, they will become dimmer. The circuit shown in the diagram is called a *series circuit* because the current must flow through all of the loads before returning to the energy source (battery).

Science activity

Dipak set up the series circuit shown below. When he turned the circuit on, he was surprised that the bulbs burned so dimly. He did not have another battery, so how do you think he could have changed the circuit to make the light brighter?

....

....

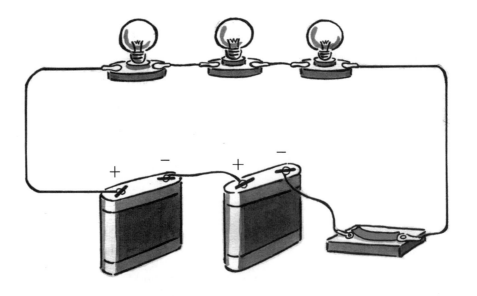

Science investigation

Build a circuit with two bulbs, in which current flows through only one light bulb before returning to its energy source. Both light bulbs must burn at the same time. This is called a *parallel circuit* because there is more than one pathway to the energy source.

What is a lever?

Background information

A lever is a rigid object that moves about a fixed point when one end is moved. The fixed point is called the fulcrum. A seesaw is a simple, or first-class, lever with the fulcrum in the middle. When the two people at the ends have the same mass and are at the same distance from the fulcrum the seesaw is balanced. The downward force that each person exerts on the seesaw is his or her weight multiplied by their distance from the fulcrum. In this diagram, the downward forces f1 and f2 are the same, so the lever is balanced.

Science activity

Carry out an experiment to find out what happens if you change the weight at one end or the other, and what happens if you change the position of the fulcrum. Using a ruler as the rigid object and a small block or rod as the fulcrum, set up a model seesaw and place two similar sized erasers on each end so that it balances. What happens if you move one of the erasers from one end to the other? Now move the fulcrum along the ruler and find a position where the lever balances again. Measure the distance from the fulcrum to each end (distances d1 and d2 in the diagram below). What answer do you get if you divide one distance by the other? The fact that a smaller weight at the long end balances a larger weight at the short end shows how a lever can give you a mechanical advantage.

Science investigation

In a first class lever, the fulcrum is between the effort and the load—you push down on one end and you can lift something at the other end. Besides the seesaw, can you think of two or three other first-class levers?

What class lever is your machine?

Background information

In a first-class lever, the effort is applied at one end, and the load is lifted on the other.

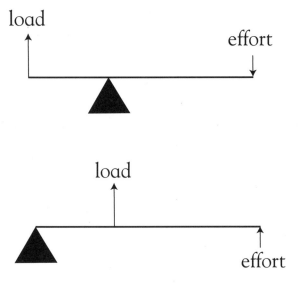

A second-class lever has the load positioned between the effort and the fulcrum. Because the effort is further from the fulcrum than the load is, a mechanical advantage is achieved. A wheelbarrow is a second-class lever.

In a third-class lever, the effort is applied between the fulcrum and the load. The effort is closer to the fulcrum than the load is, so there is no mechanical advantage here. Instead, third-class levers are used whenever a delicate grip is required, for example when using chopsticks.

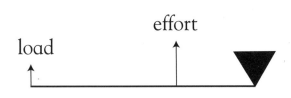

Science activity

Think about the following objects and work out what class of lever each one is. Draw each object and show where the effort, fulcrum, and load are positioned on each one.

Scissors	Shovel	Wrench
Tweezers	Crowbar	Human lower jaw
Hockey stick	Human forearm	Claw hammer
Pliers	Nutcracker	pulling a nail

Science investigation

The lids of paint cans fit tightly to prevent spills. They can be opened with a lever, using the edge of the can as a fulcrum. With the help of an adult, try to lever off the lid of a can of paint with a coin. Now try opening the lid with a small spoon, a larger spoon, and a screwdriver. Which is easier to use? Discuss, using the terms lever, effort, and force.

How do gears on a bike work?

Background information

When you ride a bike, a set of gears transmits the motion of the pedals to the rear wheel. In a car (or other motorized vehicle), gears transmit power from the engine to the wheels to make the car move. Most gears take the form of wheels with teeth cut around the edge. Gears not only transmit motion, they can also change it. Using the gears on a bike, you can pedal more easily uphill by changing to a lower gear. The gears give you a mechanical advantage that allows you to turn the back wheel with less effort.

Science activity

Find out how changing gear makes the back wheel of a bike go slower or faster while you pedal at a constant rate. You will need the help of an adult for this activity, and you will need a bike with multiple gears (such as a mountain bike), gloves, and coloured sticky tape.

A bike with multiple gears has different-sized chain wheels, to which the pedals are attached by arms called cranks. There are also several different-sized sprockets (gears) on the rear wheel. Ask an adult to help you turn the bike upside down and hold the frame steady. Make sure the bike is in low gear. In the lowest gear, the chain connects the smallest chain wheel at the front to the largest rear sprocket.

Wearing gloves to protect your fingers, slowly turn the pedals until one of the cranks is vertical. Mark a point on the rear tire with coloured tape.

Now slowly turn the crank one full turn and watch the tape mark to see how many times the rear wheel turns. How much force is needed to turn the pedals? Change into high gear (with a large chain wheel connected to a small sprocket) and turn the crank again. How many times does the rear wheel turn? How much force is needed on the pedals?

Science investigation

Mechanical clocks and watches use a series of meshing gears with precise gear ratios to turn the hands at the correct speed for accurate time-keeping. With the help of books and the Internet, learn about gear ratios. Describe what is meant by a gear ratio of two to one (2:1).

How do machines work?

Background information

The word machine is commonly used to mean a device that does useful work for us or helps us to do useful work. A car engine is a machine, but so is a corkscrew, an electric fan, or a stapler. Use resources such as dictionaries, science reference books, and the Internet to learn about the scientific principles on which different machines work.

Science activity

Compile a list of the ten different machines that might be found in the kitchen, garage, or workshop. A few are listed below as examples. In each case, describe how it works and how it helps to do a particular job more easily. Use reference resources to understand the scientific principles that are used by each machine.

Machine	Scientific principles
Axe	An axe is a machine called a wedge. The energy in the moving axe head forces the wood apart and splits the log.
Pulley	A rope, belt, or cable is passed round a pulley wheel, changing the direction of the pull.
Screw	The action of turning the head of a screw to drive it into the wood is less than that needed to knock it in directly.

Science investigation

(!) With the help of an adult, find one discarded gadget from around your home. (Be aware that some electrical equipment can be dangerous even when unplugged.) Try to figure out how it worked. Carefully take it apart. List all the parts, and number them in the order in which you removed them. Try to figure out how the parts worked together to make the machine work. Put the machine back together. Do not plug anything into a wall socket without adult supervision.

How do pulleys and cranes work?

Background information

A crane is able to lift a heavy load high in the air. It has a wheel called a "pulley" to produce a lifting force, while a "counterweight" keeps the crane from tipping over as it lifts a heavy weight. The simplest kind of pulley is a cable or rope running over a grooved wheel attached to a support. One end of the rope carries a load and the other end is pulled.

Science activity

Thinking of the principles behind how a crane works, try to build your own using materials such as string, screw hooks, a few small blocks of wood, empty spools of thread, small paper drinking cups, marbles, nails, and a small cardboard box. Gather your materials first. Include things like scissors, pen, paper, marbles, and sticky tape that you may also need. Don't forget to make a load for the crane to lift. The small paper drinking cup is lightweight and you can use marbles for the load. Use your crane to lift loads, and make improvements that help it work more easily.

Hints:
a) Study a photo of a crane from a resource book or the Internet.
b) Fill the cup with marbles and hook it to the crane. Wind the handle to lift the load of marbles.
c) Use a book as a counterweight to prevent the load from pulling the crane over. Use an empty thread spool as the pulley wheel.

Explain how your crane works and include a labelled drawing of it.

Science investigation
While a single pulley doesn't give a mechanical advantage, it does make lifting easier by changing the direction of force required. What happens when you add more pulleys? A set of pulleys (also called a block and tackle) can help you lift loads more easily.

How do you build a wheelbarrow?

Background information

When you lift a bag of stones you need to exert a lot of force. Machines can make it easier for you and give you more strength! The wheelbarrow is a second-class lever—a machine that can increase the force you use to move things.

Science activity

Build your own model wheelbarrow and experiment with it by moving some small stones. To build the wheelbarrow you might use the following materials:

A shoe box, cardboard, an empty thread spool, two equal lengths of wood (such as chopsticks), a short pencil, sticky tape, and scissors. You will also need a plastic bag and some small stones.

Use the shoe box as the body of your wheelbarrow. Use the thread spool as a wheel and the short pencil as an axle. Cut a hole in the bottom edge of one end of the box, large enough for the thread spool. Place the spool, with its pencil axle, in this hole and tape the ends of pencil to the box on either side of the hole. The two pieces of wood will form the handles. Place the bag of stones in different positions along the length of the wheelbarrow and try lifting the handles in each case. Is it easier to lift the load with the stones at the front of the wheelbarrow or the back? Record the results of your experiment and describe the function of a wheelbarrow.

....

....

....

....

....

....

Science investigation

Write up the steps of how you built your wheelbarrow. Challenge someone else to make a wheelbarrow following your directions. Does that person's wheelbarrow look exactly the same as yours?

Which light is the brightest?

Background information

Earth's brightest light source is the *Sun.* The Sun is a star. All stars are composed of gases that are constantly undergoing powerful reactions. When they do, very bright light is produced. There are billions and billions of stars, and even if you counted one star every second for 8 hours a day, after 100 years you would only have counted about a billion! Other stars don't seem as bright as the Sun because they are very far away. Astronomers use numbers called *magnitude numbers* to describe how bright stars look from Earth. Bright stars have low numbers, and faint stars have high numbers. We can see stars with a brightness between magnitudes 1 and 6.

Science activity

Here are some stars with measures of their brightness. Can you place them in order, with the brightest first and the faintest last?

Star	Magnitude
Eri	3.7
Centauri C	11.0
Ross 780	10.2
Procyon A	0.3
Kapteyn's Star	8.8
Sirius B	7.2
Polaris	2.0

Correct order of brightness

1 .... (brightest)

2 ....

3 ....

4 ....

5 ....

6 ....

7 .... (faintest)

Science investigation

(!) Suppose you are a scientist studying three stars of different sizes. Make these "stars" by covering a flashlight with a piece of black paper in which you have made three pinpricks of different sizes. Predict which star will be hardest to see as its distance from you increases. Test this out by having a friend shine the flashlight toward you. As your friend walks away from you, is there a distance from which you can no longer see any of the stars? What do you conclude? Explain.

Where will the shadow be?

Background information

The Sun is a very powerful light source. When sunlight shines on a wall, it makes the wall bright. If you place a solid, opaque object in front of the wall, the sunlight cannot pass through it and a shadow forms on the wall. Because Earth is rotating, the Sun seems to move across the sky, casting different shadows from morning (sunrise) to evening (sunset).

Science activity

The morning Sun was shining through the window in Tony's home, casting an interesting shadow of a vase on the table. Tony thought it looked great, and wanted to show his father when he came home from work. If there was still sunlight coming through the window in the afternoon, draw how the shadow looked when Tony showed it to his father.

Science investigation

On a sunny day, find your shadow on the ground. Try to change its shape. At what time in the day is your shadow the longest?

Why does the Sun appear to move?

Background information

You know that on any single day, the Sun will rise and set. However, it is Earth that is moving. It takes 24 hours for Earth to make a complete rotation on its axis. As it moves, the Sun appears to change its position in the sky. The Sun appears to rise in the east when the part of Earth you are on is turning toward the Sun, and appears to set in the west when your hometown is turning away from the Sun. In addition to rotating on its axis, Earth is also revolving around the Sun. It takes an average of 365 days, or one year, to make one complete orbit around the Sun.

Science activity

The picture shows the Sun at three times during one summer day. First it was in position A, then B, and finally C.

Which side of the picture is the east? ....

What time is it at position B? ....

What will soon happen at position C? ....

Science investigation

Make a sundial. On a sunny morning, stand a 50 cm-long stick in the ground in your garden or school. Mark the position of the end of the stick's shadow with a rock or other item that will not easily blow away. Repeat this every hour so that by evening you have at least seven marks on the ground. What pattern can you see? Explain why the shadow moved.

How much do you weigh on Mars?

Background information

Gravity is the natural force that acts between all objects in the universe. Gravity keeps all planets in orbit around the Sun. The gravitational pull between two objects is related to their masses and the distance between them. *Mass* is the amount of matter in an object. Weight is a measure of how much gravity pulls on an object or a body. If you stood on the surface of the Moon, your mass would be the same as it is on Earth, but your weight would change. The Moon's gravity is one-sixth of the Earth's, so if you weigh 60 kg on earth, your weight on the Moon you would be 10 kg. On Jupiter you would weigh 143.4 kg. The force of gravity that you feel on the surface of any object in space is called *surface gravity*.

Science activity

The chart below shows the surface gravity on the planets compared to the surface gravity on Earth. To calculate how much something would weigh on a different planet, multiply its Earth weight by the planet's surface gravity. For example, a person who weighs 80 kg on the Earth would weigh only 30.4 kg on Mercury (80 x 0.38 = 30.4). Ask friends to guess how much they would weigh on another planet. How much would your pet, favourite toy, or another object weigh? Calculate these and complete the chart.

Planet	Surface gravity	Person or object	Weight on Earth	Weight on planet
Mercury	0.38			
Venus	0.88			
Mars	0.40			
Jupiter	2.39			
Saturn	1.17			
Uranus	0.92			
Neptune	1.23			

Science investigation

Complete drawings of you and your friends jumping on different planets. On which planet would you be able to jump highest? Explain your answer.

What causes night and day?

Background information

Earth completes one rotation on its axis every 24 hours. When the part of Earth where you live faces the Sun, it is daytime. Sunrise, also called dawn, occurs when the part of Earth where you are turns just enough for you to see the Sun. At sunset, Earth has turned so that again you can only just see the Sun. When it is night where you are, it is daytime for people living on the other side of Earth.

Science activity

Early one evening, Gus, who lives in London, England, was allowed to phone his uncle who lives in Montreal, Canada. Gus was very surprised to hear that his uncle was just about to have lunch because it was only 1:00 p.m.

What is the explanation for the difference in time?

....

....

....

Science investigation

Make a model of the Sun and Earth. Use a flashlight to represent the Sun and a basketball to represent Earth. Do this experiment in a darkened room. Place the flashlight on a table so that it shines into the room. Hold the basketball about 1 metre away, and turn it around slowly. The basketball is like Earth turning on its axis. Tape a white circle onto the ball. Spin the ball slowly at a slight angle so it is tilted like Earth. See at what part of the spin the circle appears lighted. Move it to other places and repeat. Are there locations that stay lighted longer than others?

What is the Moon like tonight?

Background information

As the Moon travels around Earth, we see different amounts of the Moon lit up by the Sun. This is known as the *phases of the Moon.* When the Moon is lit up and is round, it is called a *full moon.* The amount of the Moon's sunlit side we see, gradually shrinks or wanes. When the Moon is not lit up by the Sun, it is called a *new moon.* During a new moon, you cannot see the Moon in the sky. After a new moon, the amount we can see of the sunlit side grows, or waxes, each night until it is a full moon again.

Science activity

Draw a line from each of the phases below to show its correct position in the sequence from new moon to new moon. (A gibbous phase is when about three-quarters of the Moon is lit up.)

Gibbous waxing	Crescent waxing	Crescent waning	Gibbous waning	Full moon
			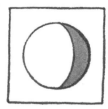	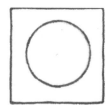

New moon   New moon

Science investigation

What does the Moon look like tonight? What phase do you think is showing? Use the Internet, a calendar, or a newspaper to check the phase of the Moon. Make your own chart of the Moon's phases over the next month.

Where is the Moon tonight?

Background information
It takes the Moon about 28 days to travel around Earth. It travels around Earth in a counterclockwise direction. It rises and sets during the night, just as the Sun rises and sets during the day. On Earth, the Moon appears to rise in the east and set in the west. Because of the way the Moon moves, we are only able to see one side of it.

Science activity
In this picture, it is evening and a boy and girl are looking at the Moon. Draw where you think they may see the Moon later that night.

Science investigation

(!) What are some of the features of the Moon? Does the Moon change shape in the evening sky? Explain. Is there a man on the Moon?

Can you hear in space?

Background information

If there were trees, would you hear one fall? Sound is created by vibrating matter, such as a liquid, solid, or gas. If there is no matter, vibrations cannot be created. Much of space is not filled with liquids, solids, or gases. It is empty, or a *vacuum*. Since you cannot hear sound in a vacuum, you would not hear a tree fall in space!

Science activity

We know that light travels much faster than sound. If a star explodes in a distant galaxy, would we hear it on Earth? Explain your answer.

....

....

Science investigation

Use the Internet to learn how astronauts talk with one another. Make a poster of your findings and share it with your friends or classmates. Research how the astronauts on the International Space Station communicate with Earth.

Can sound travel long distances?

Background information

Vibrations from sound sources travel through solids, liquids, and gases. As they travel, they lose some of their energy. We know this because a sound gets fainter the farther away it is from its source. The loudness of sound is measured in *decibels* (dB).

Science activity

The farther we are from a sound source, the fainter the sound seems to be.

Look at the chart. How does the loudness of a sound change with distance?

Distance from the source (in metres)	Loudness of the sound (in decibels)
0 m	50 dB
50 m	30 dB
100 m	20 dB
150 m	15 dB

What would the loudness be at 75 metres from the source?
Draw a graph on the grid below to work out your answer.

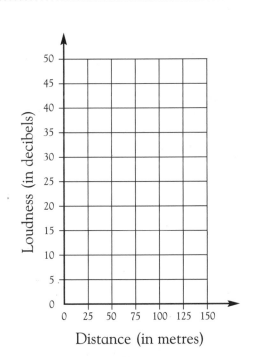

Loudness (in decibels)

Distance (in metres)

Science investigation

Before electrical amplifiers were invented, ear trumpets or megaphones were used to boost sound by collecting vibrations from a wider area than the ear could capture. Make a megaphone by rolling a sheet of paper into a cone shape. Conduct an investigation to see if the loudness of the sound is affected by the size of the cone.

Does the Moon change shape?

Background information

Did you know that the Moon is not a source of light? The light from the Moon is actually reflected light from the Sun. The Moon orbits around Earth in about 28 days. Depending on which part of its orbit it is in, you can see either a whole, round Moon reflecting light or just part of it. The different shapes you see of the Moon in the evening sky are known as the *phases of the Moon.*

The Moon's changing appearance during one month as seen from Earth.

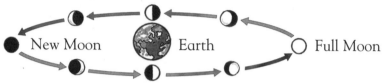

New Moon   Earth   Full Moon

Science activity

The chart below shows how the Moon appears from Earth. Can you work out the missing shapes, and complete the chart below?

Date in January	Moon's appearance
1st	●
6th	☽
10th	◑
15th	
19th	◖
24th	
28th	

Science investigation

You can model the way the Moon appears as it orbits Earth. Use a flashlight to represent the Sun and a ping-pong ball for the Moon. Ask a friend to hold the flashlight still in a darkened room. Hold the ball at arm's length in front of the flashlight. Turn around slowly in a circle, keeping your eyes fixed on the ball. Can you see the reflection of the light on the ball? How does it compare to the phases of the Moon?

Would we weigh less on the Moon?

Background information

If a man stood on the Moon, he would stay the same size. His mass would not change. However, if he weighed himself on the Moon, he would weigh less. Your weight is caused by the pull of gravity. The Moon is smaller than Earth, so it has less gravitational pull. For example, a person who weighs 700 N on Earth will weigh about 120 N on the Moon.

Science activity

Imagine that some settlers have left Earth and gone to the Moon, taking their recipe books with them. The first cake they baked was a disaster. It had far too little moisture and was about six times the size they had expected.

The cake recipe was:

1.25 N	butter
1.50 N	sugar
4	eggs
1.50 N	flour
20 ml	milk

Why was the cake so big? Why was it so dry?

....

....

....

....

....

....

Science investigation

(!) Can you catapult objects further on the Moon than on Earth? To find out, make a catapult using a thick rubber band. On Earth, objects weigh almost six times what they do on the Moon. Duct tape together 3 pennies (weight of an object on the Moon), then duct tape together 18 pennies (weight of an object on Earth). Catapult both sets of pennies. Predict which one will travel the farthest.

CONCEPT MAP GRAPHIC ORGANIZER
Example

What does the word mean?

The force that pulls things toward Earth.

Give examples:

1. A ball falls down.
2. When I jump, I fall down.
3. A rock falls to the bottom of a river.

Write the word:

Gravity

What is the word related to?

1. Forces
2. Weight
3. Mass

Use the word in sentences:

1. My weight is caused by the pull of **gravity**.
2. The pull of **gravity** is less on the Moon because it has less mass than Earth.
3. Objects fall to Earth because of the pull of **gravity**.

CONCEPT MAP GRAPHIC ORGANIZER

What does the word mean?

Give examples:

1.

2.

3.

Write the word:

Complete this organizer for each italicized word on the worksheets. This will help you better understand the science word or concept.

What is the word related to?

1.

2.

3.

Use the word in sentences:

Inquiry template
INSTRUCTIONS

Name .... Date ....

QUESTION
State your testable question.
Testable question: Who? Why? Where? When? How?
This is a question that can be answered by conducting an experiment.

PREDICTION (hypothesis)
This is a statement about what you think may happen in the experiment. It is not a guess, but is based on things you have observed or previous experiments you have conducted. Give an explanation for your prediction.

EXPERIMENTAL PROCEDURE
A well-designed experimental procedure includes:
* *Directions:* Steps to follow to conduct the experiment.
* *Materials:* A list of all materials that will be used in the experiment.
* *Variable(s):* Identified variables. (1) Which variable will you manipulate (change)? This is the independent variable. (2) What is your responding variable? This is the dependent variable. (3) Which variables will remain constant in your experiment?
* *Data collection:* Tables, graphs, charts, etc. for data organization. Include measurements in your data when you can.
* *Large sample size or repeated trials:* Good experiments have large sample sizes and/or are repeated a number of times.

RESULT
This is a statement made after analyzing the data collected. It identifies any patterns seen in the data. Do the patterns support the prediction (hypothesis)?

CONCLUSION
This is a summary that states whether the prediction (hypothesis) was supported. It explains why the prediction was supported or not supported.

COMMUNICATE RESULT
* Share your findings with others and ask for their analysis of your findings.
* Write a report or design a storyboard to tell about your investigation.

Intermediate level

Copyright © 2007 DK Publishing

Inquiry template
INSTRUCTIONS

Name _____ Date _____

QUESTION
State your testable question.

PREDICTION (hypothesis)

EXPERIMENTAL PROCEDURE

Approved by: _____

Intermediate level

Answer Section
with Notes for Adults
Grades 5-6

This section provides answers and explanatory notes for all of the science activities and investigations. Ensure that all safety precautions are carefully followed. Be aware of toxic and flammable chemicals. Proceed carefully when using an open flame or heating device.

When appropriate, use the inquiry template to guide the child through the investigations in a manner that parallels how science is done in the real world. The graphic organizer should be used to help the child to better understand scientific concepts while building vocabulary.

Why do you have a skeleton?

Background information
Your skeleton provides you with support so you have a form and shape. Otherwise you would be a blob of jelly! This support allows you to move. The skeleton also provides protection for the organs of your body. The skeleton is composed of bones. When you were born, you had about 350 bones. As you grew, some of these bones fused together. When you become an adult you will have 206 bones. The bones of your body make up your *skeletal system*.

Science activity
Draw an arrow from each label to the correct part of the skeleton.

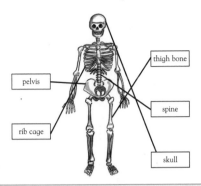

thigh bone

pelvis

spine

rib cage

skull

Science investigation

Use the Internet to learn about the skeletons of other types of living things. Make a scrapbook showing the skeletons of 5–10 different animals. Include animals that have exoskeletons. Compare and contrast the skeletons. Now use what you have learned to make your own cardboard model of a movable skeleton using round head paper fasteners to create movable parts.

Some animals, such as insects, have an exoskeleton that acts like armour on the outside of the body. Help the child appreciate the many similarities among living organisms, which provide strong evidence for common ancestry. Evolution is a unifying theme in biology.

9

Can you feel your bones?

Background information
Not all animals have bones. Animals with bony skeletons inside of them are called *vertebrates*. All vertebrates have a backbone. Vertebrates include humans, dogs, snakes, fish, and birds. Skeletons give protection and support to the body, and help it to move. Animals such as worms, insects, snails, and jellyfish do not have bony skeletons; they are called *invertebrates*.

Science activity
Here are the skeletons of a fish, a bird, and a frog. On each of the drawings, color in the part that protects the brain, and colour in the backbone.

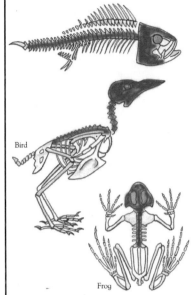

Bird

Frog

Science investigation

⚠ Ask an adult to remove the meat from a cooked beef bone and the wing, leg, and neck of a chicken. Trace the bones onto a piece of paper and label them. Draw an arrow to a joint on the chicken wing. How does a beef bone compare to a chicken bone? Is one harder than the other?

All animal skeletons protect the soft internal organs, provide anchor points for muscles, and give rigidity and support to the body. Ask the child how joints help an animal move.

10

Where are your muscles?

Background information
The muscles all over your body move your skeleton. When muscles work, they get thicker and shorter. We say that muscles *contract*. When a person "makes a muscle," you see their muscle contract. A contracting muscle pulls on a bone, making it move. Muscles need energy to work. They get their energy from sugars in your blood. Most muscles rest or relax after they have been used. They get longer and flatter. The heart is a muscle that works very hard—every time you feel a pulse, your heart muscle has contracted!

Science activity
When you move your legs, feet, hands, or arms, the muscles that move them get thicker and shorter.

On picture A, draw arrows pointing to where you think the muscles moving the foot will get thicker.

On picture B, draw an arrow pointing to where you think the muscle raising the forearm will get thicker.

Movement of arm

A   B

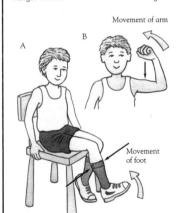

Movement of foot

Science investigation

Design and conduct an experiment to see how your muscles move your arms and legs. Which muscles thicken and shorten when you move different parts of your body? Use the Internet to learn more about muscles and bones.

Movement of leg

Limbs move when muscles contract. By flexing the lower knee, the child will feel the thigh muscles contract and relax.

11

How does the heart work?

Background information
The human heart is a powerful, muscular organ located near the centre of the chest, protected by the ribcage. The heart's main job is to pump blood throughout your body. It pumps the blood through blood vessels, which branch out to all parts of your body. In order to do this, it has very muscular walls that contract and squeeze the blood into the blood vessels. You can feel a throbbing sensation when you place your fingers on the side of your neck or on your wrist where the blood surges through blood vessels close to the surface of the skin. The throbbing is called your *pulse*. Your heart is the strongest muscle of your body. It beats from 60 to 100 times per minute, but can go much faster when necessary. It beats about 100000 times a day, which is more than 30 million times per year. A 70-year-old person's heart will have beaten about 2.5 billion times!

Science activity
The picture of the body has four empty circles. Colour the circle that represents the position of the heart. Place an X where you can locate a pulse on the body shown.

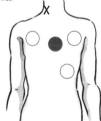

Science investigation

Fill a balloon with a small amount of air so that it can fit into your hand. Squeeze it 80 times in 1 minute. What did you learn about your heart by doing this? Now find your pulse by placing your forefinger and middle finger on your wrist. Count how many times you feel a throb in 1 minute.

The heart pumps blood around the body through arteries and veins. If your child can't feel the pulse in the wrist, try the one in the neck. Count for 30 seconds and multiply by 2 to find the pulse rate. Pulse rate is affected by age, health, and exercise.

What carries the blood?

Background information
Every time the heart beats, blood is sent throughout the body, carrying oxygen and nutrients to all of the cells. Each day, the average adult heart pumps more than 7570 litres of blood many times through about 96560 km of blood vessels. The blood that leaves the heart and goes to the body is rich in oxygen. After the oxygen is delivered to the cells, the blood returns to the heart to be sent to the lungs to pick up more oxygen. Blood vessels that carry blood away from the heart are called *arteries*. They have thick, muscular walls to help move the blood to your cells. Veins are the thin-walled blood vessels that carry blood back to the heart. Your heart, veins, and arteries are part of your circulatory system. This system delivers important substances to your cells and removes waste. You can think of your circulatory system as your blood highway.

Science activity
Fill in the missing letters in the labels for this diagram.

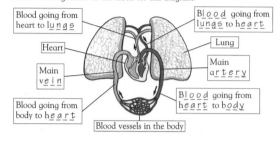

Blood going from heart to l u n g s

Heart

Main v e i n

Blood going from body to h e a r t

Bl o o d going from l u n g s to h e a r t

Lung

Main a r t e r y

Bl o o d going from h e a r t to b o d y

Blood vessels in the body

Science investigation

A *stethoscope* is a device that can listen to your heart. Obtain 30 cm of rubber tubing, some masking tape, and two small funnels. Attach a funnel to each end of the tubing with some tape. The funnel end should fit into the tube. Place one funnel over your heart and the other over your ear. How many times does your heart beat per minute? How does this compare to your pulse? Explain any similarities or differences.

The heart's sound is due to the closing of valves to prevent the back flow of blood. When the valves between the atria and ventricles close, a "lub" sound is heard. The "dub" sound is due to the closing of the pulmonary and aortic arteries.

Can you feel the pulse?

Background information
When your heart beats, it pumps blood to parts of your body through vessels called *arteries* and *veins*. Arteries carry blood away from your heart to the rest of your body, while veins return blood to your heart. Where an artery crosses a bone, you can press a finger against your skin to feel the blood pumping. This is called your pulse. It is a measure of how fast your heart is beating. A child's pulse is usually about 70 to 80 beats per minute.

Science activity
A doctor found that a girl's pulse was 80 beats per minute. After running slowly for 1 minute, her pulse went up to 120 beats per minute. After skipping for another minute, her pulse was 170 beats. After resting for 2 minutes, her pulse was 140 beats.

Using the chart below, draw a bar graph of the results. What effect does exercise have on the girl's pulse?
It makes her pulse go up.

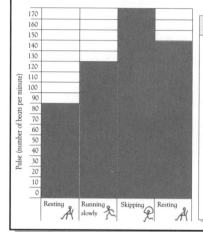

Pulse (number of beats per minute) — 170 160 150 140 130 120 110 100 90 80 70 60 50 40 30 20 10 0

Resting | Running slowly | Skipping | Resting

Science investigation

Find your pulse by pressing your first two fingers against the underside of your wrist, below the thumb. Take and measure your pulse before and after exercise. Design and conduct an experiment to see how your pulse rate changes after exercise.

Exercise makes the heart beat faster, providing more oxygen and food to muscles. The pulse rate is the same if felt on different parts of the body, such as the temple and neck. Children with respiratory ailments should be careful when exercising.

What happens when you exercise?

Background information
Your heart contracts to push blood through your body. The contractions are called heartbeats. You can feel your *heartbeat*, or pulse, by placing a finger across blood vessels close to the surface of your skin. Your pulse rate is a measure of how many times your heart beats in 1 minute. When you exercise, your muscles work harder and need more oxygen. Exercise makes the pulse rate go up so that the blood can deliver more oxygen to the muscles.

Science activity
Angela measured her pulse rate after 1 minute, 2 minutes, 3 minutes, and 4 minutes of exercise. She plotted her results on this graph.

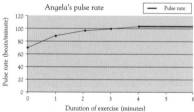

Angela's pulse rate — Pulse rate

Pulse rate (beats/minute) — 120 100 80 60 40 20 0

Duration of exercise (minutes) — 0 1 2 3 4 5 6

Describe the relationship between exercise and pulse rate. The more Angela exercises, the faster her pulse rate is.

Can Angela's pulse rate go on increasing? Give reasons for your answer. What would her pulse rate be after six minutes of exercise? Plot this on the graph.
Angela's pulse rate can't go on increasing. It will level out.

Science investigation

⚠ Mark where your pulse is with an X on your wrist so you can easily find it again. Use washable ink. Take your pulse for 15 seconds and then multiply by 4. This will give you your pulse rate for 1 minute. Try this 2–3 times for accuracy. Next, run in place for 3 minutes. Quickly take your pulse. Continue to take it until it is back to your resting pulse rate. Graph your data.

Tell the young investigator to use the forefinger and middle finger to feel a pulse. After exercise the pulse rate will go up. Someone who does not have any respiratory or heart ailments should be used to create data for the experiment.

What do our teeth do?

Background information
Humans have four different types of teeth. Young children have about 20 teeth called *milk teeth*. They have eight teeth called *incisors* at the front of the mouth (four above and four below). These are used for cutting food. The next four sharp, pointed teeth are the *canines*, which are used for tearing food. Next to these are the *premolars*, used for grinding and chewing. Between the ages of 5 and 10, these milk teeth are replaced by adult teeth, which include another 12 teeth called *molars*. These are also used for chewing.

Science activity
Animals that eat meat have canines and incisors to cut and tear meat. Animals that eat plants have large, flat teeth called molars for grinding and chewing. Humans eat both meat and plants. What sort of teeth do humans have? Label each type of tooth in the diagram below.

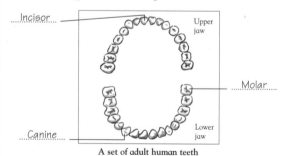

Incisor

Upper jaw

Molar

Canine

Lower jaw

A set of adult human teeth

Science investigation

Use a mirror to look inside your mouth. Then colour in all the teeth that you have of each kind in the diagram above. You may not have all of the teeth in the diagram, as it shows an adult's teeth. Check with friends and some adults to see if they have the same number of teeth as you. Use disposable rubber gloves when you check inside someone else's mouth.

Show the young investigator your molars (he or she may not have them yet). Encourage him or her to think about the purpose of teeth while eating food (chewing makes it easier to swallow food). Use disposable gloves when looking inside mouths.

16

What is in our food?

Background information
You should think about what you eat, as your health depends on it. The food groups that provide you with the most energy are *carbohydrates* (sugars and starches) and *fats,* although fats do not provide energy as quickly as carbohydrates do. Examples of foods high in carbohydrates are cereals, breads, cookies, crackers, potatoes, and rice. Oils and butter are high in fat. Foods that provides you with the raw materials you need for growth and repair are rich in a substance called *protein.* Meat, poultry, fish, eggs, and beans are all high in protein. Living things also need *vitamins* and *minerals* to remain healthy. Fruits and vegetables are foods naturally rich in vitamins and minerals.

Science activity
Classify each of the foods shown in the picture below according to what your body needs them for.

 Fish
 Cake
 Egg
 Apple
 Bread
 Cabbage
 Butter
Beans

Growth and repair	Energy	Health
Fish	Cake, Bread	Apple
Egg	Butter	Cabbage
Beans	Beans	

Science investigation

Keep a record of what you eat over two days and ask a friend to do the same. When classifying what you eat, remember that some meals you eat may have a number of foods combined into one dish. For example, pizza may have meat (growth and repair), tomato sauce (vitamins and minerals) and the crust (energy). Compare your diets. What did you learn?

Vegetables and fruit are rich in minerals and vitamins, and are a source of carbohydrates and fibre. Meats, fish, poultry, and eggs are rich in proteins and contain fats. They are needed for growth and repair. Rice, cereals, potatoes, and pasta are high-carbohydrate foods.

17

Is your diet balanced?

Background information
A healthy diet is a balanced combination of food for growth and repair, energy-giving food, and vitamins and minerals. You also need food that contains fibre. You cannot digest fibre, but it helps move food through your digestive tract. The amount of food you need depends on how active you are and how much you are growing. If you eat too little, you can suffer from *malnutrition* because your body is not getting the nutrients it needs. If you eat too much, you can become overweight, which can lead to health problems such as diabetes.

Science activity Answers may vary
Here are some meals with an item missing form each one. Decide what food item you would add to make each meal part of a balanced diet. Write the name of the item and which food group it is from.

1 • Boiled potato
  • Cabbage
  • Carrot
  • <u>Fish (protein)</u>

2 • Pizza (cheese and tomato topping)
  • <u>Salad (vitamins and minerals)</u>

3 • Boiled rice
  • Grilled lamb chop
  • Bacon
  • <u>Carrots (vitamins and minerals)</u>

4 • Chicken drumsticks
  • Peas
  • <u>Potato (carbohydrate)</u>

5 • Lettuce
  • Spring onions
  • Grated carrots
  • Bread
  • <u>Eggs (protein)</u>

6 • Fried egg
  • Bacon
  • Toast
  • Pudding
  • <u>Green beans (vitamins and minerals)</u>

Science investigation

Collect pictures of food and make a collage of a healthy dinner, by sticking them on paper plates. Label each food group. Use the Internet to learn about Health Canada's *Food Guide to Healthy Eating.*

Spend some time on the Internet to learn about the Canadian Food Guide. A healthy diet has a mixture of all of the food groups, and should be supplemented with exercise.

18

Is it a solid, liquid, or gas?

Background information
Three *phases* of matter exist naturally on Earth: solids, liquids, and gases. Generally, solids are substances that retain their shape and do not flow. Liquids flow and take the shape of the container they are in. Gases also flow and fill all of the space available. Some types of matter can exist in all phases on our planet.

Science activity
Which of these materials are solids (S), which are gases (G), and which are liquids (L)? Circle the ones that exist in all three phases on Earth. Write **S**, **G**, or **L** in each box.

Cotton S   Plastic S   Wood S   Jell-O S
Air G   Water vapour G   Wool S   Water L
Milk L   Metal S   Silk S   Oxygen G

Science investigation

Obtain a plastic zipper bag, borax, and glue. In a bowl, mix 125 mL of glue with 125 mL of water until thoroughly combined. Pour the mixture into the zipper bag. Then measure 25 mL of borax and mix it into another 125 mL of water. Pour 50 mL of the dissolved borax into the zipper bag with the other mixture. Close the bag and knead the mixtures together for 2–3 minutes, until thoroughly combined. Remove your mixture and test whether it is a liquid or solid. Also test for other properties.

Mixed borax solution and glue form a semi-solid. The child should understand that not all matter may be easily classified as a solid, liquid, or gas, and thus should take time to examine the many properties of this "slime."

What is a gas?

Background information
Some types of matter easily change into a gas. Gasoline and perfumes are examples of this type of matter. Dry ice, which is solid, can change phase directly into a gas, but it has no odour. This property of matter is called its *volatility.* Some gases flow more rapidly than others because of differences in their density. Denser gases sink under less dense gases. Less dense gases spread out faster than denser gases. You can smell dinner cooking in the kitchen because heat from the stove changes some of the food into volatile gases, which spread through your home.

Science activity

Name of gas	Density in grams per mL
hydrogen	0.00009
carbon dioxide	0.00198
helium	0.00018
nitrogen	0.00126
oxygen	0.00143

The information in the above data tables lists the density of some common gases. The density of air is 0.0013 grams per mL. According to this data table, why do helium balloons float in air?
<u>The density of helium is less than the density of air.</u>

Place the gases in order from least dense to densest. Which gas would flow the fastest? Explain.
<u>Hydrogen, helium, nitrogen, oxygen, carbon dioxide. Hydrogen would flow the fastest since it is the least dense.</u>

Science investigation

Do grapes float? You will need some soda water and grapes. Fill a glass three quarters full with soda water. Drop some grapes in the water and record what happens. Next, peel the skin off a few of the grapes and drop them into the soda water. Record what happens. Explain your observations. Make sure to include your understanding of density in your explanation.

Unpeeled grapes will rise up in carbonated water. Their skin repels the water, so they appear to float. When the grapes are peeled, they absorb water. This increases their density, so they sink.

20

⭐ What kind of material is it?

Background information

Materials can exist as solids, liquids, and gases. Liquids and gases can easily be poured to fill a space. Liquids can make a surface feel wet. You cannot easily pass your hand through a solid. Many gases have no colour. Knowing some of these things can help you identify materials.

Science activity

The table below tells you the properties of four different materials–chlorine, paraffin, mica, and margarine. Use this table to answer the questions.

Material	Chlorine	Paraffin	Mica	Margarine
Can it fill a space?	Yes	Yes	No	No
What colour is it?	Yellow	No colour	White and silvery	Yellow
Can it be poured?	Yes	Yes	No	No
Can you put your finger through it?	Yes	Yes	No	Yes
Can it make a piece of paper wet?	No	Yes	No	Yes

Which materials are solids? <u>Mica and margarine</u>
Which materials are liquids? <u>Paraffin</u>
Which materials are gases? <u>Chlorine</u>

Science investigation
Using a medicine dropper, place one drop of each of the following liquids onto wax paper: soapy water, fresh water, oil, rubbing alcohol. Have an adult help you. Can the shape of a drop of the liquid be used to identify the liquid? Explain.

All liquids tend to bubble up because of surface tension, an inward pushing force that causes them to form bubbles. The water drop will appear the roundest since it has the most surface tension; then oil, alcohol, and finally soapy water.

21

Which gas is it?

Background information

Air is a mixture of gases. The main gases in air are nitrogen and oxygen. There are also small amounts of other gases, including carbon dioxide, helium, and argon. Each of these gases has different properties that are useful to us in different ways. They can be separated from each other by cooling because each one condenses at a different temperature. *Condensation* is the phase change by which matter changes from a gas to a liquid.

Science activity

The properties of some of the gases in air are listed below. A chemically reactive gas can react with other substances to form new substances. For example, oxygen is chemically reactive; it causes iron to rust.

Gas	Properties
oxygen	chemically reactive; necessary for burning, and for living things to respire (use food for energy)
carbon dioxide	chemically reactive; extinguishes flames; quite a dense (heavy) gas; needed by plants for photosynthesis
argon	not chemically reactive (inert)

Decide which gas should be used in each of the following cases.

Filling cylinders to help people with lung disease breathe more easily
<u>oxygen</u>

Filling fire extinguishers
<u>carbon dioxide</u>

Filling light bulbs so that the filament does not react chemically
<u>argon</u>

Helium is an inert gas. It is used to fill balloons to make them buoyant. What happens when you let go of a balloon? What does this tell you about helium?
<u>The balloons float in air because they are less dense than the air.</u>

Science investigation
Fill three separate balloons with helium, air, and carbon dioxide. You can fill a balloon with carbon dioxide by placing it over a freshly opened bottle of soda (carbonated) water and letting it sit a few minutes until it inflates. Design and conduct an experiment to test differences in the density of these gases.

Make sure the type and volume of the inflated balloons are the same. The child can time how long it takes for each balloon to rise to the ceiling. The faster balloon will be the least dense (most buoyant).

22

⭐ Do all liquids flow equally well?

Background information

Liquids flow and take the shape of the container into which they are poured. Some liquids feel "thin" and flow quickly, while others feel "thick" and flow slowly. This property of resistance to flow is called *viscosity*.

Science activity

Hunter tested the viscosity of different liquids by pouring each one into a tall jar and timing how long it took for a small lump of modelling clay to drop to the bottom.

Using the chart below, number the liquids in order of their viscosity. Write **1** for the least viscous liquid and **7** for the most viscous.

Liquid	Time taken (for modelling clay to fall)	Order
water	2 seconds	
vegetable oil	4.5 seconds	
olive oil	6 seconds	
nail polish remover	1 second	
golden syrup	90 seconds	
motor oil	10 seconds	
dishwashing liquid	7 seconds	

How long do you think the modelling clay would take to fall through apple juice? Explain.
<u>The modelling clay would probably take just over 2 seconds to fall through apple juice because apple juice is mostly water.</u>

Science investigation
Collect different liquids in your home such as liquid soap, molasses, or one of the liquids noted in the above chart. Design and conduct an experiment to see which liquid has the greatest viscosity.

Be sure to use a tall glass in the investigation so liquids don't overflow. The more viscous the liquid, the slower an object will fall through it. The young investigator should drop the same object in each liquid for the most valid comparisons.

How runny is it? ⭐

Background information

Liquids are materials that make things wet. All liquids flow. This means that they are runny and you can pour them. If you spill liquids, they spread out. If you pour a liquid into a container, it takes the shape of the container. If you leave a liquid to stand, its surface will flatten, with the edges a bit higher than the centre. You can easily push your finger through a liquid.

Science activity

Lauren and Tai did an experiment to find out which of the five liquids below was the runniest. The same amount of each liquid was poured from a pitcher into a glass. Each pitcher was held in the same position over the glass. The time it took to fill each glass was written down.

Water
5 seconds

Honey
25 seconds

Liquid soap
8 seconds

Jam
42 seconds

Oil
9 seconds

Which liquid is the runniest? Explain.
<u>Water because it filled up the glass the fastest.</u>

Science investigation
Design and conduct an experiment to see which of the following liquids is runniest: water, juice, maple syrup, soda, and liquid soap. Drop a small object, such as a marble, into each liquid to help you determine this.

Objects will drop more slowly in the more viscous (thicker) liquids. Use an unbreakable container for this investigation so that none of the liquids leak.

24

Will they mix?

Background information
When solids are added to some liquids, the solid dissolves into very tiny particles and seems to disappear. A mixture in which one material dissolves in another is called a *solution*. When you add sugar to a cup of tea, the sugar dissolves in the tea to form a solution. Some solids will not dissolve in liquids. For example, flour will not dissolve in water. Materials that dissolve in liquids are called *soluble*. Materials that do not dissolve in liquids are called *insoluble*. Water is a liquid that can dissolve many types of materials.

Science activity
Read the sentences below and decide which ones are true and which ones are false. Circle the right answers.

Sand dissolves in boiling water.   True (False)
Sugar dissolves in lemon juice.   (True) False
Soil dissolves in water.   True (False)
Salt dissolves in tomato soup.   (True) False
Sugar dissolves in sand.   True (False)
Oil is soluble in vinegar.   True (False)

Boiling water

Sand

Science investigation
Design and conduct an experiment to see if a sugar cube dissolves faster in hot water or cold water.

The sugar cube will dissolve fastest in hot water. The sugar dissolves into particles that are too small to be seen, but we know they are still there because the water tastes sweet.

25

How fast do things cool down?

Background information
Hot water will cool down until it reaches the temperature of its surroundings. There is a pattern in the way things cool down.

Science activity
Look at the axes on the graph below. Estimate the shape of a line showing how hot water cools down. Draw this line on the graph. Francesca did an experiment to see what really happens. Her results are shown in the table on the right. Plot the results on the graph using a different colour pencil. Do a line graph and connect all of the points. Does it match the drawing you made? Explain.

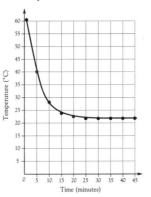

Time (minutes)

Cooling time	Temperature of water
0 minutes	60°C
5 minutes	40°C
10 minutes	28°C
15 minutes	24°C
20 minutes	23°C
25 minutes	22°C
30 minutes	22°C
35 minutes	22°C

Predict the temperature after 45 minutes. *22° C – room temperature*
Explain.

Science investigation
Design and conduct your own experiment to measure the change in the temperature of refrigerated water that is placed in room temperature. Create a data table and graph your results.

Use a Celsius thermometer. The water can be slightly frozen to begin. If the water is frozen it may take a while for the temperature to change, since when matter undergoes a phase change its temperature does not change.

26

How quickly does it evaporate?

Background information
Water left in a bowl will slowly disappear. The water evaporates into water vapour, the gas phase of water. The water vapour mixes with the air. *Evaporation* is a type of phase change in which matter changes from a liquid to a gas. Some liquids evaporate more quickly than others. Liquids with high boiling points (those that boil at very high temperatures) tend to evaporate more slowly than those with lower boiling points.

Science activity
Number the liquids listed below in order of how fast you would expect them to evaporate at room temperature. Explain why you think this is so.

| 2 | water | 1 | rubbing alcohol | 3 | vegetable oil |

Alcohol, water, oil. Since you can smell alcohol, it is more volatile. It has a lower boiling point than water or oil. Oil has the highest boiling point of the liquids.

How do you think you can make the water evaporate more quickly?
The water could be made to evaporate more quickly by heating it.

Science investigation
(!) What happens when a liquid evaporates from your skin? Gently rub some water on your upper arm. Wait a few minutes and describe what you feel on your arm. Repeat this experiment, but this time apply some rubbing alcohol on your upper arm. Wait a minute and describe what you feel. You can try this with other liquids.

When a liquid evaporates from your skin, it removes heat. This causes the sensation of cooling. The more volatile the liquid, the faster the evaporation and cooling effect. Alcohol feels cooler because it evaporates faster.

Can you separate salt from sand?

Background information
Filtering removes *insoluble* particles from water (particles that do not dissolve). Salt is *soluble* in water, but sand is insoluble (it is not soluble). The water in a salt solution will evaporate if it is left uncovered. Rock salt is a mixture of salt and sand.

Science activity
Using the information above and the equipment shown below, explain how you would separate the salt in rock salt from its insoluble parts. You may add other equipment that is not shown here. You may want to draw a flow chart to show the steps in your procedure.

Draw your flow chart here.

    Stir the rock salt in water.
    Heat the mixture to dissolve all salt.
    Pour the mixture through a filter to remove the sand.
    Leave the salt solution to evaporate.
    You will be left with the salt.

Science investigation
A lot more matter would be recycled if it could be separated from a mixture. Try out your skills. Mix together some sand, aluminum paper clips, and pennies in a bowl (and anything else you want to add). Design a procedure to separate the mixture. Test out your procedure to see if it works.

Materials could be filters, magnets, or water. Scientists often work on methods to separate mixtures. Recycling has improved by separating plastics by density. Each plastic is thus purer and can then be recycled into objects with specific properties.

28

Can we filter it?

Background information
Sometimes it is necessary to separate a mixture. For example, coffee filters are used to keep the coffee grinds out of the coffee. When you pour your coffee into a filter, the holes in the filter are large enough for the water to drain away, but too small for the grinds to pass through. The coffee grinds are trapped by the filter. When the materials in a mixture are *insoluble* in water, you can use a filter to separate them.

Science activity
Here are some lentils, peas, and marbles all mixed up in a pot. Pictures A and B show the bottom of the pot. On A, draw the sizes of the holes you must make to separate the lentils from the peas and marbles. On B, draw the holes you would need to make to separate the lentils and peas from the marbles.

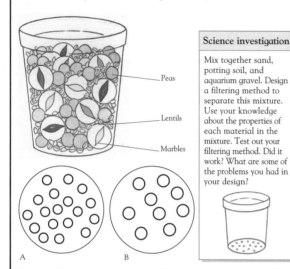

Peas

Lentils

Marbles

A   B

Science investigation

Mix together sand, potting soil, and aquarium gravel. Design a filtering method to separate this mixture. Use your knowledge about the properties of each material in the mixture. Test out your filtering method. Did it work? What are some of the problems you had in your design?

Encourage the child to make a filtering device. Cut holes in old fabric, or use colanders or other draining devices. Emphasize the relationship between the size of the openings in the filter and its ability to separate mixtures of a certain particle size.

29

Are some changes reversible?

Background information
When ice is warmed, it melts to form water. When water is heated further, it boils to form *water vapour*, a colourless, odourless gas. These changes from solid to liquid to gas can be reversed by cooling water vapour. The water vapour will condense to form liquid water, and if cooling continues the water will eventually freeze.

| Ice | melts → ← freezes | Water | boils → ← condenses | Water vapour |

Science activity
Explain what is happening to the water in each picture.

The water vapor is condensing to form water on the cold window pane.

The water in the wet washing is evaporating to form water vapor.

The water vapor in the air is changing to water, then quickly to ice on a very cold day.

Science investigation

Look at weather maps in different parts of the country. Find some cities in which it is snowing. What is the temperature in these cities? Find some cities in which it is raining. What is the temperature in these cities? Create a data table to summarize the data you collected. What is the relationship between temperature and weather?

Point out the different symbols on maps that represent each type of precipitation. Some examples of precipitation symbols are the raindrop, representing rain, and the snowflake, representing snow.

30

How can we separate mixtures?

Background information
Mixtures are two or more materials combined together. They can be separated in many different ways. To find out which is the best way to separate a mixture, you must first ask yourself some important questions. For example, are the materials in the mixture soluble? Are the materials attracted to a magnet? Do the materials change when they are heated? What size are the particles in the mixture?

Science activity
On the left, you can see four mixtures. On the right are four different methods for separating mixtures. Draw a line between each mixture and the best separation method. On a separate piece of paper, explain your choice.

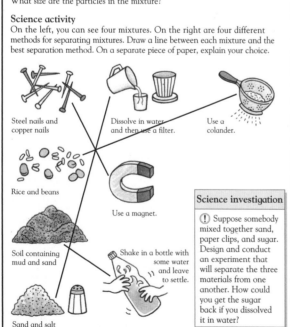

Steel nails and copper nails

Dissolve in water and then use a filter.

Use a colander.

Rice and beans

Use a magnet.

Soil containing mud and sand

Shake in a bottle with some water and leave to settle.

Sand and salt

Science investigation

(!) Suppose somebody mixed together sand, paper clips, and sugar. Design and conduct an experiment that will separate the three materials from one another. How could you get the sugar back if you dissolved it in water?

Sugar dissolves in water while sand does not. If water is added to the mixture, the sand can be separated with a coffee filter. The sugar can be separated from the water by boiling off the water—be careful not to burn the sugar.

Are some changes irreversible?

Background information
When you mix substances together, they may change to form a new substance. Sometimes the change is *reversible*, while at other times it is *irreversible*. For example, when vinegar is mixed with baking soda, the two fizz and a new substance is formed. This change is irreversible. A change is more likely to be irreversible if there is a reaction such as a fizz, colour change, or a change in temperature.

Science activity
Are the following mixing processes reversible or irreversible?

1. Dissolving sugar in water — Reversible

2. Shaking together vinegar and oil — Reversible

3. Mixing sand and sugar — Reversible

4. Adding lemon juice to red cabbage juice (the colour changes from bluish-purple to red) — Irreversible

(a colour change often signifies a permanent change)

Science investigation

Try mixing the following substances together, and decide whether the change is reversible or irreversible. Do any mixtures result in a temperature change? Explain.
1. Lemon juice added to baking powder
2. Vinegar added to chalk
3. Vinegar added to salt
4. Lemon juice added to sugar

Borax mixed with glue makes an irreversible change. An irreversible change is always a chemical change since the matter takes on new properties. A reversible change is a physical change, since the individual properties of the matter are still present.

What happens when it burns?

Background information
Oxygen from the air is needed for something to burn. *Burning* is an irreversible process that forms new substances. Some of these substances are solids, such as ash or soot, and some are gases, such as water vapour and carbon dioxide. When paper burns, it produces soot (mostly carbon), water vapour, carbon dioxide, a small amount of other gases, and ash (minerals that do not burn).

Science activity
Look at the drawing. It shows a candle burning inside an upturned jam jar.

- Soot
- Water droplets
- Candle goes out

What is produced when a candle burns? What is a possible explanation as to why the candle went out?

When a candle burns, water vapour, ash, and carbon dioxide are produced. The water is seen when it condenses on the sides of the bottle. The candle went out because there was not enough oxygen to support its burning.

Science investigation
(!) Light a candle and place a jar over it. Time how long it takes for the candle to go out. When the flame goes out, let the jar cool down a bit. Carefully lift the jar, keeping the open end facing downward and placing it quickly on a table. Relight the candle. Place the jar over the candle. Does the candle burn now? If so, time how long it burns. Explain your observations.

The investigator will learn that the candle will still burn in the second scenario, but not for as long as before, since the amount of oxygen in the jar continues decreasing while the carbon dioxide builds up.

33

How does the water cycle work?

Background information
The process by which water changes from one phase to another is called the *water cycle*. *Evaporation* is when water (a liquid) turns into water vapour (a gas). *Condensation* is when water vapour turns back into liquid water. Evaporation increases with heating while condensation increases with cooling. The Sun causes water to evaporate into the atmosphere. Cooling of the atmosphere results in the formation of clouds (water droplets). Rain occurs when the droplets become too heavy for the clouds. Rainwater then soaks into the ground and eventually ends up back in the rivers and oceans.

Science activity
Place a check mark (✔) by the correct statements and a cross (✘) by the incorrect ones. Then decide whether or not statement 1 happens because of statement 2.

Statement 1	(✔) or (✘)	Statement 1 happens because of Statement 2 – True or False	Statement 2	(✔) or (✘)
Rain falls when clouds are formed.	✘	False	Water vapour condenses to form water when cooled.	✔
Water only evaporates from oceans.	✘	False	Water vapour is formed faster when water is warmed.	✔
Water vapour condenses faster in the higher regions of the atmosphere.	✔	True	It is colder in the higher regions of the atmosphere.	✔

Science investigation
(!) Make your own cloud chamber with a 250 mL glass jar filled 2 cm high with tap water, a large rubber balloon with the mouth end cut off, a match, a rubber band, and a flashlight. Add water to jar. Light match over the jar and blow it out. Place balloon over jar and secure in place with rubber band. Wait 2 minutes. Darken the room. Push down on balloon while shining flashlight on jar. Observe and record what you see when you let go of the rubber balloon. Do this a number of times. Explain your observations.

The lit match provides particles on which the cloud will form. Pressing on the balloon increases pressure in the jar, which facilitates cloud formation. Water droplets should be seen on the sides of the jar after the balloon has been pushed a number of times.

34

How does a condenser work?

Background information
Condensers are devices that turn gases into liquids by cooling the gas quickly. You can find condensers in many places, such as air conditioners, power stations, and laboratories. A condenser can change water vapour to a liquid. The water vapour comes in contact with a cold surface and condenses back into liquid water. It is important to keep the surface cold. The surface normally gets heated by the vapour and so becomes less efficient. In a laboratory condenser, this warming up is prevented by placing the cold surface inside a jacket of cold, flowing water.

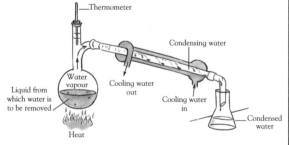

- Thermometer
- Condensing water
- Water vapour
- Cooling water out
- Liquid from which water is to be removed
- Cooling water in
- Condensed water
- Heat

Science activity
When Juan gets out of the shower, he notices that the mirror is all "steamed up." He also notices that when he drinks iced tea, there is moisture on the outside of the glass. Explain Juan's observations.

Juan is observing condensation. When water vapour in the air touches a cold surface, it condenses as moisture.

Science investigation
Design and conduct an experiment to determine the best surface for condensing water vapour. Predict which surface you think will be best and explain why you think so. One suggestion is to place water in paper cups and place a cover made of a different type of matter over each cup.

Colder surfaces, such as metals, are better at condensing water vapour. Some surfaces feel cooler than others because of a property called specific heat. Matter with high specific heat does not change temperature as quickly as matter with low specific heat.

How soluble are materials?

Background information
Substances that can be dissolved in a liquid are said to be *soluble*. Substances that do not dissolve are *insoluble*. The liquid in which a substance dissolves is called the *solvent*. The substance that dissolves is called the *solute*. When mixed together, they make a solution. Water is an excellent solvent. It dissolves many substances. Sugar and salt are very soluble in water, while substances such as sand and chalk are insoluble.

Science activity
Rosa collected two different plant fertilizers from a garden centre. The directions said to mix each fertilizer with water and to sprinkle the solution on her plants. When she mixed the first fertilizer in the water, it seemed to disappear. However, when she mixed the second fertilizer, she noticed it sank to the bottom of the watering can.

Which fertilizer should Rosa use for her plants? Explain.

Rosa should use the one that dissolves to ensure that the plants obtain the fertilizer's nutrients when they are watered.

Science investigation
(!) Design and conduct an experiment to test which common household substances are soluble in water. Always add the substance to water and not the water to the substance, as there could be a strong reaction. Wear safety glasses. You might try flour, baking soda, alcohol, or cooking oil.

The investigator should find that the amount of water used will affect how easily something dissolves. The same amount of water and solute should be used for each matter tested to ensure valid comparisons.

36

Are all substances equally soluble?

Background information
All soluble substances do not dissolve equally well. Sugar dissolves very easily, while other substances, such as salt, dissolve less easily. The amount of solute that will dissolve in a solvent is a measure of its *solubility*.

Science activity
Below is a graph showing the solubility of different substances.

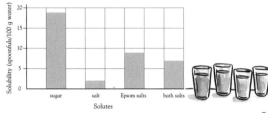

About how many spoonfuls of salt dissolve in the water? ......2......

About how many spoonfuls of bath salts dissolve in the water? ......7......

Another substance is more soluble than bath salts but less soluble than Epsom salts. What range of spoonfuls would you expect to dissolve? ...7–9...

List the solutes in the bar graph in order of their solubility.
Write the name of the most soluble substance first.

.....sugar...... .....Epsom salts..... .....bath salts...... ......salt......

Science investigation
Does the size of a sugar particle affect its solubility? Obtain sugar cubes, powdered sugar, and granulated sugar. Design and conduct an experiment to see which type of sugar is most soluble.

The child should place the samples of sugar in water, then time how long each takes to dissolve. The larger the particle of sugar, the longer it will take. Children often confuse dissolving with melting. Sugar does not melt in the water; it dissolves.

37

Is water really pure?

Background information
Tap water contains substances (solutes) already dissolved in it. The amount and type of dissolved substances depend on where you live. This is one of the reasons that tap water tastes different in different areas. You can find out how much solute is dissolved in water by pouring a small amount into a glass and allowing it to evaporate. The white ring or scale left behind in the glass contains minerals that were dissolved in the water. Water that contains a lot of dissolved substances is called *hard water*, while water that contains very few dissolved substances is called *soft water*.

Science activity
Tiah had a fish tank. As the water evaporated, she would add more water. She noticed a line of white scale on the inside of the fish tank where the water had evaporated. Explain Tiah's observation.

Tap water has minerals in it. When the water evaporates, the minerals are left behind, forming white scale on the fish tank.

Science investigation
Obtain a black, water-soluble marker. Cut a white paper coffee filter into a circle just a bit larger than the opening of a glass. Draw a circle 2 cm wide in the middle of the filter. Now place the filter on top of a glass. With an eyedropper, place one small drop of water in the centre of the marker circle, making sure not to get any water on the marker. Observe what happens as the water moves across the paper. Explain your observations.

Try different water-soluble markers. Ink in these markers is a colour mixture; black ink is composed of a number of dyes such as red, blue, yellow, and green. The paper separates the ink mixture because the ink solutes are absorbed at different rates.

38

Does temperature affect solubility?

Background information
It is easier to dissolve soluble substances in warm water than in cold water. However, heat increases the solubility of some substances more than of others.

Science activity
Make a line graph to plot the data from the table. Be sure to connect all the points after they are plotted. The data shows the solubility of table salt and of Epsom salts as temperature increases.

Temperature (°C)	Amount dissolved per jug (in grams)	
	Salt	Epsom salts
20	10	20
30	12	30
40	14	40
50	16	50
60	18	55

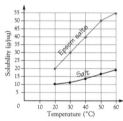

1 Do you see a relationship between temperature and the solubility of table salt? Explain.
Yes, as the temperature increases, the salt becomes more soluble.

2 Is this relationship the same for Epsom salts? Explain.
Yes, the relationship is the same for Epsom salts.

3 Describe any differences temperature has on the solubility of Epsom salts as compared to table salt.
Temperature has more effect on the solubility of Epsom salts.

Science investigation
⚠ You can make rock candy by dissolving 2 cups of sugar in a cup of boiling water. Let the solution cool and pour it into plastic cups, filling each half way. Tie 12 cm of plain dental floss in the center of a pencil. Place the pencil over a cup and let the floss drop into the solution. Repeat for the other cups. Observe what happens over two weeks. Draw diagrams and explain your observations.

Rock candy is made from a supersaturated sugar solution. Document candy formation in daily observations and diagrams. Food colouring can be used to colour the candy. Some heat packs are supersaturated solutions that release heat when crystallizing.

Does adding salt change water?

Background information
Mixing substances together can cause their properties to change. Adding salt to water makes the water salty. Salt water boils at a higher temperature than fresh water and freezes at a lower temperature. *Buoyancy* is the upward pushing force of a fluid. Objects float more easily in salt water than in fresh water, because salt water is more buoyant. This is also why it is easier to swim in salt water than in fresh water.

Science activity
Look at the pairs of pictures. Which picture in each pair shows sea water and which shows fresh water?

......fresh water...... ......sea water......

......fresh water...... ......sea water......

If you added sand to water, would it boil at a higher temperature? Explain.
No, because sand will not dissolve in water.

Science investigation
Obtain a small toy boat. Design and conduct an experiment to see the effect of different concentrations of salt on the buoyancy of the boat.

Prepare salt solutions with different concentrations, then place the boat in each solution to see how high it floats. The more salt added to the water, the greater its buoyancy (density). As the water's density increases, its buoyant force increases.

When do liquids freeze?

Background information
Pure water freezes at 0°C. Water with substances dissolved in it (a solution) freezes at a lower temperature. Some substances, such as candle wax, freeze (solidify) at temperatures above 0°C. Other substances, such as vegetable oil, freeze at a temperature below 0°C. The temperature at which a substance freezes is called its *freezing point*.

Science activity
The freezing points of different liquids are shown in the bar graph below.

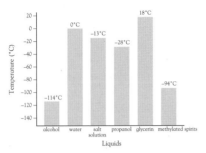

Looking at the bar graph, which substance will be a solid on a winter's day but a liquid on a summer's day? The rhyme below will help you.

"Minus 5, plus 10 and 21 – winter, spring, and summer sun."

Water and glycerin

Science investigation
Design and conduct an experiment to determine the effect of different concentrations of salt on the freezing of water. Note down the temperature of the salt water when it begins to freeze. *Hint:* Slush or ice crystals will begin to form.

Prepare different solutions of salt water and time how long it takes each to freeze. The water can be placed in the freezer and checked at regular intervals. Use a Celsius thermometer to take the solution's temperature when it begins to freeze.

41

Is it a thermal insulator?

Background information
Matter that allows heat to pass through it is a *thermal conductor*. Metals are excellent thermal conductors, though the best thermal conductor is diamond. Diamonds are crystals made of carbon. Glass, water, wood, and air are poor thermal conductors. Matter that is a poor conductor of heat is called a *thermal insulator*. Some types of matter are better thermal insulators than others.

Science activity
Five glasses containing water at 60°C were each wrapped in different types of matter. After 10 minutes, the water temperature in each glass was recorded. The results are shown in the table below.

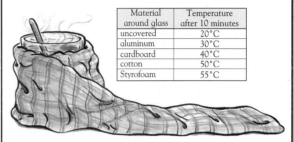

Material around glass	Temperature after 10 minutes
uncovered	20°C
aluminum	30°C
cardboard	40°C
cotton	50°C
Styrofoam	55°C

Which type of matter is the best insulator? Explain. Why was one glass uncovered?

Styrofoam is the best insulator, since the temperature of the water in the Styrofoam glass decreased the least.

Science investigation
Animals that live in cold climates have thick layers of fat. Fats and oils have similar properties. Using vegetable oil, design and conduct an experiment to test the purpose of the fatty layers.

Place an equal amount of heated water into a number of cups. Add different amounts of oil (to vary the thickness of the "fat"). One cup should have no oil (control). The oil models the fat on an animal.

42

Which metal is it?

Background information
A metal is a type of matter. Most metals are shiny and *malleable* (can be hammered into shapes), *ductile* (can be pulled into wires), and can conduct heat and electricity. There are different types of metals like iron, copper, gold, lead, and tin. Each metal has a set of additional properties that make it unique. These properties can be used to identify the type of metal. For example, some metals are denser than other metals. *Density* has to do with how much matter can occupy a given amount of space.

Science activity
Use the branching key below to identify each of the five metals in this chart. Write the correct letter for each metal below its name.

Metal	Properties
A	hard; brown in colour; good conductor of electricity
B	relatively soft; yellow colour; does not rust; very good conductor of electricity
C	soft; silver colour; tarnishes quickly; very heavy; weak conductor of electricity
D	hard; silver colour; magnetic; tarnishes easily (rusts)
E	hard; silver colour; not magnetic; does not tarnish easily

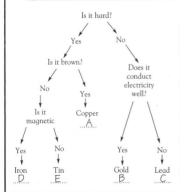

Is it hard?
Yes → Is it brown? No → Is it magnetic → Yes → Iron D / No → Tin E
Yes → Copper A
No → Does it conduct electricity well? Yes → Gold B / No → Lead C

Science investigation
1. Collect 10 small pieces of metal.
2. Create a poster chart to show the properties of each metal and some of their possible uses. You may have to design an experiment to determine some properties.
3. Use a magnet to determine which metals are magnetic.

Samples of metal matter can easily be collected around the home. Broken objects and parts of old toys work very well. Properties such as magnetism, colour, lustre (ability to reflect light), conductivity, and texture can be tested.

What makes things fall?

Background information
Gravity is a pull or force of attraction between two objects, and is a property of all matter. The more mass an object has, the bigger its attraction to another object. Earth is a huge object with a lot of mass. Everything on Earth is pulled towards its centre. Our weight is caused by the pull of gravity. The more mass we have, the greater our response to the pull of gravity. Our weight is a force that is measured in units called *Newtons* (N). The force of gravity on one kilogram of mass equals about 10 Newtons. The force of gravity does not change on Earth. What changes is an object's response to the force. Prove this by dropping a heavy book and a light book from the same height. Since the force of gravity is the same on both objects, they will hit the ground at the same time.

Science activity
Draw an arrow to show the direction of the force extending the spring.

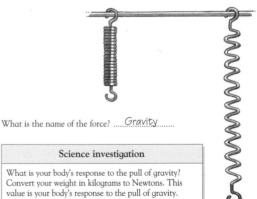

What is the name of the force? Gravity

Science investigation
What is your body's response to the pull of gravity? Convert your weight in kilograms to Newtons. This value is your body's response to the pull of gravity. Who in your family has the greatest response to the pull of gravity? Use the following conversion: 1 kg = 10 N.

The spring will stretch about double in length (Hooke's Law). The child only needs to understand that it stretches more.

Does a force have a direction?

Background information

A *force* is a push or pull. Forces can start or stop an object from moving. They can increase or decrease the speed of a moving object. The force that opposes motion is called *friction*. Forces can also make things change their direction of motion. For example, the force of the wind can blow a boat off course. A force acts in one direction. This direction is shown in the diagrams by using arrows. A longer arrow is used to show a bigger force.

A gentle kick

A hard kick

Science activity

Examine the diagrams below. On each diagram, draw an arrow to show the direction of each force mentioned.

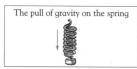
The pull of gravity on the spring

The force of friction slowing the rolling can

The force of the hammer

The force exerted by each team (two arrows)

Science investigation

Using the spring balance that you made in the last investigation or a store-purchased spring balance, investigate the amount of force needed to: lift a cookie, lift a cup, brush your teeth, write with a pen or pencil, or another activity of your choice.

Connect the object to be measured to the spring. A cabinet door may work better than a room door. Balances used to weigh fish can be used, but if they are not metric, the child will need to convert the measurement to metric units.

45

What effect does friction have?

Background information

Friction is a force that slows things down. When two surfaces come in contact with one another, there is a frictional force. The amount of friction depends on a number of factors. Rougher surfaces create more friction than smooth surfaces. It is a lot easier to ride a bike on a newly paved road than on a dirt trail. The weight of an object pushing on the surface causes friction. The amount of surface in contact with another surface also affects the amount of friction. For example, wheels reduce the amount of surface contact.

Science activity

Gail covered a ramp with different materials and measured how far a wooden block slid on each surface before coming to a halt. Here are her results.

Type of surface	How far the block slid after being pushed
sandpaper	50 cm
glass	500 cm
wood	100 cm
plastic	300 cm
cardboard	90 cm

Which is the smoothest surface, and which is the roughest surface?
Glass is the smoothest surface and sandpaper the roughest.

Explain how you worked out the answers to the question above.
Rough surfaces slow things down because of more friction.
The block slid farthest on glass, so it must be the smoothest.

Science investigation

Using a spring balance, test out the friction of various objects on a wooden ramp. Keep in mind that if you want to test the effect of different surfaces, the same object must be tested each time. Make sure to explain how you will use the spring balance to measure friction.

The spring balance can be used to measure friction, since the force needed to pull the object up a ramp will be greater when there is more friction. Ask the child to make reasoned predictions, such as, "Rougher surfaces will require more force due to increased friction."

46

What makes boats float?

Background information

Boats are built so they can float on water. A boat builder must consider both the shape and weight of the boat. Remember, weight is an object's response to the pull of gravity. When an object is placed in water, the water pushes upward against it. This upthrust is known as *buoyancy*. The force of gravity pulls the boat down. In order for the boat to float above water, the buoyant force must be greater than the force of gravity.

Upthrust   Gravity

Science activity

Objects weigh less in water than in air because of the buoyant force. Marcos used a spring balance to measure and compare the weights of different objects in air and in water. His results are given in the table below.

Object	Weight in air (N)	Weight in water (N)
stone	130 N	6 N
wood block	20 N	0 N
plastic hair clip	5 N	1 N
metal pan	500 N	0 N

Use the table above to work out which objects will float. Explain your conclusions.
The wood block and metal pan will float because they weigh nothing in water.

Science investigation

Build a boat out of about 30 square centimetres of aluminum foil. Obtain about 200–300 pennies. Predict how many pennies your boat can hold before sinking. Explain your design. If you don't have pennies, substitute with something like rice, beans, or macaroni.

The penny boat activity is excellent for learning about buoyancy. Encourage the child to think of a design that will allow for the greatest buoyant force. Ask other family members to build a boat. Hold a competition to see which boat holds the most pennies.

How much does it weigh?

Background information

Scientists measure the weight of objects using its metric weight. The unit is called a Newton (N). All matter has weight due to the force of gravity. Since a 1 kg (1000 g) mass weighs 10 N, a 100 g mass is 1 N. A metric spring balance or scale can be used to measure force.

Science activity

What is the weight in Newtons of each objects in the pictures below?

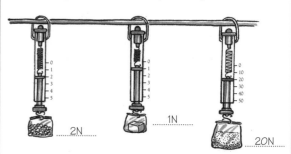
2N   1N   20N

Science investigation

Build and calibrate your own spring balance. Use white heavy board, a large adhesive hook, a large rubber band, and a paper clip bent into a hook. Attach the hook to the heavy board near the top. Hang the rubber band off the hook. Hang the paper clip from the rubber band to create another hook. Attach a sandwich-size plastic bag or cup to this hook so you can add objects for calibration. Instead of Newtons, create your own unit: pennies, marbles, etc. Every time you add one of these objects, draw a line for calibration. Make sure to decide where the 0 unit will be. Once completed, try measuring different objects in this unit. Can you use your unit to tell which object weighs more?

In order to calibrate accurately, use objects of the same mass, such as marbles, paper clips, or pennies. The child can now measure objects in pennies or marbles, etc.

48

Which is the strongest wood?

Background information

Tensile strength is an important property of matter. It measures the amount of force a type of matter can withstand before breaking. Since wood is a material often used in construction, it is important to know its tensile strength. One simple way to compare the strength of different materials is by hanging increasingly heavier weights from them until they break.

Science activity

Dylan hung weights on strips of wood until the wood broke in the middle.

Type of wood	Weight needed to break wood (in Newtons)
beech	2000 N
oak	3000 N
walnut	2600 N
ash	2500 N
pine	500 N
sycamore	2500 N

Based on the data you have collected, which wood would you choose for constructing a bridge? Explain your choice.

Oak is the best choice, since it has the highest tensile strength of the woods tested.

> **Science investigation**
>
> Thread can be made of different type of materials such as nylon, rayon, or silk. Design an experiment to test the strength of different types of thread. If Spiderman had to purchase thread to climb buildings, what type of thread would he choose based on your data? Explain.

The child might try hanging the same weight from different types of thread to see which one breaks first. Each approach must test the different thread samples in exactly the same way to ensure the validity of results.

49

Which fabric will stretch the most?

Background information

There are many properties that can be used to describe matter. Fabrics are a type of matter. Some fabrics stretch more than others. A property of matter in which it can stretch and return to its original shape is called *elasticity*. Some fabrics are more elastic than others. You can compare the elasticity of two types of fabric by hanging equal weights off each and measuring how much they stretch.

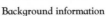

Science activity

Lauren tried to compare the stretch in five different fabrics. All of the fabrics were the same length at the beginning of the experiment. Her data table of results is shown below. A Newton (N) is a metric measurement of weight.

Fabric	Weight hung from fabric	Amount of stretch
cotton	10 N	3 cm
wool	100 N	40 cm
nylon	100 N	55 cm
polyester	500 N	200 cm
denim	10 N	3 cm

According to this data table, which fabric stretched the most? (Hint: Consider both the weight hung and the amount of stretch for each fabric.) Explain.

Nylon stretched the most at 5.5 cm for each 10 N.

How could Lauren have improved this experiment?

If Lauren had used the same weight in each trial, she wouldn't have to make a conversion to compare the results.

> **Science investigation**
>
> Design and conduct an experiment to test which pair of your socks stretches the most. Use the results of the science activity to guide your investigation. Incorporate your suggested improvements for Lauren's experiment.

Socks are made of many different fabrics. A good experiment tests all of the sock fabrics using the same weight (force). The results of the first activity can be used to formulate a hypothesis.

50

Is it elastic?

Background information

One of the properties of matter is *elasticity*. This is its ability to stretch and then go back to its original shape. Rubber is elastic. Metals can be made into springs that behave as if they were elastic. When you pull a spring to stretch it, you can feel a force pulling in the opposite direction. When you push a spring together, you can feel a force pushing against you.

Science activity

Rubber bands stretch when they are pulled. The graph shows how much a rubber band stretched when different forces were applied.

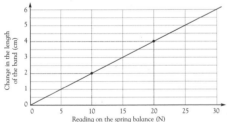

By how much is the rubber band stretched when pulled by a force of 20 N? ...... *4 cm*

By how much do you think the band would stretch if the spring balance read 30 N? ...... *6 cm*

The rubber band was 15 cm long to start with. How long was it when the spring balance read 10 N? ...... *17 cm*

> **Science investigation**
>
> Make a spring by coiling some thin, bare copper wire around a pencil, and then removing the pencil. Use a ruler to measure how long the spring stretches when first 5, then 10, and finally 15 paper clips are hung on it. How much would you expect it to stretch with the weight of 30 clips?

For the activity, tell your child that the wire will need about 30 twists around a pencil. You may need to change the number to get good results, but you should see that the spring stretches evenly before it reaches a point where it overstretches.

Is it crushable?

Background information

Force can change the shape of an object as it pushes or pulls on it. Some shapes can withstand greater forces than others. For example, you can easily crush a Styrofoam cup by squeezing its sides, but it is more difficult to crush the cup by squeezing it from top to bottom.

Science activity

A scientist tested how much force differently shaped pillars could withstand before they collapsed. Here are her results.

Shape of pillar base	Weight supported before collapsing
triangular	550 N
square	450 N
circular	900 N
rectangular	430 N

Which shape of pillar would best support the roof of a building?

A pillar with a circular base would best support the roof.

Explain how you worked out the answer to the question.

The cylindrical pillar with a circular base was able to support the most weight before collapsing, so it must be the strongest.

> **Science investigation**
>
> Use three pieces of paper and 30 cm of clear tape to build a support for a cup filled with rice, beans, or pebbles. How many of the objects can your support take before it collapses? Describe the design you used.

Ask the child to consider the shape of most skyscrapers and stadiums. A stadium's round shape allows for an even distribution of weight, which provides the most strength. The triangular shape of tall buildings is also strong.

Are all microbes harmful?

Background information

Not all microbes are harmful; some are extremely useful. Microbes help the remains of plants and animals to decay. This returns important nutrients to the soil that plants will use to grow. Some microbes are used to make foods such as yogurt and cheese. A microbe called yeast is used to make bread. Yeast is also used to make alcohol. Bacteria convert sugars in some fruit juices to vinegar that is used in salad dressing.

Science activity

Put a check mark (✔) beside the drinks that are made with the help of useful microbes.

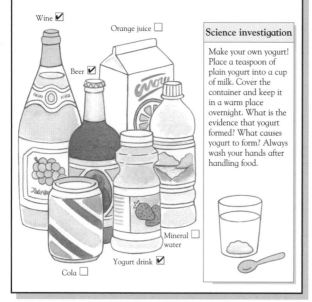

Wine ✔
Orange juice ☐
Beer ✔
Mineral water ☐
Cola ☐
Yogurt drink ✔

Science investigation

Make your own yogurt! Place a teaspoon of plain yogurt into a cup of milk. Cover the container and keep it in a warm place overnight. What is the evidence that yogurt formed? What causes yogurt to form? Always wash your hands after handling food.

Supervise the making of yogurt. Make sure the child is aware of why the texture of the food has changed. Help the child make a yeast bread to understand how yeast makes bread rise by producing gas.

53

What are the causes of disease?

Background information

Microbes such as viruses, bacteria, and fungi can infect living things and make them sick. They can cause illness and disease in humans. In some cases, the illness can kill people. Our bodies have special cells that fight microbes and help us get better. Medical doctors can give us medicines called *antibiotics* to help our bodies fight some harmful microbes. Antibiotics cannot treat viral infections.

Science activity

Write the letter **M** in the box beside each person infected with a microbe.

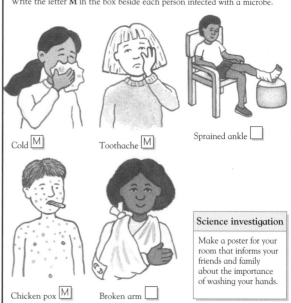

Cold M
Toothache M
Sprained ankle ☐
Chicken pox M
Broken arm ☐

Science investigation

Make a poster for your room that informs your friends and family about the importance of washing your hands.

Encourage the use of the Internet to learn about the cause and effect relationship between microbes and disease.

54

What are vertebrates?

Background information

The animal kingdom is divided into two types: animals with backbones are called vertebrates; animals without backbones are called invertebrates. People are vertebrates. So are snakes, goldfish, ducks, cats, and frogs. Scientists divide vertebrates into different classes–reptiles, fish, birds, mammals, and amphibians.

Science activity

Using the Internet and other resources, look for the key features of each vertebrate class. Some features of each class are given below. Add the results of your research to this information.

Vertebrates	Key features
Reptiles	Are cold blooded; breathe air using lungs; may be found in water but live on land
Fish	Are cold blooded; live in water; breathe by means of gills
Birds	Have hollow, light bones; bodies are covered with feathers; develop from eggs
Mammals	Are warm blooded; breathe air using lungs; have body hair or fur
Amphibians	Are cold blooded; have smooth, loose wet skin; return to water to breed

Science investigation

What is the main difference between warm-blooded and cold-blooded animals?

Warm-blooded animals have a body temperature that stays the same, even if it gets hotter or colder outside. Cold-blooded animals have a body temperature that is influenced by the temperature of their bodies.

55

What are invertebrates?

Background information

All animals that are not vertebrates are called invertebrates. Invertebrates do not have a backbone. All invertebrates are cold blooded. Like vertebrates, invertebrates are divided into classes.

Science activity

Using the Internet and other resources, look for the key features of each invertebrate class. See how many features you can add to the ones below.

Invertebrates	Key features
Porifera	Simplest of animals; stiff bodies; filter feed through their bodies
Cnidaria	Soft and jelly-like; have hollow, sack-like bodies with one opening
Nemertea	Flat worm; very long, up to 27m
Platyhelminthes	Simple animals with only one opening—the mouth; most are no more that 1 mm wide
Nematoda	Many are parasites in humans; more complex than flatworms
Annelida	Round worms (segmented worms); have a mouth and an anus
Echinidermata	Have tough spiny skin; body parts are arranged in fives or multiples of five
Arthropoda	Jointed legs; hard skin or shell (cuticle); have an outer skeleton (exoskeleton)
Mollusca	Soft body surrounded by a hard shell; most are marine animals, some live on a land

Science investigation

What kind of animals are crabs and lobsters? How many legs do they have?

Encourage your child to use the many resources and Internet sites that have beautiful photos and virtual reality videos of the animal kingdom.

56

What is yeast?

Background information
Scientists place yeasts, mushrooms, moulds, and other fungi together in their own kingdom. Yeast is a one-celled, microscopic member of the fungi kingdom. Fungi cannot make food for themselves like plants can.

Science activity
Below is a table to show how yeast cells were grown over a period of 12 hours. Show this same data using the bar graph below. If you have access to a computer, enter the data into a spreadsheet or graphing program. Explain what your graph tells you.

Time	Number of yeast cells
2 hours	50 yeast cells
4 hours	95 yeast cells
6 hours	190 yeast cells
8 hours	360 yeast cells
10 hours	500 yeast cells
12 hours	700 yeast cells

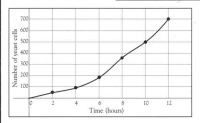

Science investigation
Try feeding some yeast with sugar. Pour a small amount of warm water into a small plastic ziplock bag. Then add a teaspoon of yeast. In another ziplock bag, put the same amount of warm water and yeast but add 3 teaspoons of sugar. Squeeze the air out of the bags and zip them up. Place them in a pail of warm water and observe. Discuss your findings.

The mixture becomes foamy. The yeast cells become active when they use the sugar for food. They also produce carbon-dioxide gas that inflates the bags.

57

What kind of animal is this?

Background information
There are many different animals that make up the animal kingdom. Scientists often use keys to help identify an unknown animal. Being able to use keys is an important skill. One type of key is called a *dichotomous key*. This is a branching key in which there are two choices in each branch. The last choice in the key will identify what the scientist is trying to determine. A dichotomous key can be used to identify animals.

Science activity
Arthropods are small animals with jointed legs and other appendages to their body. The word arthropod actually means "jointed feet."

.....Spider.....Millipede.....Insect.....Centipede.....Crustacean

Use the dichotomous key to identify the arthropods shown above.

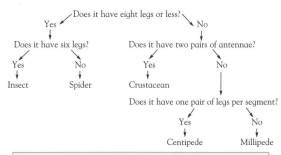

Science investigation
(!) Create your own dichotomous key to identify eating utensils (knives, forks, spoons, soup spoons, salad forks, steak knives, etc.). Try this key out on your friends and/or members of your family. How well does it work? Did you have to make any changes? Explain.

Answers will vary. Encourage the young investigator to try the key on friends or members of his or her family. Make sure the key is set up to ask yes and no questions.

58

How do you describe an arthropod?

Background information
Arachnids, crustaceans, and insects are part of the arthropod class of invertebrates. Insects are by far the largest of these three groups. All arthropods have a jointed body with a tough body case. The case is shed as the animal grows.

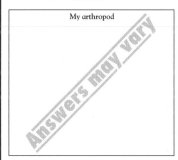

Science activity
Creative people, such as computer designers and moviemakers, often invent lifelike creatures that don't really exist. Your challenge is to create a realistic arthropod for a science fiction movie. Plan your design and draw your creature in its own habitat. Label all of its features. Now, create your arthropod from your design using household materials, such as empty plastic containers, packaging, paper, and cardboard.

My arthropod

Answers may vary

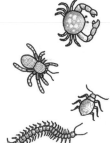

Science investigation
Write a description of your arthropod including all its features. Include a name for it and explain how it adapts to its surroundings. What does it eat? How does it protect itself and survive in the environment? Get creative and write a storyline for a movie based on your creature.

Together collect recycled materials to create your arthropod creature. Encourage your child to be creative with paints or a different media and make a poster to advertise their creature.

59

How long is a life cycle?

Background information
Animals and plants have life cycles. The period of development before birth is called *gestation*. It is followed by a period of growth leading to adulthood. Adults can then reproduce and repeat the cycle. In humans, the gestation period and the time taken to reach maturity are very long. The growth phase can be divided into: infancy (birth to age 2); childhood (age 2 to before puberty); adolescence (puberty to adulthood); and adulthood (after puberty to old age).

Science activity

Animal	Gestation period (days)	Average age of maturity
human	270 days	14 years
bear	230 days	4 years
horse	336 days	2 years
dog	63 days	15 months
cat	60 days	9 months
elephant	624 days	14 years
mouse	20 days	6 weeks

Which animal has the longest gestation period? Elephant

Which animal reaches maturity in the shortest time? Mouse

Is there a relationship between the age of maturity and the size of the animal? Generally, the bigger the animal, the longer the time taken to reach maturity.

Science investigation
Make a booklet that shows the life cycle of a human. Make four sections for each life stage: *infancy, childhood, adolescence,* and *adulthood.* Under each section, describe the major characteristics of that stage of life. Find pictures of people from magazines or your own family and friends and include them in each section. Note down any similarities or differences among people who are the same age. What do you conclude?

This activity will allow the child to identify the major characteristics of each stage of development. Gather a number of pictures for each stage, including family pictures. The child should not only note physical changes, but also compare when they occur.

60

How quickly do we grow?

Background information

Most animals have similar patterns of growth—they grow when they are young and stop at adulthood. Girls and boys grow at different rates. Rates of growth and size at maturity are also affected by things such as diet and heredity. For example, tall parents are more likely to have offspring who grow into tall adults.

Science activity

These charts show the heights of some girls and boys. They are measured in Year 1, then in Year 3 and in Year 5. Find out how much each child has grown by working out the difference between their heights in Year 1 and Year 5. Fill in each growth chart.

Girls	Height in cm				Boys	Height in cm			
Name	Year 1	Year 3	Year 5	Growth	Name	Year 1	Year 3	Year 5	Growth
Susan	110	116	128	18	Jack	110	115	126	16
Dela	109	116	130	21	John	112	119	126	14
Rachel	102	110	121	19	Dave	112	120	131	19
Jasmine	112	118	126	14	Peter	100	105	111	11

Which child grew the most in four years? ..... Dela grew the most.

What was the average growth of the girls? ..... 18 cm

What was the average growth of the boys? ..... 15 cm

Did all the girls grow at the same rate? ..... No

Did all the boys grow at the same rate? ..... No

Did the girls or the boys grow faster? ..... The girls grew faster.

Science investigation

 Soak 10 lima beans in water overnight. Obtain five paper cups filled with soil and plant two beans in each cup about 3 cm apart. Repeat this set up for 10 pea seeds. Measure the growth of each plant after it sprouts. Create data tables to record your information. Make a bar graph to compare the growth of the bean plant with the growth of the pea plant.

Some plants grow faster than others. A good experiment measures both fast- and slow-growing plants at the same frequency and time, and records results in a data table. Make sure the young investigator comes to some conclusions regarding the growth rate of the two plants.

61

Are plants and animals similar?

Background information

Animals and plants need water, air, and nutrients. They also live best under certain temperatures. For example, while an iguana and a rubber tree prefer warm climates, polar bears and certain pines prefer very cold climates. Plants and animals grow, reproduce, move and/or respond to things in the environment, such as sunlight and water. However, while animals are dependent on other living things for their food, plants make their own food. Plants have a green substance (mostly in their leaves) that helps them use the energy from the sun to make food. Plants have roots that anchor them into the soil. Plants reproduce by producing seeds. Animals reproduce by laying eggs that hatch into their young or by giving birth to live offspring.

Science activity

These numbered words and phrases are features of plants and animals. Write the numbers under the correct heading in the chart below (some phrases are true for both plants and animals).

1 Move   2 Respond   3 Grow
4 Make food   5 Form seeds   6 Reproduce
7 Need air   8 Lay eggs or have live young   9 Need nutrients
10 Need sunlight   11 Contain chlorophyll   12 Eat

Animals		Plants	
1	7	2	6
2	8	3	7
3	9	4	9
6	12	5	10
		11	

Science investigation

 Obtain a large paper cup and add soil. Plant one or two sunflower seeds in the cup. Try to begin this experiment in the spring. Describe and do what is needed to keep the plant healthy. Sketch the plant to keep a record of its growth, or if you have a camera take regular pictures. Measure your plant's growth. Record it in a data table and graph it. Which characteristics of plant life did you observe? Explain.

The young investigator should measure the sunflower's growth and keep track of the watering schedule. A data table should be generated to record growth. Growth diagrams or digital pictures are also helpful. Avoid over-watering. Transplant the sunflower outdoors in spring.

62

How do plants get food?

Background information

A plant needs sunlight, carbon dioxide, and water to make food. A green substance in plants called *chlorophyll* traps the energy from the Sun needed to make food. Chlorophyll is mostly found in the leaves of a plant. The leaf can be thought of as a food factory. Leaves of plants vary in shape and size, but they are always the plant organ best suited to capture solar energy. Once the food is made in the leaf, it is transported to the other parts of the plant such as the stem and roots.

Food moving to rest of plant — Carbon dioxide — Sunlight — Water from roots

Science activity

Kenny found a plant that had been put in a cabinet by accident. It looked very unhealthy. Some of its leaves were yellow and drooping, and others had fallen off. Kenny decided to put the plant on the windowsill to see if it would revive.

What else will Kenny need to do to help the plant recover?

Kenny should place the plant in sunlight and water the plant.

What do you predict would happen after several days? Give reasons for your ideas.

The plant will become more rigid. The plant will also turn greener as it produces chlorophyll again.

Science investigation

 Obtain a geranium plant. Design and conduct an experiment to see what happens to a leaf when it does not get sunlight. One suggestion is to fold some black paper over one of the leaves. Make sure to place the plant near the sunlight and water it when the soil becomes dry. Predict what you think will happen.

The part of the plant that was covered with black paper will no longer produce chlorophyll and so will appear whitish in colour. Plants need chlorophyll to make food and need sunlight to make chlorophyll. Without chlorophyll, they will die.

Can you make a bird key?

Background information

Dichotomous keys work best when they are divided into groups and then further divided into smaller groups. When putting birds into groups, you could first divide them into wading birds (those with webbed feet) and non-wading birds, then think of some subsets, such as size, shape, or colour of the beak. Charles Darwin, who developed the present-day theory of evolution, studied the many types of beaks found on the finch, each adapted to eating different types of food.

Science activity

Swan   Blackbird   Duck   Coot   Magpie

On another piece of paper, make your own dichotomous key for the birds pictured above. Make sure the questions are based on clear differences. For example, "Does the bird have webbed feet?" A poor question would be, "Does the bird have large wings?"

 Answers may vary

Science investigation

 Identify birds in your yard, nearby park, or school. Use the Internet and reference books for help. Make a bird feeder out of recycled material to attract birds to your garden or school. Create a booklet of birds in your area. Include their names and the types of bird feeder that should be used to attract them.

This is a great way for the young investigator to learn how to recycle materials to support wildlife. As the birdfeeder is built, the child should also learn a lot about the bird.

64

Can you make a plant key?

Background information
Some *dichotomous keys* used to identify plants and animals ask *yes or no* questions. They also rely on looking for clear differences. Questions are numbered and answered in order. Look at the three pictures. A simple key would be:

1　Is the plant over 200 cm tall?
　　If yes, go to 2; if no, go to 3.
2　It is an oak tree.
3　Does the plant have a flower?
　　If yes, go to 4; if no, go to 5.
4　It is a daffodil.
5　It is moss.

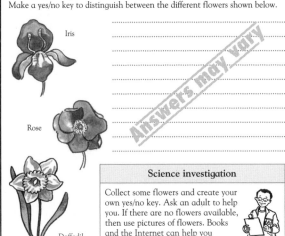

Science activity
Make a yes/no key to distinguish between the different flowers shown below.

Iris

Rose

Daffodil

....
....
....
....
....
....

Answers may vary

Science investigation
Collect some flowers and create your own yes/no key. Ask an adult to help you. If there are no flowers available, then use pictures of flowers. Books and the Internet can help you identify some common garden flowers.

Answers will vary. Make sure the key questions are clear enough to make decisions about the flower's classification. Test the key. If it does not work well, encourage the young investigator to revise it. This is how real science works.

65

What sort of plant is this?

Background information
Trees are plants. There are many different types of trees. A *dichotomous key* can be used to identify different species of trees.

Science activity
Look at the pictures of the four twigs below. Use the dichotomous key to identify each one. Write your answer on the dotted line.

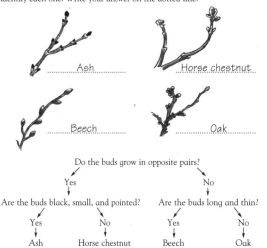

.... Ash ....　　.......... Horse chestnut ....

.... Beech ....　　.......... Oak ....

Do the buds grow in opposite pairs?

Yes → Are the buds black, small, and pointed?
　Yes → Ash
　No → Horse chestnut

No → Are the buds long and thin?
　Yes → Beech
　No → Oak

Science investigation
During spring, collect some twigs and create your own key to identify the twigs. During fall, collect and identify tree leaves. Make a booklet. Use the Internet and reference books for more information on tree identification.

Answers will vary. Make sure the young investigator uses a key that always has two choices. Suggest to the child to try the key out on friends, family, or classmates.

66

How do microbes help?

Background information
Microbes, or micro-organisms, are living things that are often too small to be seen. Common types of microbes are bacteria, viruses, and some fungi. These organisms need food, warmth, and moisture to grow and reproduce. Some microbes feed on things that were once living, such as fallen leaves and dead animals, causing them to breakdown or decay. The decayed materials mix with soil, providing essential nutrients for plants to use. Without this process, the nutrients in the soil would run out. These types of organisms are called *decomposers*. They are the natural recyclers of living things on our planet. Microbes also help us make some of our foods, such as bread, cheese, yogurt, beer, and wine. They feed on the sugar in grain, fruit, or milk, giving these foods a special texture and taste.

Science activity
Donna put the following items into a large plastic bag. She took them out again after two weeks. In the boxes below, write **D** for the items that would have decayed and **U** for those that would be unchanged.

D	Grass	D	Tangerine
U	Plastic spoon	D	Bread
D	Apple peel	D	Leaves
U	Pop can	U	Nylon tights

Why have some of the items not decayed?
The items in the bag that were non-living could not be decayed by the microbes. Those were the items still in the bag.

Science investigation
Take a large coffee can and obtain some soil, food samples, and non-food items. Bury the food and non-food items in different layers of soil placed in the coffee can. Add about 60 mL of water. Place a cover with punched holes on top of the can so air can get in. After 2–3 months, determine what has decayed.

The child should carefully record observations of selected items in a data table before burying them. Generally, only dead things decay. Let the items sit for about 1–3 months or longer. The child should then note how the buried items have changed.

How are microbes harmful?

Background information
Some microbes, often called germs, can cause illness or disease. Chickenpox, mumps, and measles are caused by microbes. They are infectious diseases. Some microbes can cause food to decay. Moldy bread or fruit, sour milk, and rotten meat are examples of decayed food. If eaten, this rotten food and drink can cause stomach upsets. Other microbes cause tooth decay. You can protect yourself from harmful microbes by storing and preparing food properly, cleaning your teeth, washing your hands, and by avoiding close contact with ill people.

Science activity

Look at the picture above. It shows a number of unhygienic ways in which germs can travel into food and cause illness. List all of the ways this could happen in the picture.
Uncovered rubbish attracts flies, which spread germs to uncovered food. The dog, dirty laundry, and potty could all carry germs.

Science investigation
(!) Design and conduct an experiment to see what type of bread grows mould the best. Obtain different samples of bread. Make sure to wash your hands before and after each time you experiment or use rubber gloves. Explain why mould grows better on some bread than on others.

The child may try placing the bread in an airtight container or refrigerating it. Refrigeration slows the growth of microbes. Good experiments have a large but manageable sample size. Use a control in the experiment; in this case, non-refrigerated food.

What is friction?

Background information

When an object travels across a surface, there is friction between the object and the surface. Friction is the force that resists the movement of one surface over the other. It's much easier to slide on something smooth, such as ice, than on a rough surface. This is because rough surfaces create more friction than smooth ones, and friction slows things down.

Science activity

Test for friction. Lean a piece of wood against two books so that it makes a ramp. Roll a marble down the ramp. Keep adding books to increase the angle and make the slope steeper. What difference does this make to the way the marble rolls down the ramp?

Replace the marbles with a small block of wood or a toy car and compare. If you have to make the ramp steeper to make the object slide, what does this tell you about the friction? How does putting a little oil or water on the ramp affect what happens? Record your findings.

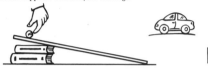

The steeper the ramp, the faster the marble rolls.
If you have to make the ramp steeper to make the object
slide, this means there is more friction holding the object
back. Oil reduces the friction. Water also reduces the friction,
but not as much as the oil does.

Science investigation

Investigate friction. Describe two ways of reducing friction. How can friction help you complete tasks? List at least three situations in which friction works against what you are trying to do. What can you do to reduce the friction in each case?

Bearings and wheels and lubricants such as oil and grease are two ways to reduce friction. Experiment together and discuss different situations that friction helps and works against what we are trying to do.

69

How do parachutes work?

Background information

Gravity is a pulling force. It pulls objects toward Earth. *Air resistance* is a pushing force. It is a source of friction because it opposes motion. When parachutes fall to Earth, air resistance pushes against them. The fabric of a parachute has a lot of surface on which air can push. The effect of this force is to slow the parachute down. The larger the parachute, the slower it will fall, because there is more air resistance.

Air resistance

Gravity

Science activity

Examine the drawing of two people jumping with parachutes.

Which person will fall to Earth faster? Explain your answer.

The person with the smaller parachute will fall to Earth faster
because there is less air resistance.

Describe all of the forces acting on the parachute. Make sure to state the direction of the force.

Air resistance acts upward. Gravity pulls the parachute down.

Science investigation

Obtain five pieces of paper of the same size. Leave one piece of paper unfolded. Fold one in half and tape it closed. Repeat this, but fold and tape two pieces of paper together. Fold one piece of paper in half two times and then tape it closed. Design and conduct an experiment to see which paper falls first when they are dropped from the same height.

Unfolded paper has more air resistance than folded paper, so should fall the slowest. Since gravity pulls on all objects with the same force, the paper's weight should not affect its rate of fall.

70

What are the four forces of flight?

Background information

Gravity is the force that acts on all objects and pulls them toward the centre of the Earth. The greater the mass of an airplane, the more it is affected by gravity. *Thrust* is the force that moves a plane forward. Experiment with a toy airplane or glider. When you throw the plane, you provide the thrust. In a real airplane, the thrust comes from the propellers or the jet engine. The forward movement produced by the thrust causes air to move across the surface of the wing, and this creates *lift*, an upward force that keeps the plane in the air. This is how an airplane can fly.

As the airplane moves forward, the air creates *drag* on the plane and slows it down. A disadvantage of drag is that it is a force that tries to prevent motion. A plane needs more thrust than drag if it is to fly.

Drag can be used by the pilot to control the plane. An airplane has flaps on the wings and the tail, and the pilot turns these to increase the drag on one side of the plane or the other in order to steer it. When it comes in to land at an airport, the flaps are used to deliberately slow the airplane down. Planes that must land in a short distance, such as on an aircraft carrier, use parachutes to increase the drag on the plane and slow it down suddenly.

Science activity

On the drawing of the airplane, draw arrows that show the direction in which each of the forces—gravity, thrust, lift, and drag—is acting. Describe the effect of each force on an airplane.

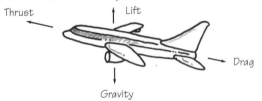

Thrust

Lift

Drag

Gravity

Science investigation

Like planes, birds and insects make use of the four forces of flight. List the similarities and differences between an airplane and a bird or insect.

An airplane is made of metal and holds people. Birds and insects are living; lighter than planes; and get their thrust and lift from beating their wings. Birds have muscles to help them turn.

What is Bernoulli's Principle?

Background information

Aero means "air" and dynamics means "motion." Aerodynamics is the study of gases (particularly air) in motion and of objects moving through them. The work of Daniel Bernoulli was instrumental in the study of aerodynamics. In 1738, he published his first article explaining that moving fluids exert less pressure than do stationary fluids. This was found to be true for moving air as well, and today this discovery is called Bernoulli's Principle. It means that the faster the air moves over an object, the lower the pressure it exerts.

Science activity

Take a hairdryer set to cool, and hold it pointing upward. Place the ping-pong ball in the middle of the air stream and observe and describe what happens. Draw a picture of the experiment. Use Bernoulli's Principle to explain how we are able to make a ping-pong ball hover in the air.

My drawing

Answers may vary

Science investigation

To make a mini hovercraft, wash a glass in hot soapy water and place it upside down on a wet, smooth surface. Now give the glass a little push, and it will slide easily as the expanding warm air escapes. How is this like a mini hovercraft? Investigate hovercrafts on the Internet.

The ping-pong ball will stay put. In the middle, the air flows faster (less pressure) than it does at the edges (higher pressure). The higher pressure always pushes the ball back. Relate how the investigation is like a mini hovercraft. Encourage your child to research hovercrafts on the Internet.

How do you fly a plane?

Background information
When birds and aircraft fly, moving air around their wings helps carry them high into the sky. Building and flying a model plane will help show you how moving air lifts up a wing and keeps it airborne.

Science activity
Fold a sheet of paper to make a simple paper dart or model plane. If you don't know how to do this, ask an adult or look on the Internet for folding instructions. Experiment with throwing your plane and see how it flies. Record your findings.
Now make adjustments to its shape and balance to see how these affect the way it flies. Start by bending up the back edge of both wings. What effect does this have? Now bend up the back of just one wing. Does it still fly straight? What happens if you bend one flap or both flaps downward?
To change the balance of the plane, attach a paper clip to the front of it. How does this affect the flight pattern? Attach the paper clip to the tail of the plane instead and see what difference this makes. Can you make your plane loop the loop or fly in a circle?
After your investigation, write a report summarizing your results. Add flying tips that would make the plane fly better.

....

....

....

....

....

Science investigation

Tape cotton threads to two lightweight balls and hang them about 15 cm apart. Try blowing air through the space between the balls. Describe what happens.

Instead of separating the balls, the moving air draws them together. The balls move toward the lower pressure, so they swing together.

How does a jet engine work?

Background information
Airplanes fly around the world at high speed. They have large jet engines that produce a powerful stream of air to push the airplane through the sky. The engine that powers a space rocket works on the same principle.

Science activity
Make your own simple jet engine to show how it produces a force that propels an object through the air. You will need the following materials:
1. A piece of thread long enough to stretch across your room.
2. Two pieces of sticky tape.
3. A drinking straw.
4. A balloon.

Feed one end of your thread through the drinking straw. Attach one end of the thread to one side of the room, and the other end to the other side of the room at the same height from the ground. Make sure that the thread is stretched tight. Slide the straw to one end of the thread, and stick the two pieces of tape across the straw so that they stick out on both sides of it. Now blow up the balloon and hold onto the neck of it tightly so that no air escapes. Position the balloon under the straw with the neck pointing at the wall, and attach the balloon to the straw with the tape. Now let go of the balloon. What happens? *Escaping air propels the balloon forward.*

Science investigation

Do you think a jet engine could be used to propel an object across the land or over water? Describe how this would work. Search the Internet to find out whether jet engines have been used to power cars or boats.

Jet engines power the fastest cars in the world as well as high-speed aircraft. A jet engine sucks in air at the front and heats this air with burning fuel. It then sends the hot air blasting out from the back of the engine. This forces the aircraft or car forward at very high speeds.

How do you design a parachute?

Background information
When a moving object travels through air, the air causes friction. This is called air resistance. If people want to travel *faster* through the air, they must **reduce** air resistance. **Increasing** the air resistance *slows* moving objects down. This can be done by increasing the area of the moving object that pushes against the air. A parachute is a good example of increasing air resistance. Parachutes have many uses such as for the sport of skydiving; dropping supplies for people; slowing down space capsules and racing cars.

Science activity
Design your own parachute. Think about what important factors you should consider when designing your parachute. What material would you use? The top of a parachute resembles that of an umbrella and is usually made from nylon or silk. They must be light weight but strong enough to prevent tearing while catching the air and supporting the person's body mass. Using materials that you already have, create your own parachute from your design. Experiment with your parachute by dropping it from various heights to hit a target. Can you improve your design? Draw your final design and label the materials used.

My parachute design

Science investigation

Do you think there is friction when an object travels through a liquid? Make a variety of paper boats with differently shaped bottoms. Test the theory that there is friction between the surface of a moving object and a liquid by pushing your boats across water in the sink or bathtub.

Provide materials such as different types of cloth, silk, cotton, and plastic. Tie string and a weight to the parachute. The best design for the boat to glide more easily is one with a keel (the main timber or steel piece that extends the length of the bottom of a boat).

Is it an electrical conductor?

Background information
Matter that allows electricity to pass through it easily is called an *electrical conductor*. Electricity passes through a conductor to turn on a TV or computer, for example. Metals can conduct electricity, but some are better conductors than others. Solutions that have dissolved charged particles in them can also conduct electricity.

Science activity
An electrical circuit was set up to test the conductivity of different types of matter. A bulb was placed in the circuit. If the matter conducted electricity, the bulb lit up.

Material tested	Status of bulb
gold	very bright
copper	bright
plastic	not lit
wood	not lit
graphite	fairly bright
lead	fairly bright
paper	not lit
salt water	bright
distilled water	not lit

What factor was used to determine the conductivity of the matter?
The brighter the bulb, the better the conductor.

Which sample(s) of matter are the best conductors? *Gold and copper*

What types of matter are the best conductors of electricity?
Metals are the best conductors of electricity.

Why do you think salt water can light the bulb but distilled water cannot?
Salt water has charged particles in it, and so it can conduct electricity.

Science investigation

(!) Build your own circuit using a 6-volt battery as your source of electricity and a LED light bulb. Test other types of matter for conductivity. Create a data table to record your observations.

LED lights, batteries, and alligator wires can be purchased from stores such as Radio Shack. Answers will vary as the child tests different matter samples for conductivity.

76

Will it conduct electricity?

Background information

When you build an *electric circuit*, all of the parts of the circuit must be connected. Each part must also let electricity flow through it before the circuit will work. A working circuit can light a bulb or ring a bell, for example. Materials that allow electricity to flow through it are called *electrical conductors*. Materials that block the flow of electricity are called *electrical insulators*.

Science activity

Which of the following objects will make the buzzer sound when they are connected to the alligator clips in the circuit? Place a check mark (✔) beside each one that makes the buzzer sound.

☐ PVC-coated wire not stripped at the end
☑ PVC-coated wire stripped at the end
☐ Spaghetti
☐ String
☐ Nylon fishing line
☑ Iron wire
☐ Paper drinking straw
☐ Wooden rod

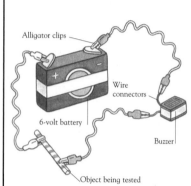

Alligator clips
Wire connectors
6-volt battery
Buzzer
Object being tested

Science investigation

(!) Build your own circuit with alligator clip wires, a 6-volt battery, a switch, and an object that will use electricity, such as a bulb, buzzer, or bell.

Make sure that the load (bell, buzzer, bulb, etc.) can take a 6-volt battery. Use alligator clip wires since they are easy to attach to a battery. All of these materials can be purchased at an electrical supply company or a hardware store.

77

What does a circuit diagram show?

Background information

Electricity always flows in a circuit from the negative pole of a battery to its positive pole. The flow of electricity creates an electric current. Electrical circuits can be represented by special diagrams. There is a symbol for each electrical component in a circuit.

Battery   Buzzer
Bulb   Motor
Switch (open ⸺ and ⸺ closed)   Wire

Science activity

Look at the circuit diagram shown below.

Battery   Bulb
Switch   Buzzer   Motor

Label each of the five components shown in the circuit.

Complete the following sentences about the circuit shown above.

The electric current leaves the battery and passes through the ....bulb.... .

It then travels through the ....motor...., next through the ....buzzer....,

and finally passes through the ....switch...., before returning to the battery.

Science investigation

Create a model of a parallel circuit that contains two bulbs, one motor, and one buzzer. You might draw the symbols on small cards and then arrange them into the circuit. Connect the circuit with wires.

The investigator can make drawings, use the Internet for pictures, or trace the ones in this book. Ask the child to trace the direction of the circuit. Electricity always moves from negative to positive.

78

Can you draw a circuit diagram?

Background information

A simple circuit diagram often looks like a rectangle. It shows how the loads, batteries, wires, and switches are linked together, and how the circuit is organized.

Science activity

Look at the two pictures of circuits.

Draw a circuit diagram for each of the circuits shown.

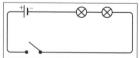 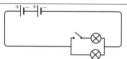

What will happen in the second circuit when the switch is off and when it is on?
When the switch is off, only one bulb will light up, but when the switch is on, both bulbs will light up.

Science investigation

(!) Using small cards, create a game to teach your friends about circuits. Draw different parts of the circuit on each card. One card can be a lamp and another can be a connecting wire. Players can pick cards and the first player with enough cards to make a complete circuit wins. Try the game out with your family and friends.

One possible game is to make a deck of cards with circuit components. The players draw from a deck, always keeping a certain number of cards in their hand. The first player to have all the cards needed to set up a circuit wins.

Will it switch on or off?

Background information

Electricity will only flow through a circuit that has no gaps in it. A switch is a useful device because it allows you to open or close a circuit. When a circuit is open, electricity cannot flow through the circuit to run a load in it. When a switch is turned on, it closes the circuit so that loads in the circuit can operate. Loads such as light bulbs and appliances in your home are turned on and off with switches.

This is the symbol for an open switch. ⸺⸱⸺ It is off.
This is the symbol for a closed switch. ⸺•⸺ It is is on.

There are different types of switches.

This switch is closed by pressing down the metal bar   This one is closed by turning the lever and slotting it into the clip.

Science activity

Look at this circuit diagram.

Battery
Switch 4   Bulb
Switch 3
Switch 1   Switch 2

What is the least number of switches you would need to light up the bulb? ......Two switches......

Identify the switches you would need ......Switches 1 and 4......

Science investigation

One type of switch is called a *pressure switch*. You have to press the switch to close it. Design and build your own pressure switch and then connect it to a circuit with a load on it, such as a buzzer or light bulb. Some pressure switches work by stepping on them. Can you name any common pressure switches in your home?

Homes have many pressure switches, such as the doorbell. Remind the child that switches must be made of metal. One simple pressure switch is made with cotton balls separating two metal strips. The circuit is closed when the metal strips touch.

What do batteries do?

Background information
Batteries are a source of electricity because they contain charged particles that can flow. The amount of energy provided by a battery depends on its *voltage* and is measured in units called *volts*. For example, a 1.5-volt (V) battery has less energy than a 6-V battery. If a lower voltage battery is used in a flashlight, the bulb will be less bright than in a flashlight using a battery with higher voltage. A battery has two ends called *poles*. One end is called the positive (+) pole and the other, the negative (−) pole. When wires connect the poles, an electric circuit is created. *Current electricity* is produced, which lights up the light bulb. This flowing electricity can be turned on or off by a *switch*. When more batteries are added to a circuit, the current is also increased. The circuit has more electrical power.

Science activity
The drawings below show two electric circuits.

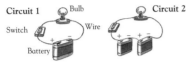

What will happen to the flow of electricity when the switch is opened in circuit 1 and circuit 2?

Electricity will not flow to the bulb, so it will not light up.

In which circuit is the bulb brighter when the switch is closed? Explain.

The light will be brighter in circuit 2 because the extra battery will increase the amount of electric current to the light bulb.

Science investigation
⚠ Roll a lemon to release its juices. Cut two slits in the lemon about 5 cm apart. Stick half of a shiny penny (the + pole) into one slit and half of a shiny dime (the − pole) in the other slit. Create a circuit. Use wires with alligator clips to connect the coins and bulb. If the bulb does not light up, add more lemons to the circuit. Why can a lemon light a bulb?

Use a low voltage LED light. Lemon juice contains charged particles, but is a much weaker acid than battery acid. Clean the coins with a metal cleaner so the zinc and copper are in direct contact with the lemon's acid.

81

Why change the length of wire?

Background information
Conductors are a type of matter through which electricity can flow. Most metals are good conductors of electricity. Copper is used to make wires because it is a very good conductor. When current flows through a conductor, friction can reduce its flow. Some metals cause less friction than others. It is friction that makes wires feel hot. The type of wire conductor and its length and thickness affect current. Longer wires offer more resistance to flow than shorter wires, while thicker ones offer less resistance. This knowledge can be used to control the speed of a motor. For example, speed controllers on electric car tracks and dimmer switches on lights work by varying the length of wire in a circuit.

Science activity
Susan made a model electric windmill by attaching toy windmill blades to a motor in a homemade circuit. She wanted to change the speed at which the blades turn, to show what happens when the wind blows in the blades of a real windmill. She found that she could do this by changing the length of wire in the circuit. Here are her results. Can you fill in the missing values?

Length of wire in the circuit	Number of turns in 5 seconds
25 cm	80
50 cm	70
100 cm	50
150 cm	30
200 cm	10

Science investigation
⚠ Use the Internet to provide you with a materials list and directions to build a motor. You can experiment with how the length of the wire affects the speed of the motor by varying the number of coils in the copper wire.

The child will learn the effect of wire length on motor speed, as well as the main principles about motors. Current electricity produces a magnetic field. The motor turns as the magnet repels the like magnetic field generated by the copper wire.

82

Do more bulbs mean more light?

Background information
A light bulb is a fairly simple device that has not changed much since its invention by Thomas Edison in 1879. Inside a bulb is a filament. When current flows through the filament, some of the electrical energy is converted into light energy. The devices on a circuit using the electricity are called *loads*. The more loads added to the same circuit, the slower the flow of electricity. If the load is a light, as more lights are added, they will become dimmer. The circuit shown in the diagram is called a *series circuit* because the current must flow through all of the loads before returning to the energy source (battery).

Science activity
Dipak set up the series circuit shown below. When he turned the circuit on, he was surprised that the bulbs burned so dimly. He did not have another battery, so how do you think he could have changed the circuit to make the light brighter?

He could have made the light brighter by removing one or two of the bulbs and their bulb holders from the circuit.

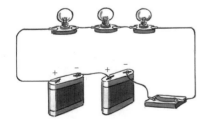

Science investigation
Build a circuit with two bulbs, in which current flows through only one light bulb before returning to its energy source. Both light bulbs must burn at the same time. This is called a *parallel circuit* because there is more than one pathway to the energy source.

Small lamps can be purchased at stores like Radio Shack. Make sure the bulb's voltage capacity is equal to or greater than that of the battery. The investigator can include a switch.

What is a lever?

Background information
A lever is a rigid object that moves about a fixed point when one end is moved. The fixed point is called the fulcrum. A seesaw is a simple, or first-class, lever with the fulcrum in the middle. When the two people at the ends have the same mass and are at the same distance from the fulcrum the seesaw is balanced. The downward force that each person exerts on the seesaw is his or her weight multiplied by their distance from the fulcrum. In this diagram, the downward forces f1 and f2 are the same, so the lever is balanced.

Science activity
Carry out an experiment to find out what happens if you change the weight at one end or the other, and what happens if you change the position of the fulcrum. Using a ruler as the rigid object and a small block or rod as the fulcrum, set up a model seesaw and place two similar sized erasers on each end so that it balances. What happens if you move one of the erasers from one end to the other? Now move the fulcrum along the ruler and find a position where the lever balances again. Measure the distance from the fulcrum to each end (distances d1 and d2 in the diagram below). What answer do you get if you divide one distance by the other? The fact that a smaller weight at the long end balances a larger weight at the short end shows how a lever can give you a mechanical advantage.

Science investigation
In a first class lever, the fulcrum is between the effort and the load—you push down on one end and you can lift something at the other end. Besides the seesaw, can you think of two or three other first-class levers?

In the Science activity, the child should find that if the load on one end is 3 times that on the other, the lever will balance when the fulcrum is 3 times as far from the light end as it is from the heavy end. First class levers include oars for rowing, a bottle opener, and a shoehorn.

What class lever is your machine?

Background information
In a first-class lever, the effort is applied at one end, and the load is lifted on the other.

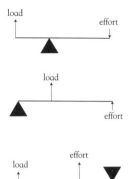

load

effort

A second-class lever has the load positioned between the effort and the fulcrum. Because the effort is further from the fulcrum than the load is, a mechanical advantage is achieved. A wheelbarrow is a second-class lever.

load

effort

In a third-class lever, the effort is applied between the fulcrum and the load. The effort is closer to the fulcrum than the load is, so there is no mechanical advantage here. Instead, third-class levers are used whenever a delicate grip is required, for example when using chopsticks.

load

effort

Science activity
Think about the following objects and work out what class of lever each one is. Draw each object and show where the effort, fulcrum, and load are positioned on each one.

Scissors	1	Shovel	3	Wrench	2
Tweezers	3	Crowbar	1	Human lower jaw	3
Hockey stick	3	Human forearm	3	Claw hammer	
Pliers	1	Nutcracker	2	pulling a nail	1

Science investigation

The lids of paint cans fit tightly to prevent spills. They can be opened with a lever, using the edge of the can as a fulcrum. With the help of an adult, try to lever off the lid of a can of paint with a coin. Now try opening the lid with a small spoon, a larger spoon, and a screwdriver. Which is easier to use? Discuss, using the terms lever, effort, and force.

Because the coin is so short, you can't get much leverage to magnify the effort you apply. The longer the lever is, the easier it is to open the can. You apply less effort, but your hand had to move much further to produce enough force to lift the lid.

How do gears on a bike work?

Background information
When you ride a bike, a set of gears transmits the motion of the pedals to the rear wheel. In a car (or other motorized vehicle), gears transmit power from the engine to the wheels to make the car move. Most gears take the form of wheels with teeth cut around the edge. Gears not only transmit motion, they can also change it. Using the gears on a bike, you can pedal more easily uphill by changing to a lower gear. The gears give you a mechanical advantage that allows you to turn the back wheel with less effort.

Science activity
Find out how changing gear makes the back wheel of a bike go slower or faster while you pedal at a constant rate. You will need the help of an adult for this activity, and you will need a bike with multiple gears (such as a mountain bike), gloves, and coloured sticky tape.
A bike with multiple gears has different-sized chain wheels, to which the pedals are attached by arms called cranks. There are also several different-sized sprockets (gears) on the rear wheel. Ask an adult to help you turn the bike upside down and hold the frame steady. Make sure the bike is in low gear. In the lowest gear, the chain connects the smallest chain wheel at the front to the largest rear sprocket.
Wearing gloves to protect your fingers, slowly turn the pedals until one of the cranks is vertical. Mark a point on the rear tire with coloured tape. Now slowly turn the crank one full turn and watch the tape mark to see how many times the rear wheel turns. How much force is needed to turn the pedals? Change into high gear (with a large chain wheel connected to a small sprocket) and turn the crank again. How many times does the rear wheel turn? How much force is needed on the pedals?

Science investigation

Mechanical clocks and watches use a series of meshing gears with precise gear ratios to turn the hands at the correct speed for accurate time-keeping. With the help of books and the Internet, learn about gear ratios. Describe what is meant by a gear ratio of two to one (2:1).

In high gear, you need more force on the pedals, but the rear wheel turns faster. In low gear, you need less force and the wheel turns slower. A 12-tooth gear must turn twice in order to turn a 24-tooth gear just once. Therefore, the ratio is 2:1.

How do machines work?

Background information
The word machine is commonly used to mean a device that does useful work for us or helps us to do useful work. A car engine is a machine, but so is a corkscrew, an electric fan, or a stapler. Use resources such as dictionaries, science reference books, and the Internet to learn about the scientific principles on which different machines work.

Science activity
Compile a list of the ten different machines that might be found in the kitchen, garage, or workshop. A few are listed below as examples. In each case, describe how it works and how it helps to do a particular job more easily. Use reference resources to understand the scientific principles that are used by each machine.

Machine	Scientific principles
Axe	An axe is a machine called a wedge. The energy in the moving axe head forces the wood apart and splits the log.
Pulley	A rope, belt, or cable is passed round a pulley wheel, changing the direction of the pull.
Screw	The action of turning the head of a screw to drive it into the wood is less than that needed to knock it in directly.

Science investigation

(!) With the help of an adult, find one discarded gadget from around your home. (Be aware that some electrical equipment can be dangerous even when unplugged.) Try to figure out how it worked. Carefully take it apart. List all the parts, and number them in the order in which you removed them. Try to figure out how the parts worked together to make the machine work. Put the machine back together. Do not plug anything into a wall socket without adult supervision.

Encourage your child to use other resources and the Internet to find out how each machine listed works. Discuss the principles of science behind each machine and then have your child record his or her findings.

How do pulleys and cranes work?

Background information
A crane is able to lift a heavy load high in the air. It has a wheel called a "pulley" to produce a lifting force, while a "counterweight" keeps the crane from tipping over as it lifts a heavy weight. The simplest kind of pulley is a cable or rope running over a grooved wheel attached to a support. One end of the rope carries a load and the other end is pulled.

Science activity
Thinking of the principles behind how a crane works, try to build your own using materials such as string, screw hooks, a few small blocks of wood, empty spools of thread, small paper drinking cups, marbles, nails, and a small cardboard box. Gather your materials first. Include things like scissors, pen, paper, marbles, and sticky tape that you may also need. Don't forget to make a load for the crane to lift. The small paper drinking cup is lightweight and you can use marbles for the load. Use your crane to lift loads, and make improvements that help it work more easily.

Hints:
a) Study a photo of a crane from a resource book or the Internet.
b) Fill the cup with marbles and hook it to the crane. Wind the handle to lift the load of marbles.
c) Use a book as a counterweight to prevent the load from pulling the crane over. Use an empty thread spool as the pulley wheel.

Explain how your crane works and include a labelled drawing of it.

Answers may vary

Science investigation

While a single pulley doesn't give a mechanical advantage, it does make lifting easier by changing the direction of force required. What happens when you add more pulleys? A set of pulleys (also called a block and tackle) can help you lift loads more easily.

Adding other pulleys increases the force applied, which means less effort is required–a mechanical advantage. A building crane gets much of its lifting power from a multiple pulley system.

88

How do you build a wheelbarrow?

Background information

When you lift a bag of stones you need to exert a lot of force. Machines can make it easier for you and give you more strength! The wheelbarrow is a second-class lever—a machine that can increase the force you use to move things.

Science activity

Build your own model wheelbarrow and experiment with it by moving some small stones. To build the wheelbarrow you might use the following materials:

A shoe box, cardboard, an empty thread spool, two equal lengths of wood (such as chopsticks), a short pencil, sticky tape, and scissors. You will also need a plastic bag and some small stones.

Use the shoe box as the body of your wheelbarrow. Use the thread spool as a wheel and the short pencil as an axle. Cut a hole in the bottom edge of one end of the box, large enough for the thread spool. Place the spool, with its pencil axle, in this hole and tape the ends of pencil to the box on either side of the hole. The two pieces of wood will form the handles. Place the bag of stones in different positions along the length of the wheelbarrow and try lifting the handles in each case. Is it easier to lift the load with the stones at the front of the wheelbarrow or the back? Record the results of your experiment and describe the function of a wheelbarrow.

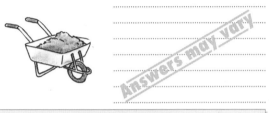

Answers may vary

Science investigation

Write up the steps of how you built your wheelbarrow. Challenge someone else to make a wheelbarrow following your directions. Does that person's wheelbarrow look exactly the same as yours?

Use household materials to make your wheelbarrow. If you have the opportunity, study a real wheelbarrow or good photos to help you create yours.

89

Which light is the brightest?

Background information

Earth's brightest light source is the *Sun*. The Sun is a star. All stars are composed of gases that are constantly undergoing powerful reactions. When they do, very bright light is produced. There are billions and billions of stars, and even if you counted one star every second for 8 hours a day, after 100 years you would only have counted about a billion! Other stars don't seem as bright as the Sun because they are very far away. Astronomers use numbers called *magnitude numbers* to describe how bright stars look from Earth. Bright stars have low numbers, and faint stars have high numbers. We can see stars with a brightness between magnitudes 1 and 6.

Science activity

Here are some stars with measures of their brightness. Can you place them in order, with the brightest first and the faintest last?

Star	Magnitude
Eri	3.7
Centauri C	11.0
Ross 780	10.2
Procyon A	0.3
Kapteyn's Star	8.8
Sirius B	7.2
Polaris	2.0

Correct order of brightness
1 _Procyon A_ (brightest)
2 _Polaris_
3 _Eri_
4 _Sirius B_
5 _Kapteyn's Star_
6 _Ross 780_
7 _Centauri C_ (faintest)

Science investigation

⚠ Suppose you are a scientist studying three stars of different sizes. Make these "stars" by covering a flashlight with a piece of black paper in which you have made three pinpricks of different sizes. Predict which star will be hardest to see as its distance from you increases. Test this out by having a friend shine the flashlight toward you. As your friend walks away from you, is there a distance from which you can no longer see any of the stars? What do you conclude? Explain.

Make sure the paper is opaque so that the only light coming through is from the three different-sized pinpricks. Have the child stand at different distances from the simulated starlight to see how distance affects seeing a star. The child should work with a peer.

90

Where will the shadow be?

Background information

The Sun is a very powerful light source. When sunlight shines on a wall, it makes the wall bright. If you place a solid, opaque object in front of the wall, the sunlight cannot pass through it and a shadow forms on the wall. Because Earth is rotating, the Sun seems to move across the sky, casting different shadows from morning (sunrise) to evening (sunset).

Science activity

The morning Sun was shining through the window in Tony's home, casting an interesting shadow of a vase on the table. Tony thought it looked great, and wanted to show his father when he came home from work. If there was still sunlight coming through the window in the afternoon, draw how the shadow looked when Tony showed it to his father.

Science investigation

On a sunny day, find your shadow on the ground. Try to change its shape. At what time in the day is your shadow the longest?

The child will learn that his or her outdoor shadow moves as the day progresses. As the Sun appears to move across the sky, the position and length of the shadow will change. Shadows in the morning and evening are longer than those cast at midday.

Why does the Sun appear to move?

Background information

You know that on any single day, the Sun will rise and set. However, it is Earth that is moving. It takes 24 hours for Earth to make a complete rotation on its axis. As it moves, the Sun appears to change its position in the sky. The Sun appears to rise in the east when the part of Earth you are on is turning toward the Sun, and appears to set in the west when your hometown is turning away from the Sun. In addition to rotating on its axis, Earth is also revolving around the Sun. It takes an average of 365 days, or one year, to make one complete orbit around the Sun.

Science activity

The picture shows the Sun at three times during one summer day. First it was in position A, then B, and finally C.

Which side of the picture is the east? _The left side is east._

What time is it at position B? _Midday – 12 o'clock_

What will soon happen at position C? _The sun will set._

Science investigation

Make a sundial. On a sunny morning, stand a 50 cm-long stick in the ground in your garden or school. Mark the position of the end of the stick's shadow with a rock or other item that will not easily blow away. Repeat this every hour so that by evening you have at least seven marks on the ground. What pattern can you see? Explain why the shadow moved.

The apparent movement of the Sun is caused by Earth's rotation. For this activity, the child should notice that the shadow gets shorter as midday approaches. It then appears to move to the other side and become longer again.

How much do you weigh on Mars?

Background information

Gravity is the natural force that acts between all objects in the universe. Gravity keeps all planets in orbit around the Sun. The gravitational pull between two objects is related to their masses and the distance between them. *Mass* is the amount of matter in an object. Weight is a measure of how much gravity pulls on an object or a body. If you stood on the surface of the Moon, your mass would be the same as it is on Earth, but your weight would change. The Moon's gravity is one-sixth of the Earth's, so if you weigh 60 kg on earth, your weight on the Moon you would be 10 kg. On Jupiter you would weigh 143.4 kg. The force of gravity that you feel on the surface of any object in space is called *surface gravity*.

Science activity

The chart below shows the surface gravity on the planets compared to the surface gravity on Earth. To calculate how much something would weigh on a different planet, multiply its Earth weight by the planet's surface gravity. For example, a person who weighs 80 kg on the Earth would weigh only 30.4 kg on Mercury (80 x 0.38 = 30.4). Ask friends to guess how much they would weigh on another planet. How much would your pet, favourite toy, or another object weigh? Calculate these and complete the chart.

Planet	Surface gravity	Person or object	Weight on Earth	Weight on planet
Mercury	0.38			
Venus	0.88			
Mars	0.40			
Jupiter	2.39			
Saturn	1.17			
Uranus	0.92			
Neptune	1.23			

Answers may vary

Science investigation
Complete drawings of you and your friends jumping on different planets. On which planet would you be able to jump highest? Explain your answer.

One would jump higher on planets with lower surface gravities, since the gravity on those planets is not pulling one down as much as Earth's gravity.

93

What causes night and day?

Background information

Earth completes one rotation on its axis every 24 hours. When the part of Earth where you live faces the Sun, it is daytime. Sunrise, also called dawn, occurs when the part of Earth where you are turns just enough for you to see the Sun. At sunset, Earth has turned so that again you can only just see the Sun. When it is night where you are, it is daytime for people living on the other side of Earth.

Science activity

Early one evening, Gus, who lives in London, England, was allowed to phone his uncle who lives in Montreal, Canada. Gus was very surprised to hear that his uncle was just about to have lunch because it was only 1:00 p.m.

What is the explanation for the difference in time?

Montreal is west of England. Sunrise in Montreal is about 5 hours after England. Therefore, when it is 5:00 p.m. in England, it is lunchtime in Montreal.

Science investigation
Make a model of the Sun and Earth. Use a flashlight to represent the Sun and a basketball to represent Earth. Do this experiment in a darkened room. Place the flashlight on a table so that it shines into the room. Hold the basketball about 1 metre away, and turn it around slowly. The basketball is like Earth turning on its axis. Tape a white circle onto the ball. Spin the ball slowly at a slight angle so it is tilted like Earth. See at what part of the spin the circle appears lighted. Move it to other places and repeat. Are there locations that stay lighted longer than others?

Ask the child to describe what is happening at the circle's place on the model of Earth. This model should help the child understand why when it is day where he or she lives, it is night somewhere else.

94

What is the Moon like tonight?

Background information

As the Moon travels around Earth, we see different amounts of the Moon lit up by the Sun. This is known as the *phases of the Moon*. When the Moon is lit up and is round, it is called a *full moon*. The amount of the Moon's sunlit side we see, gradually shrinks or wanes. When the Moon is not lit up by the Sun, it is called a *new moon*. During a new moon, you cannot see the Moon in the sky. After a new moon, the amount we can see of the sunlit side grows, or waxes, each night until it is a full moon again.

Science activity

Draw a line from each of the phases below to show its correct position in the sequence from new moon to new moon. (A gibbous phase is when about three-quarters of the Moon is lit up.)

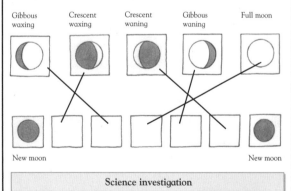

Gibbous waxing · Crescent waxing · Crescent waning · Gibbous waning · Full moon

New moon · New moon

Science investigation
What does the Moon look like tonight? What phase do you think is showing? Use the Internet, a calendar, or a newspaper to check the phase of the Moon. Make your own chart of the Moon's phases over the next month.

The child learns that the Moon changes as it orbits Earth. Encourage the child to visit sites on the Internet that show what the Moon looks like in real time and some of the simulations of the Moon.

95

Where is the Moon tonight?

Background information

It takes the Moon about 28 days to travel around Earth. It travels around Earth in a counterclockwise direction. It rises and sets during the night, just as the Sun rises and sets during the day. On Earth, the Moon appears to rise in the east and set in the west. Because of the way the Moon moves, we are only able to see one side of it.

Science activity

In this picture, it is evening and a boy and girl are looking at the Moon. Draw where you think they may see the Moon later that night.

Science investigation
⚠ What are some of the features of the Moon? Does the Moon change shape in the evening sky? Explain. Is there a man on the Moon?

The child learns that the Moon makes one complete rotation on its axis during each orbit around Earth. The Moon does not produce its own light. It reflects light from the Sun. The Moon changes shape in the evening sky during a month.